THE ACCIDENT
OF COLOR

ALSO BY DANIEL BROOK

A History of Future Cities

The Trap: Selling Out to Stay Afloat in Winner-Take-All America

THE ACCIDENT OF COLOR

A STORY OF RACE IN RECONSTRUCTION

DANIEL BROOK

W. W. NORTON & COMPANY

Independent Publishers Since 1923

New York | London

For information about special discounts for bulk purchases, please contact
W. W. Norton Special Sales at specialsales@wwnorton.com or 800-233-4830

Manufacturing by Worzalla Publishing Company
Book design by Chris Welch
Production manager: Beth Steidle

ISBN 978-0-393-24744-2

W. W. Norton & Company, Inc., 500 Fifth Avenue, New York, N.Y. 10110
www.wwnorton.com

W. W. Norton & Company Ltd., 15 Carlisle Street, London W1D 3BS

1 2 3 4 5 6 7 8 9 0

FOR OUR REPUBLIC

CONTENTS

PREFACE: DOWN THE MEMORY HOLE   XIII

INTRODUCTION: *LES AMBASSADEURS*   XIX

1.   MISFIT METROPOLISES   1

2.   STRANGE CONFEDERATES   29

3.   LEGALLY BLACK   57

4.   FREEDOM RIDERS   81

5.   PROGRESS ON PARCHMENT   105

6.   BROWNS VERSUS BOARD OF EDUCATION   123

7.   RADICAL UNIVERSITY   151

8.   LAWS AND OUTLAWS   173

9.   THE GREAT BETRAYAL   213

10.   FADE TO BLACK AND WHITE   243

CONCLUSION: LIVING THE LIE   283

Bibliographic Note   291

Acknowledgments   293

Notes   297

Index   331

A Note on Language: This work contains quotations from eighteenth- and nineteenth-century sources. Spelling, italics, underlining, punctuation, and capitalization have been rendered in the original, even when they do not conform to contemporary norms of written American English. Offensive language in quotations has also been rendered in the original.

DOWN THE MEMORY HOLE

Emancipated Americans in New Orleans during the Civil War.

(Courtesy of the Charles L. Blockson Afro-American Collection,

Temple University Libraries, Philadelphia, PA)

When Williston Henry Lofton, a history major at Howard University, decided to earn a master's degree in tandem with his bachelor's, he had all he needed except a thesis topic. Fishing around, Lofton became captivated by an odd subject: the history of the civil rights movement.

It was an unfashionable, even anachronistic, choice. The civil rights struggle of five decades past was not something most anyone was interested in. Its victories had faded and the landscape for African-Americans was bleak. In official Washington, just beyond the gates of the Howard campus, hostile forces held sway in the White House, in Congress, and on the Supreme Court. Voter suppression was rampant and police shootings of African-American youth commonplace. But as young Williston dove into the archives, he discovered remarkable material. He went on to write a fine survey of the protests, boycotts, sit-ins, test cases, and legislation of the civil rights era.

Lofton submitted his thesis in the spring of 1930 and entitled it "Civil Rights of the Negro in the United States, 1865–1883." The monograph opened with these words: "A study of the civil rights of the Negroes in the United States in the two decades following the Civil War reveals surprising information to the investigator. The surprise exists not so much in the denial of civil rights to the Negro, for that is expected, but rather in the great degree to which civil rights were accorded the Negro by both the State and the Federal governments."

In unearthing the achievements of this forgotten civil rights movement, Lofton faced twin challenges. First, he was at odds with the view of leading historians who saw the granting of civil rights to African-Americans during Reconstruction as a tragic mistake and Klan terrorism as a necessary evil in revoking those rights. Pioneered by white supremacist historians besotted with the latest racial pseudoscience—men like William A. Dunning of Columbia University—this view had been popularized through Thomas Dixon Jr.'s pulp fiction and D. W. Griffith's subsequent blockbuster screen adaptation of it, *The Birth of a Nation*.

Williston Henry Lofton was also up against rampant historical document destruction; white reactionaries had covered up the most stunning achievements of the postwar integrationists. Even if the undergraduate Lofton had had the time, the funds, and the freedom to scour Southern archives for original documentation— many were held by whites-only institutions that barred researchers of color—he would have hit numerous walls. In New Orleans, the school board records for the district's integrated period from 1870 to 1877 had long ago been expunged from the archives. At the University of South Carolina, the records of the student debating society from the school's integrated era, from 1873 to 1877, had been defaced page by page with black-ink tombstone pictographs inscribed "Negro Regime." To try to fill these gaps in the primary source records, Lofton was forced to reconstruct America's first attempt at interracial democracy as best he could through newspaper coverage of civil rights activism and court records of civil rights cases.

Facing these obstacles, even when W. E. B. Du Bois tried his hand at a history of Reconstruction, which he published in 1935, the nation's preeminent African-American scholar lamented that "the material today . . . is unfortunately difficult to find. Little effort has been made to preserve the records of Negro effort and speeches [and] actions. . . . The loss today is irreparable, and this present study limps and gropes in darkness."

In the depths of segregation, even with complete information, it would have been hard to properly process the antiracist activism of the Reconstruction era. Under the system known as "Jim Crow," named for a minstrel show's blackface stereotype of a slave, Americans were pressed into legal categories of "white" and "colored" with rights and restrictions allocated accordingly. Jim Crow's widening of whiteness, the one-drop rule of blackness, and retroactive complete conflation of blackness with servitude made it difficult to comprehend the leading Reconstruction activists on their own terms. These were men and women who defied binary racial categorizations and, indeed, fought against them. That such a disproportionate number of pioneering Reconstruction-era civil rights activists sprang from the distinctive, long free, openly biracial communities of New Orleans and Charleston is no coincidence. For generations, New Orleans's "Creoles of color" and Charleston's "Browns" had been resisting the imposition of race-based rights and challenging America's black-or-white notion of race itself. Only in light of these communities' unique histories and self-conceptions can their cities' outsized civil rights achievements be understood.

Just as an historian of medieval France must keep in the front of her mind that in the Middle Ages there was no France, only a smattering of feudal lands that would one day become France, so a student of Reconstruction must be cognizant that the firm racial binary Americans accept to this day is a result of Jim Crow, not a cause of it. The one-drop rule—the concept that any trace of African ancestry at all makes an American "a negro"—was not even conjured until the 1850s and was not widely accepted until the early twentieth century. It is only because mixed-race activists were defeated in their valiant effort to stop a regime of race-based rights that contemporary Americans view society through the racial blinders that we do. Today, decades after the dismantling of Jim Crow, Americans still see our society and ourselves in binary terms of "white" and "colored." That our racial system is second nature to us but incomprehensible to the rest of the world—even to people from other New World societies that once practiced slavery but never instituted Jim Crow—should highlight for us how peculiar it is.

Most Americans still live their lives trapped in these outdated and scientifically unjustifiable notions. On the Right, white nationalists patrol the ever-hazier borders of whiteness while some on the Left see any questioning of Jim Crow's racial categories as an attempt to shirk responsibility for historical wrongs. This book does not wish to be such an attempt. Nor does it wish to gloss over the flaws of its flawed heroes. Scores of the activists profiled, who fought for civil rights after the Civil War, had been silent on the evils of slavery before it. Some even held slaves themselves. But telling their stories on their own terms can help remove our own blind spots about the long, imperfect struggle to build the world's most diverse democracy and about the racial system that still mars our national life. In our ever more multihued society, we may finally be able to hear these voices from the past, recovered from yellowed newspaper clippings and dusty court records, and heed their plea that there can never be full emancipation from American racism until we put the American system of race itself on trial.

INTRODUCTION

LES AMBASSADEURS

E. Arnold Bertonneau of New Orleans.

(Courtesy of Thomas F. Bertonneau)

On March 12, 1864, a pair of Southern gentlemen, E. Arnold Bertonneau and Jean Baptiste Roudanez, arrived at the White House to lobby President Abraham Lincoln. They hailed from New Orleans, a city that had been retaken by the Union just one year into the Civil War and had become a testing ground for what the multiracial nation might look like when the war was won. The visitors were leaders of the city's distinctive openly mixed-race Afro-French community, and they presented the president with a petition signed by one thousand of their fellow property-owning free men of color demanding the right to vote. At the time, this was an audacious ask.

Though the petitioners addressed the president as "Citizens of the United States," technically this was no longer true. Seven years before their visit to the White House, the nation's highest court had revoked their citizenship. In the *Dred Scott* case, a dispute ostensibly over slaves' rights, the Supreme Court of the United States had declared that an African-American, whether enslaved or free, had "no rights which the white man was bound to respect [and] is not a 'citizen' within the meaning of the Constitution of the United States." This sweeping ruling was a vicious attack on free people of color nationwide. But the ongoing war was opening up new possibilities. The Union army now brimmed with African-American soldiers, and on New Year's Day, 1863, Lincoln had issued the Emancipation Proclamation. Yet when Lincoln had recently announced a plan for Reconstruction in Louisiana, it barred African-Americans from voting.

According to the Supreme Court, the petitioners had no rights that Lincoln was bound to respect but they were hardly his inferiors. Lincoln had been born in a log cabin in Kentucky and, though whip-smart, he had completed just a single year of formal schooling. By contrast, Roudanez was a trained engineer. Before the war, he had worked as a food scientist on a sugar plantation, pioneering methods to turn raw cane into salable commodities like molasses. And even with those accomplishments, he was the underachiever in his family. His brother, Louis Charles, was a medical doctor with degrees from Dartmouth and the Sorbonne.

Bertonneau, for his part, made his living as a wine merchant, that most refined of professions. In aristocratic fashion, this son of a French father and an Afro-Cuban mother went by his middle name; Lincoln was so lowborn that he didn't even have one. While the wine merchant kept tabs on the Paris auction house prices of the latest Loire Valley vintages, the rail-splitter-turned-commander-in-chief's entire international experience amounted to visiting the Ontario side of Niagara Falls once. In fact, it was Lincoln's youthful trips down the Mississippi River to New Orleans, especially his month-long sojourn there in 1831, that constituted the deepest cosmopolitan immersion of his life. For Lincoln, the meeting with Bertonneau and Roudanez may well have felt like a visit from foreign dignitaries, if not interplanetary ambassadors.

But the strangest thing of all about these visitors was their racial identity. Though these men were light enough to pass for white—Roudanez was just one-eighth African; Bertonneau, with his rakish wave of dark hair, looked like a stereotypical Frenchman—they clearly had no interest in doing so. Bertonneau and Roudanez were of partial African descent and they were completely unabashed about it, willing to go to the White House as community representatives of African-Americans in their state. They didn't feel that their African heritage made them any less American than their French heritage did. Lincoln, by contrast, with his dark features and anomalous height, had spent his entire political career dodging scurrilous rumors that he secretly had African ancestors.

There are no transcripts of the meeting in the White House that spring day. One presidential aide later quoted Lincoln as saying, "I regret, gentlemen, that you are not able to secure all your rights [and] that circumstances will not permit the government to confer them upon you." Still, the visitors clearly impressed the president. The day after their visit, Lincoln wrote a private letter to the governor of Louisiana, Michael Hahn, urging him to bestow the right to vote on "some of the colored people . . . as, for instance, the very intelligent, and especially those who have fought gallantly in our ranks."

Hahn ignored the president's request, and only when the war ended in 1865 did Lincoln finally go public with his controversial position on limited African-American suffrage. Standing at a second-floor window with a crowd gathered on the White House lawn two days after General Robert E. Lee's surrender at Appomattox, the president discussed the terms of Louisiana's readmission to the Union. He urged that the ballot be "conferred on the very intelligent [African-American men], and on those who serve our cause as soldiers." His phrasing was nearly identical to what he'd written to Governor Hahn a year earlier after being lobbied by Bertonneau and Roudanez.

For at least one person in the crowd, even this was a step too far. "That means nigger citizenship," a Maryland-born actor named John Wilkes Booth reportedly remarked to a friend. "Now, by God, I'll put him through," he vowed. "That will be the last speech he ever makes." Two days later, the actor shot the president dead at Ford's Theatre and leapt to the stage ranting in Latin about tyranny.

The Civil War was over but its meaning was in dispute. The fight for equal rights was just beginning and in its way stood an ambivalent voting public, a Supreme Court packed with elderly racists, and some unknown number of potential white supremacist terrorists, like John Wilkes Booth. Across the rural South, plantation owners schemed to resurrect something akin to slavery by assigning Americans different rights based on race. They hoped to rally those deemed white, whether rich or poor, immigrant or native-born, Northerner or Southerner, to their side and to conflate African heritage with ignorance and barbarism.

If equal rights were to be won, it would be with heavy reliance on people like Bertonneau and Roudanez who gave the lie to these bigoted and fallacious racial concepts. Concentrated in the cosmopolitan Southern port cities of New Orleans and Charleston, their mixed-race, freeborn community had the education, wealth, and connections to press for equal citizenship in the corridors of power. Now they were uniquely threatened by a *Dred Scott*–style race-based inequality that would make no distinction between freemen and freedmen, between wine merchants and cotton pickers. But they also had a mass constituency on the streets—the millions of new free people of color emancipation had created.

1.

———

MISFIT METROPOLISES

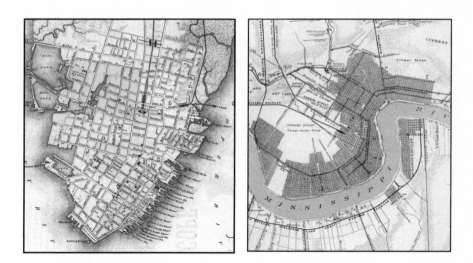

Charleston (left) and New Orleans (right)
in the mid-nineteenth century.

(Courtesy of Hargrett Rare Book and Manuscript Library / University of Georgia Libraries;

The Historic New Orleans Collection, 1974.25.18.122)

In colonial times, Charleston, South Carolina, the peninsula at the confluence of the Ashley and Cooper rivers and the Atlantic Ocean, was the South's leading seaport. Goods from all over the world flowed in but the most important inflow was people—slaves and slave drivers, indentured servants and skilled free laborers, refugees and get-rich-quick schemers. Together these newcomers groped over the decades to forge a new society in the New World.

Before American independence, Charleston was more closely linked to the Caribbean than were other Anglo-American outposts. Fully six of the governors of the Charleston-headquartered Carolina colony between 1670 and 1730 were immigrants from Barbados not England and many of the planters were West Indian transplants as well. On the islands, these future Carolinians had imbibed more flexible Latin-inflected notions of race than were common in the rest of colonial America. The Latin American racial system was still a racist one—the lighter one was, the better; green eyes trumped brown eyes and life was easier with tan skin than brown skin—but its foundational assumption was that in the New World there was precious little racial purity. With people from all continents living jumbled together for generations, virtually everyone was mixed and the only question was what the proportions of one's particular mixture were.

While the New World Spanish term *la raza* looks like a cognate of the New World English word *race*, it's more like its antonym. *La raza* denotes the human being the New World created, a mixture of all the world's ethnic groups, while *race* is based on the supposition that despite living together in the New World for centuries, each group somehow remains distinct.

Race mixing is, of course, a one-way street. Each generation spent in the New World was more mixed than the last. Slavery, with its rampant sexual exploitation, made race mixing more common, not less. This was true everywhere in the New World, but Anglo-American colonists, steeped in Puritan traditions that frowned on sex in general and promiscuity in particular, became skilled in the art of not seeing what was right in front of their eyes.

In Charleston, meanwhile, with its Caribbean-tinged outlook, mixing was more openly acknowledged than elsewhere. When a 1736 editorial in the *South Carolina Gazette* pleaded that mixed-race relationships at least not be flaunted—"Certain [white] young Men," it proposed, should "frequent less with their black Lovers the open Lots" of the city—it took just a week for the paper to publish a poet's retort. *"Kiss black or white,"* he urged, *"why need it trouble you?"*

At the time, the poet had the upper hand. Loath to give their wives any power to thwart their affairs, the rice-plantation aristocrats who ran South Carolina simply did not permit divorce. And loath to hem in their sexual privileges or, more worrisome still, prompt the precise adjudication of their own racial makeups, they never outlawed interracial marriage either.

In every slave society, solving the social riddle of what to do with the oft-freed mixed-race children of masters and slaves and their descendents presented a conundrum. In the Caribbean, the masters opted to enlist the ever-growing mixed-race free population as a middle-class buffer between themselves and their slaves. Colonial Charleston initially embraced this strategy as well. But in most of America, the demographic math was different than it was in Barbados or South Carolina with their slave majorities. In the American colonies as a whole, poor, slaveless European immigrants and their descendants were the single largest social group.

Political stability hinged on these impoverished Americans not overturning a system that left them poor. They would be won over to identification with the master class through race.

The American Revolution supplanted an empire built upon the eternal inequality of monarchs and subjects, nobles and commoners, and masters and slaves with a republic based on the self-evident truth that all men are created equal. Against this new egalitarian backdrop, the peculiar institution of slavery became a glaring contradiction. In the years after the Revolution, slavery, which had initially been justified on grounds of religion (imported Africans weren't Christian) and nationality (imported Africans weren't English), increasingly came to be justified through a new theory of supposed African racial inferiority. European immigrants and their descendants, though they came from tribes that had fought each other back home for centuries would become, in America, a single unified people through the alchemy of race. And they would set themselves above and against a second category of American, those from the warring tribes of sub-Saharan Africa who would be similarly reconstituted into a single racial group.

This bifurcation became more convincing in the new republic as white indentured servitude died out. Even as the first federal census in 1790 still enumerated what it called "free white people"—free and white not yet being completely synonymous in the American mind—the cost of emigrating from Europe was declining, so there was less need for immigrants to sell themselves into terms of unfreedom to finance the trip. With each passing year, whiteness was more fully conflated with freedom and blackness with servitude. In time, white men were universally deputized as slave patrollers throughout the South, packing side arms and demanding passes from African-Americans they found off the plantation. (In Charleston, as in the Caribbean, free, mixed-race people were never fully boxed out of this role.) Eventually whiteness—a category that grew to encompass ever more disparate ethnic groups from Europe, West Asia, and North Africa—would harden into a kind of inherited aristocratic status in America.

Ill-matched to American realities, where racial lines grew blurrier with each generation, in Charleston, the black/white binary was particularly anathema. But after the nation was founded, the Caribbean-inflected distinctiveness of early Carolina waned. In 1790, not fifteen years into American independence, St. Phillip's Episcopal Church, the oldest and most prestigious congregation in Charleston, where the white elite and their free mixed-race relatives had worshipped for generations under the same roof, announced that it was prohibiting its mixed-race members from being buried in the church graveyard. Mixed-race people might be free but they wouldn't be equal.

In response to their church's decree that they were good enough to worship, even marry, in the church but not good enough to be buried there, the mixed-race relatives of Charleston's leading white families organized themselves into a separate subcongregation, the Brown Fellowship Society. Formed by five biracial freemen who dubbed themselves the "Originators," the preamble to the group's "Rules and Regulations" declared, "We, free brown men, natives of the city of Charleston, in the State of South Carolina . . . holding it an essential duty of mankind to contribute all [we] can towards relieving the wants and miseries, and promoting the welfare and happiness of one another, and observing the method of many other well disposed persons of this State, by entering into particular societies for this purpose . . . have freely and cheerfully entered into a society in Charleston, and State aforesaid, commencing the first of November, 1790." By October 1794, the Brown Fellowship Society had raised enough money to purchase a plot of land to use as a burial ground, solving the immediate crisis that had sparked its founding, and it threw open the new cemetery to the entire free mixed-race community of Charleston. Taking on a broad communal responsibility, over time the Society sponsored a school, founded a credit union, and organized a life insurance fund.

For all the institutions it created—it soon spun off a literary society and a debating club as well—the Brown Fellowship Society's greatest creation was the community itself. The Society made brownness a communal identity, elevating it into a racial category, at least within the city limits of Charleston. By doing so, the Originators hoped to carve out a space for their community in the social and political minefield that was being free and mixed-race in an America with a looming Manichaean racial order.

As that order grew sharper every year, Charleston's "Browns," as they were known, confronted the choice every middle class eventually faces: cozy up to the elite or make common cause with the masses. In the antebellum era, the Browns sought the former path before, pivotally, breaking ranks during Reconstruction. In part, family ties led the Browns in their initial identification with the elite. After all, they were the blood relatives of the city's wealthiest whites. But, more crucially, they were living in a society where the distinction between slave and free mattered far more than gradations of skin color.

Counterintuitively, Charleston's Browns were indifferent to the evils of slavery precisely because they lived in a city where those evils were so openly on display. Antebellum Charleston was littered with slave auction houses, the backs of which were jails where the human merchandise was imprisoned prior to sale. After a brief stay packed in the pen—slave traders paid the jailer-auctioneers on a per-head, per-day basis, so churn meant money—families were sold on the block. Nearly all were bound for plantations in the hinterlands but different family members were often sold to different buyers, never to see one another again. If free Brown Charlestonians entered these grotesque human auction houses at all, it was as purchasers, not as the purchased.

For Charleston's free people of color, the barbarism in the slave pens only underscored how utterly different they were from the enslaved, no matter how closely their complexions sometimes matched. No doubt there was a social gulf between even the wealthiest Browns and their white relatives. But it paled in comparison to the social distance between their freeborn selves and the enslaved strangers coursing through their city in chains.

Charleston's Brown community gained its only American analogue by happenstance when President Thomas Jefferson purchased the Louisiana Territory and its capital, New Orleans, from France in 1803. By the time of its annexation, the city of New Orleans, built on a natural levee at a crescent-shaped bend in the Mississippi just upriver from the Gulf of Mexico, had existed for eighty-five years. Having spent nearly a century as a possession of, alternately, France and Spain, the Crescent City's social fabric reflected its Latin lineage. While the British typically tried to enforce a strict color line in their colonies, building their colonial outposts with a "white town" separate from a "black town," the French were less punctilious; the Spanish, who usually sent single men as their colonizers, eagerly mixed with whomever they found in the lands they conquered.

In colonial New Orleans, under French and Spanish rule, a system of recognized, institutionalized race mixing had been established. Though pre-American New Orleans never became as fully *mestizo* as Spanish Mexico, there was little impetus to hide interracial relationships; mixed-race couplings might not be the paragon of Christian matrimony but they were not considered unnatural or particularly shameful. Indeed, in New Orleans interracial relationships were even more open than those in British colonial Barbados or Charleston. The mixed-race children that resulted—either born free or set free ("manumitted") by their free fathers—came to constitute a mixed-race middle class in the city. As the mixing continued down the generations, a system known as *plaçage*, in which married European men would take on free women of color as their official concubines and provide for the education and sustenance of the resulting children, was quietly recognized by church and state.

Even more than in Charleston, the mixed-race free population of New Orleans constituted a distinct community. In colonial times, the New World–born descendants of the original colonists had dubbed themselves Creoles (or, in Spanish, *Criollos*); their mixed-race descendants, born in the New World but with roots in both Europe and Africa, were dubbed "Creoles of color." By 1788, these free people of color (*gens de couleur libres,* in French) constituted more than a third of New Orleans's population. Outside the Anglo-American world, a free mixed-race middle class was no anomaly, so there was no need to form anything as blatant as a Brown Fellowship Society in New Orleans. The community's identity and status was not threatened until Creoles of color awoke one day in 1803 to learn that their city had been sold to the United States of America.

When the first American governor of Louisiana, William C. C. Claiborne, a friend of Louisiana purchaser Thomas Jefferson and, like him, a slaveholding Virginian, took office, the Creole of color community put him on notice. In their 1804 letter, "An Address from the Free People of Color," they informed the governor that they expected the rights they had enjoyed under French rule would be preserved under American power. After all, the bilateral purchase treaty had explicitly promised that free inhabitants of the Louisiana Territory would enjoy "all the rights, advantages and immunities of citizens" of the United States. As the petitioners wrote, "We are duly sensible that our personal and political freedom is thereby assured to us for ever . . . and we are also impressed with the fullest confidence in the Justice and Liberality of the Government towards every Class of Citizens which they have taken under their Protection." Claiborne never responded. Privately, he schemed to chip away at the community's rights and privileges, slowly making his new territory conform to American racial norms.

In spite of the new governor, at annexation Louisiana became unique among Southern states in that its laws presumed biracial individuals to be free rather than enslaved. Even the post-Purchase influx of ambitious Anglo-American transplants, derisively called *Américains* by the established Francophone Creoles, could not fully upend this atypical racial system.

Just as America's binary racial system was beginning to press down on Charleston and New Orleans, world events conspired to impede it. The year of the Louisiana Purchase coincided with the final collapse of the slave society on the French colony of Saint-Domingue (modern-day Haiti). What had been France's most valuable possession, a fertile colony packed with sugarcane slave-labor camps, had won its independence through a slave revolt that grew into an abolitionist revolution. On the island, the tiny minority of European slave owners had always been too small to rule alone and they had long relied on mixed-race free people as overseers and runaway slave catchers. Some mixed-race people had even become wealthy slaveholders themselves. When the revolt came, free biracial Haitians were divided and those defending slavery were targeted alongside the Europeans. As they fled the island, slave owners of all colors came ashore as refugees in nearby slave societies, including Cuba and the United States. The largest American-bound group went to New Orleans; as a Francophone city, it was the easiest place in America for a French-speaking refugee to settle. A smaller but still significant contingent landed in Charleston. In the United States, the slaveholding refugees of color were an anomaly: African-Americans who came to the United States voluntarily because they wanted to live in a country where slavery was legal.

Yet their influx was greeted with suspicion by proslavery

Anglo-Americans. With thousands of additional *gens de couleur libre* flocking to New Orleans as refugees from Haiti, Governor Claiborne, who already had strained relations with the existing community, ordered refugees of color banned from landing in Louisiana. When enforcement proved impossible, Claiborne lobbied the American consul general in Cuba to cut off the flow of refugees who had stopped there en route to America. "We have already a much greater proportion of that population, than comports with our interest," Claiborne informed the diplomat.

The mayor of New Orleans similarly smarted at the influx of "many worthless free people of color or persons calling themselves free [who] arrive here daily without our being able to prevent it, or drive them away after they had come." In the New Orleans city council, one paranoid legislator warned, "men with their hands still reddened with the blood of our fellow countrymen [white Frenchmen] are arriving daily in great numbers. . . . Tomorrow their smoking torches will be lighted again to set afire our peaceful homes." Many Americans assumed all nonwhite Haitians must sympathize with the slave revolt, discarding the logic that, by definition, those who came to America were fleeing the victors of the revolution.

Even those who understood that the mixed-race newcomers held proslavery views thought their presence in itself could be destabilizing. Like all oppressive social structures, slavery was preserved by maintaining the illusion that society could not be structured any other way. Simply by arriving from Haiti, the refugees would alert enslaved Americans to the reality that the slaves on Saint-Domingue had successfully overthrown their masters and founded their own republic. Considering the Haitian influx to Charleston, one native-born Carolinian fretted,

> The circumstances which occasion'd their introduction gave new ideas to our slaves which the opportunities of conversation with the new comers could not fail to ripen into mischief.

It may be perhaps true that the generality of those admitted were not immediately concerned in the revolt—their hands were free from blood but they had wittnessed all the horrors of the scene—they saw the dawning hope of their countrymen to be free—the rapidity with which the flame of liberty spread among them—the enthusiasm with which it was cherished had scarcely perceiv'd it, before they saw too, that their triumph was complete, that it needed but the wish of a trifling struggle to effect their freedom.

Despite fulminations against them, the Haitians stayed and integrated into the Southern port cities. As much as Charleston's white elite complained about "the French negroes," the Haitian refugees quickly adopted the English language and assimilated into the Browns. In New Orleans, where cultural space already existed for biracial French-speakers, the influx of wealthy slave owners of color reinforced the city's un-American, tripartite racial system. The first federal census taken in purchased Louisiana, in 1810, revealed that New Orleans's free people of color population had more than tripled from the Haitian migration. Faced with America's racial paranoia, the free mixed-race communities in both cities decided their best hope of protecting their status was in proving their loyalty to the white slaveholding elite, even if the loyalty did not always run in both directions. In the slave revolts that rattled New Orleans in 1811 and Charleston in 1822, free people of color largely sided with the slaveholders and some actively helped put down the insurrections.

Brown Charlestonians, a middle class that was neither black nor white, could fit into their hometown because, from its founding, Charleston was one mixed-up city. Only a single city neighborhood, the Battery, mimicked the social structure of the rural South. Sited at the tip of the eight-square-mile Charleston peninsula, the Battery boasted grand homes where the city's wealthiest white families resided with their slaves. The vast verandahs of these mansions overlooked the placid natural harbor, sheltered by barrier islands and guarded by federal troops at Fort Sumter out on the horizon. In summer, the Battery filled up as slave owners from the countryside flocked to the city hoping the Atlantic Ocean breezes would protect them from the malarial miasmas inland. The rest of the year, the Battery was a veritable ghost town.

Walking back from the Battery, things got less grandiose but more interesting. Mansions gave way to modest row homes. With each block back towards the narrowing part of the peninsula called "the Neck," spaces grew tighter and rents lower. Lines of carved-wood doorways, pressed up to the sidewalk, formed a unified wall along the street front and gave each home, no matter how crowded, a middle-class dignity. These front doors opened not into buildings but onto breezeways where ground-floor porches were squeezed in between the tightly packed townhomes. Though hidden from the street, these secret porches were an ingenious and attractive solution to the Carolina coast's formidable heat and humidity. They also provided a place to socialize in comfort, safe from the prying eyes on the street. Being shielded from the judgments of bigoted strangers was particularly useful since these dense blocks of the Neck were packed with families of every color and creed from all over the world, sometimes even in the same house, broken up into apartments or taking in boarders.

The foundation for Charleston's cosmopolitan mix had been laid in the seventeenth century when Lord Ashley Cooper, the rivers' namesake and a leading investor in the Carolina colony, hired the liberal political theorist John Locke to craft a constitution for the settlement. Locke's colony was based on a class system of free people, enslaved people, and indentured servants. For the free at least, this arrangement was progressive in an age of peasants and kings. Tolerant Lockean South Carolina became one of the only spots on the face of the earth where religious tolerance was guaranteed for all and even Jews were granted full civil rights. Voting with their feet, European, Caribbean, and Latin American migrants would make Charleston the most Jewish city in early America. Free people of color from other American colonies, Haiti, and beyond flocked to Charleston as well. As the Carolina economy boomed on the exportation of rice, grown by the people Lord Ashley Cooper did not see fit to grant human rights, other immigrants followed. Visitors often remarked on the foreign languages heard on the city's streets. It was not until the eve of the Civil War that Charleston became majority white and this was only on account of international immigration from Europe. Rooted in the colony's vaunted tolerance, Charleston's skyline sprouted steeples of all denominations, giving the settlement its nickname, the Holy City.

Layered into this cosmopolitan mix, Charleston Browns thrived economically. Anyone arriving by boat would encounter a waterfront district teeming with free people of color working as barrel makers, rope makers, ironworkers, and teamsters. One visitor to the city noted the "sleek, dandified negroes" who look down on the "cracker[s]," while Edward Laurens, the scion of a wealthy slave-trading family, complained that anyone "walk[ing] through the streets of our ill-fated city [can] see how . . . all mechanical arts [are] becoming overstocked by persons of colour."

By the eve of the Civil War, free people of color constituted 8 percent of the city's population and dominated the skilled crafts. Three-quarters of Charleston's millwrights, the specialists who crafted mill gears and waterwheels, were free African-Americans, as were half of its butchers and tailors, a third of its coopers, and a quarter of its carpenters. Elite Brown Charlestonians prospered through entrepreneurship and investment, with some families attaining significant wealth in the form of real estate.

With a nonwhite population that was unusually well represented in the middle class and diverse communities drawn from all over the world, Charleston's neighborhoods were remarkably integrated. An 1861 city survey found only fifteen streets in the entire municipality that were all white. It found a similar paucity of streets with no whites. Free people of color lived in every neighborhood of the city, but there were always more in the Neck.

The middle of the peninsula, dominated by the merchant class, was particularly diverse. There, for example, in 1860, a well-to-do German-born grocer and a wine merchant from New England lived alongside a prosperous African-American hairstylist. Further up in the Neck a sixty-year-old African-American grocer owned her own home along with the property next door, which she rented to a white engineer from New York. According to city records, there were seventy-five whites who were renting their homes from free people of color that year, making the practice not exactly common but hardly unheard of. The more widespread deviation from American racial norms was the city's peculiar take on the peculiar institution: the 1860 census recorded over a hundred slave owners of color in Charleston.

The strangeness of this city where race and class did not line up in the typical American way was lost on international immigrants. Foreign-born grog-shop owners, raised without America's racial concepts and seeking to prosper in the New World, were famous for serving all customers on an equal basis. As one native-born white Carolinian sniffed, the city's immigrants "become courteous to the negro and submit to an equality of sociability." The root of nativists' distrust of Charleston was that it was a city where too many whites didn't behave like proper whites and too many people of color didn't know their place, a polyglot metropolis that refused to conform to American norms. As a British visitor to the United States noted with surprise, "the negroes here [in Charleston] have certainly not the manners of an oppressed race."

As New Orleans grew from the Haitian influx and the early nineteenth-century cotton-exporting boom, *plaçage*, the social phenomenon W. E. B. Du Bois later termed the city's "systematic common law marriages between whites and mulattoes," transformed the urban fabric. The proliferation of mixed-race families was becoming a spatial reality on the map of New Orleans. At its founding in 1718, the original city encompassed solely the seventy-eight square blocks of the French Quarter but, as the population grew after the Louisiana Purchase, surrounding farmland was sold off and transformed into new neighborhoods (called *faubourgs* in French). To the north and east of the French Quarter, Faubourg Tremé and Faubourg Marigny became dotted with the homes of the *plaçées* (biracial concubines) and their children. The faubourgs' street names, such as Rue d'Amour (Love Street) and Rue des Bons Enfants (Good Children Street), flaunted their purpose. When neighborhood children reached adulthood, they typically inherited the family home, creating a middle class of mixed-race homeowners. In the period between annexation and the Civil War, roughly three-quarters of the lots in the Tremé and Marigny neighborhoods were owned at some point by a free person of color. Well-to-do Haitian refugees naturally concentrated in these mixed-race, Francophone neighborhoods where they built "Creole cottages," modest homes with the gables peaking parallel to the street like a country house instead of in the typical urban perpendicular style. With their bright colors, floor-to-ceiling windows, and louvered shutters, these Haitian immigrants' homes augmented the city's Caribbean look and feel.

The whites who lived alongside the Creoles of color in these neighborhoods tended to be European immigrants less steeped in America's racial codes. With each block back from the Mississippi riverfront, where the elegant cathedral and government buildings stood, land grew less desirable. In the flood-prone "back of town" neighborhoods carved out from the swamps, New Orleans became a jumble of peoples of all colors and creeds from all over the world.

Back of town was a place with no analogue in America save the Neck in Charleston.

As mixed-race people and European immigrants settled downriver from the French Quarter and directly behind it, Anglo-Americans settled upriver. There they built a business district that resembled the downtown of any other American city where they conducted their affairs in English. Meeting on the "neutral ground" median of the city's central artery, Canal Street, *Américains* traded with French-speakers by day while retreating to separate social worlds after dark. The poshest residential sections of Anglophone Uptown mimicked the racial and social structures of the rural South, much like the Battery in Charleston. For decades after annexation, New Orleans was essentially two cities, side by side but culturally distinct, speaking different languages and abiding by different racial codes.

Sheltered from the harshest expressions of Anglo-American racism and benefiting from the established system of inheritance, the Creole of color community's prosperity survived Americanization. The community educated its children in private academies in New Orleans and Paris, and maintained near-universal literacy. Creoles of color dominated the skilled building trades, like carpentry and brick making, and even elite professions were within reach. Free people of color worked as physicians, engineers, and architects. With their valuable skills and their wealthy fathers, select Creoles of color amassed real estate empires in the city. Many owned slaves as well. The 1830 census recorded hundreds of slave owners of color in greater New Orleans—more nonwhite slave owners than were found in the states of Alabama, Mississippi, and Florida combined.

The Francophone downtown wards that were the heart of the Creole of color community were free of systematic segregation; each business made its own rules about whom it would serve. The taverns along Bourbon Street famously welcomed all comers. As one newspaper noted, the barrooms at the corner of Bourbon and Orleans streets were "distinguished for the equality which reigns between black and white—all was hail fellow well met, no matter what the complexion." Even less concerned with color lines were the city's brothels. Wags quipped that they were the most integrated places in all of America.

As the decades passed, free communities of color came to be seen more starkly as a threat to the white power structure despite their often vocal support for slavery. As justifications for slavery became increasingly race-based, the mere presence of people of color who were free and successful became an implicit argument for abolition. Accomplished free people of color gave the lie to the notion that people's aptitudes and abilities were predetermined by their racial backgrounds. From this perspective, even a slave owner of color was not an argument for slavery but an argument against it. After all, if a person of African descent could own and successfully run a plantation, how could one argue that Africans were, by nature, slaves?

As race came to supersede class in the Jacksonian era—albeit as a way to safeguard the power of the wealthiest whites—free people of color found themselves increasingly stripped of their historic rights on racial grounds. When the American colonies declared themselves independent in 1776, African-Americans had been permitted to vote in all but two states (provided they met the other qualifications—being free, being male, and owning property—which few of them did). But as property qualifications for voting were dropped, racial barriers were raised. In time, whiteness became a qualification for voting in nearly every state.

Even in Charleston, restrictions grew. Legislation passed in the 1820s required free people of color to register twice a year with the authorities, account for all time spent away from the city, enlist a white "guardian," and pay a special fifty-dollar-a-head tax. An

1835 South Carolina law forbidding its citizens to educate slaves also cracked down on free African-Americans' schools. Academies for free children of color had existed in Charleston for nearly a century, but the new law required them to be supervised by a white person, present in the classroom during all instruction to ensure no slaves were being taught. In response, some schools complied, submitting to a white minder; others went underground.

As restrictions grew more draconian, Charleston came to rely on an ad hoc system of carve-outs for the most elite mixed-race people. An 1835 South Carolina state supreme court decision afforded Charleston authorities plenty of racial leeway. In *State of South Carolina v. Cantey*, the court ruled that one need not be physically white to be legally white, i.e., entitled to the ever-increasing rights and privileges of whiteness. An individual's status, the court explained, "is not to be determined solely by the distinct and visible mixture of negro blood, but by reputation, by his reception into society, and his having commonly exercised the privileges of a white man . . . [A] man of worth, honesty, industry and respectability should have the rank of a white man, while a vagabond of the same degree of blood should be confined to the inferior caste."

The most elite Browns generally escaped the full brunt of the laws as city authorities turned a blind eye to the officially illegal activities of prominent biracial individuals. William Rollin, for example, the mixed-race owner of a lumberyard worked by a crew of slaves and white employees, routinely went north unannounced on business trips—a blatant violation of restrictions on movement the legislature had mandated for free people of color. And Charleston mayor Robert Y. Hayne specifically exempted the Brown Fellowship Society from an edict that African-Americans could not meet without a white man present. A rising politician who would go on to serve as South Carolina governor and senator, Mayor Hayne had read the minutes of the Brown Fellowship Society and personally vouched for the organization.

But with each passing year, as racial categories hardened, more restrictions were proposed. In 1850, the governor of South Carolina floated the idea expelling all free people of color who didn't own either real estate or slaves. Later that decade, a bill was introduced to strip free people of color of their right to slave ownership. Though the measure never passed, its impetus—to complete the racialization of slavery—was clear.

Shortly before the Civil War, the state legislature, responding to a petition by white citizens who urged a crackdown on interracial cohabitation, attempted to ban the conception of biracial babies. The petition was dismissed after one legislator quipped that "the evil complained of cannot be prevented by legislation." The closest antebellum Charleston ever got to American-style denial of interracial relationships was the supposition that they were rampant—but only in other people's families. As Charleston society lady Mary Boykin Chesnut put it in her diary, "Like the [biblical] patriarchs of old, our men live all in one house with their wives and concubines; and the mulattoes one sees in every family partly resemble the white children. Any lady is ready to tell you who is the father of all the mulatto children in everybody's household but her own. Those, she seems to think, drop from the clouds."

Over the decades after its annexation, New Orleans, too, was increasingly pushed towards a system where race would be a black-or-white proposition and it would supersede class. With their business acumen and live-to-work mindset, the *Américains* were on the rise. Part and parcel of the city's Americanization was pressure to reduce the status of its anomalous well-to-do, free, mixed-race citizens. Shortly after the Purchase, Louisiana's newly American legislature had issued an overarching statement on the coming racial order when it passed a law that "Free people of color ought never insult or strike white people, nor presume to conceive themselves equal to whites." The first clause of the law was actionable if abhorrent, but it was the second part, with its creation of an Orwellian thought-crime, that spoke to the legislators' deeper motivations. To the shock and rage of the *Américain* representatives, the state's *gens de couleur libres* did not believe themselves to be in any way inferior to whites.

In 1816, the New Orleans city council passed its first segregation law, an ordinance that applied to seating in theaters and exhibition halls. But in a city with such a range of complexions, it was only because people's ancestry was widely known that there was any hope of enforcing these boundaries.

Visitors to New Orleans, especially foreigners, found its intricate racial system puzzling. Traveling through America on his famed 1831 research trip, Alexis de Tocqueville noted in his travel diary the "faces with every shade of colour" on the streets of New Orleans as well as the paradox of white-skinned residents classed as "coloured [on account of] a trace of African blood." His research partner, Gustave de Beaumont, recorded his befuddlement at length.

> The first time I attended a theater in [New Orleans,] I was surprised at the careful distinction made between the white spectators and the audience whose faces were black. In the first balcony were whites; in the second, mulattoes; in the third, Negroes. An American, beside whom I was sitting, informed me that the dignity of white blood demanded these classifications. However, my eyes were being drawn to the balcony where sat the mulattoes, I perceived a young woman of dazzling beauty, whose complexion, of perfect whiteness, proclaimed the purest European blood. Entering into all the prejudices of my neighbor, I asked him how a woman of English origin could be so lacking in shame as to seat herself among the Africans.
>
> "That woman," he replied, "is colored."

"What? Colored? She is whiter than a lily!"

"She is colored," he replied coldly; "local tradition has established her ancestry, and everyone knows that she had a mulatto among her forebears."

He pronounced these words without further explanation, as one who states a fact which needs only be voiced to be understood.

At the moment I made out in the balcony for whites a face which was very dark. I asked for an explanation of this new phenomenon; the American answered:

"The lady who has attracted your attention is white."

"What? White! She is the same color as the mulattoes."

"She is white," he replied; "local tradition affirms that the blood which flows in her veins is Spanish."

For all the confidence of the locals that they could unerringly track everyone's bloodlines, the streets of the city presented a confounding rainbow of complexions. Joining the bronzed Iberian-Americans were new immigrants from a wide swath of the Old World. An international arrival port, by the mid-nineteenth century nearly half of New Orleans's white-classified population was foreign-born. Even decades after the city became part of America, *Scribner's Monthly* correspondent Edward King described the French Quarter as "not an American scene" but rather a "unique" and "cosmopolitan" space. The Northern reporter noted that the city clothing market was presided over by "lively Gallic versions of the Hebrew female." In the produce market King gawked at all the mixed-race people—the "mulatto fruitseller"; the "face in which the struggle of Congo with French and Spanish blood is still going on"; and the "mulatto girl hardly less fair than the brown maid[s of] Sorrento [or a] little mountain town near Rome." Spotting a flaxen-haired, pasty-complected young man, King assumed he must be a Yankee tourist, as did the locals. The fellow was immediately surrounded by "black urchins [who] grin confidingly and solicit alms as the blond Northerner saunters by." In this municipality of racial misfits, it was the so-called all-American—fair-haired and pale-faced—who didn't fit in.

The color continuum of the cosmopolitan city with a century-long tradition of open interracial coupling rendered the strict enforcement of race-based restrictions a challenge. Shortly after annexation, the city council made whiteness a requirement for voting with a statute reading that only those "designated by this single phrase—free and white [may vote. There is] no ambiguity in these expressions." Out on the streets, however, there was plenty of ambiguity, and as late as 1844 the fairest-skinned Creoles of color were still casting ballots. In the antebellum period this cohort of African-Americans met as the Clay Club, so named because they had all successfully managed to vote for Henry Clay in the 1844 presidential election.

Attempts to cut off the mixed-race population's growth at its source were similarly stymied. The Louisiana Civil Code of 1808 barred free biracial people from marrying whites or blacks, restricting them to marrying one another. Thus, even in its attempt to stanch Louisiana's tripartite racial scheme, the legislature recognized the local system rather than the American racial binary. Despite the new law on the books, the Catholic Church continued to quietly unite interracial couples in "marriages of conscience." Civil authorities refused to recognize these unions and the courts railed against them as "illicit connexions" and "abominations" but to little effect. In 1825, still hoping to stamp out *plaçage*, the Louisiana Civil Code made it impossible for a child of color to legally claim a white man as his or her father. But fifteen years later, when a bill was proposed to bar women of color from inheriting portions of their white lovers' estates, a

Louisiana legislator stopped it with the argument that African-American women who lived with white men were clearly faithful and virtuous enough to deserve an inheritance, since doing so now required a love that defied the law. An official ban on "quadroon balls," where wealthy white men were paired with mixed-race concubines, was passed in 1828, but it was never enforced. Officially, it was a crime for a white man to attend "dressed or masked balls composed of men and women of color" but the practice continued as an open secret.

Despite spotty enforcement, the restrictions piled up. When New Orleans became one of the first cities in the South to create a public education system, its schools were explicitly for white children only. In 1835, the New Orleans city council segregated the city's burial grounds for the first time. Henceforth, half of each cemetery was to be relegated to whites, one quarter to slaves, and one quarter to free people of color. An 1840 city ordinance required all free African-Americans to register at the mayor's office, though most mixed-race, French-speaking Creoles of color ignored the law, secure in their wealth and their close, often familial, relationships with the city's elite whites. In an attempt to better track who was white and who wasn't, in 1847 city authorities began requiring doctors and midwives to record the race of newborns and parents, ending their reliance on church baptismal records. To the civil authorities, the Catholic Church, with its Mediterranean roots and its "marriages of conscience," was notoriously unreliable and unscientific when it came to racial matters.

By the 1850s, the rising tide of American racism threatened to drown New Orleans. While an 1855 Louisiana state supreme court ruling reiterated that "there is . . . all the difference between a free man of color and a slave, that there is between a white man and a slave," it added a laundry list of caveats: "the exception[s]

of political rights, of certain social privileges, and of the obliga-
tions of jury and militia service." A pair of New Orleans city ordi-
nances passed in 1856 and 1857 aimed to stamp out the integrated
gambling halls in African-American-owned coffeehouses. Tavern
owners were even barred from allowing "white persons and colored persons [to] play cards together." Another 1857 ordinance
attempted to segregate brothel employees by race, mandating that
houses be wholly staffed by either white women or women of color;
it further specified that the white brothels be run exclusively by
white madams rather than madams of color. These segregation
laws were famously unenforced in the back of town, where people
of all colors continued to eat, drink, play, and sleep together. But,
on paper, the racial system in New Orleans was growing more
American with each passing year.

In 1858, the Supreme Court finished the decades-long erosion
of the rights of free people of color with a bang of the gavel. In
its *Dred Scott* decision, the high court revoked all rights held by
African-Americans *in toto*. From Washington, the decision cast a
long shadow over the unusual social structures and economies of
New Orleans and Charleston. If Louisiana and South Carolina
were to follow the federal logic with state-level legislation, business relations across the color line would become impossible. A
white man renting from a landlord of color could stop paying rent
with impunity, since the landlord could no longer sue him. An
African-American blacksmith could purchase a load of coal from
a white supplier, but the white man's company would be under no
obligation to actually deliver it.

Their American citizenship now revoked by the nation's highest court, few came to the defense of free people of color. In the
aftermath of John Brown's attempt to spark a slave revolt with
his raid on Harper's Ferry, Virginia, in 1859, several bills were

debated in the South Carolina legislature mandating the enslave-
ment of free African-Americans either as a punishment for certain
crimes or simply for refusing to leave the state by a certain date.
Only action by the Charleston delegation prevented its passage. In
New Orleans that same year, the local *Daily Picayune* newspaper
was a lonely voice still maintaining that "our free colored population form a distinct class from those elsewhere in the United
States. Far from being antipathetic to the whites, they have followed in their footsteps. . . . [T]he 'creole colored people,' as they
style themselves . . . are a sober, industrious and moral class, far
advanced in education and civilization." But there were precious
few defenders left.

With the election in 1860 of Abraham Lincoln, a president
pledged to halting the expansion of slavery, an emergency political
convention was called in Charleston. On December 20, South Carolina issued a secession ordinance. With all the grandiosity South
Carolina's puffed-up aristocracy could muster, the proclamation
concluded, "The union now subsisting between South Carolina
and other States, under the name 'The United States of America,'
is hereby dissolved."

Four days later, the convention released its "Declaration of the
Immediate Causes Which Induce and Justify the Secession of
South Carolina from the Federal Union." It listed many reasons,
including that the Northern states "have denounced as sinful the
institution of slavery [and elected] a man to the high office of President of the United States, whose opinions and purposes are hostile
to slavery." But, clinging to Charleston's waning and ever more
anomalous tradition as a city where slaveholders were not universally white, the declaration never explicitly mentioned race.

In March 1861, with Lincoln inaugurated and a shooting war
looming, it fell to the Georgia-born vice president of the Confederacy to explicitly give voice to the race-based nature of the new
regime. In a speech delivered in Savannah, Alexander Hamilton

Stevens, a man so unimpeachably white he was nicknamed "The Little Pale Star from Georgia," proposed that the United States of America had been founded upon Thomas Jefferson's big lie that all men are created equal. And the new Confederacy would be a corrective to it.

As Stevens intoned,

> The prevailing ideas entertained by him [Jefferson] and most of the leading statesmen at the time of the formation of the old constitution, were that the enslavement of the African was in violation of the laws of nature; that it was wrong in principle, socially, morally, and politically. It was an evil they knew not well how to deal with, but the general opinion of the men of that day was that, somehow or other in the order of Providence, the institution would be evanescent and pass away. . . . These ideas, however, were fundamentally wrong. They rested upon the assumption of the equality of races. This was an error. . . .
>
> Our new government is founded upon exactly the opposite idea; its foundations are laid, its corner-stone rests, upon the great truth that the negro is not equal to the white man; that slavery subordination to the superior race is his natural and normal condition. . . .
>
> Anti-slavery fanatics . . . assume that the negro is equal, and hence conclude that he is entitled to equal privileges and rights with the white man. If their premises were correct, their conclusions would be logical and just but their premise is wrong; their whole argument fails.

For the free people of color of Charleston and New Orleans, this was terrifying rhetoric. How long could their self-conception that they weren't "negros" but "Browns" and "Creoles of color" placate bald-faced white supremacists like Stevens? Perhaps, they gambled, their last best hope of reclaiming their eroded rights lay in definitively proving themselves loyal to their states' white power structures by supporting the Confederacy. As the South left the Union, the Charleston Browns and New Orleans Creoles of color embarked on a path as unlikely Confederates, but they soon found themselves pushed into a new and pivotal role.

2.

STRANGE CONFEDERATES

Confederate general Pierre Gustave Toutant Beauregard
of New Orleans after the Civil War.

(Photography Collection, Miriam and Ira D. Wallach Division of Art, Prints and Photo-

graphs, The New York Public Library, Astor, Lenox and Tilden Foundations)

The secession crisis deepened in early 1861 as Mississippi, Florida, Alabama, Georgia, Louisiana, and Texas followed South Carolina out of the Union. Charleston remained the cradle of the rebellion. Locals had convinced themselves that they were no longer part of the United States—indeed that the United States itself had been dissolved—and they wanted the federal presence excised from their city. Viewed from the verandahs on the Battery, the federal garrison on Fort Sumter, the tiny manmade island at the gateway to Charleston harbor, looked like a bothersome mosquito that could be easily flicked off the map.

Fort Sumter was truly vulnerable; fewer than a hundred federal troops were stationed on it. But they were commanded by an experienced veteran of the Mexican-American War, Major Robert Anderson, a onetime slaveholder from Kentucky who remained loyal to the Union. To oust Anderson and his modest crew, the newly tapped Confederate president, Jefferson Davis, sent a Louisiana Creole named Pierre Gustave Toutant (P. G. T.) Beauregard. The Union major on whom Beauregard now fixed his cannon's sights had taught him the science of artillery at West Point. He had been Beauregard's favorite teacher.

Anderson had trained Beauregard well; the cadet graduated second in his class. This achievement was all the more impressive for a south Louisianan for whom West Point constituted an immersion program in Anglo-American culture. Beauregard had been born in 1818 on a Mississippi River sugarcane plantation named Contreras and baptized in St. Louis Cathedral in New Orleans's

French Quarter, twenty miles away. His father, Jacques Toutant-Beauregard, traced his roots to medieval France. The dark features of his petite mother were explained away by her ostensible Italian roots. Though her family had immigrated to Louisiana from France, they claimed to be a branch of the De Reggios, a noble family in Italy. At Contreras, young Pierre was raised by an enslaved Caribbean-born wet nurse and when he learned to speak, as a toddler, it was in French. Pierre inherited his mother's dark features. Though accepted as a "white Creole" by lineage, he was physically darker than many of the region's Creoles of color.

Born fifteen years after Louisiana was sold to the United States, Pierre grew up wary of the *Américain* interlopers but cognizant of their ascendance. At age eleven, Pierre's father transferred him from a Francophone private school in New Orleans to a French-language school in New York City. Living in New York as an adolescent, Pierre finally learned to speak English. Upstate at West Point, hoping to better blend in with the Anglos, he dropped the hyphen in his name, enrolling as cadet Toutant Beauregard rather than Toutant-Beauregard. The assimilationist Pierre had no interest in remaining a hyphenated American. Still, Beauregard's exotic background remained a source of ribbing from his Anglo classmates. They dubbed their diminutive co-cadet "Little Creole," "Little Frenchman," and the redundant, "Little Napoleon." (In truth, standing five feet seven inches, Beauregard had a good inch on *le petit caporal*.) After graduation, Beauregard married the aristocratically named Marie Antoinette Laure Villeré. It was a savvy match. The bride was of unimpeachable French Creole stock—her grandfather had been governor of Louisiana—but she didn't look it. With her fair complexion and light eyes, she possessed what one Jim Crow–era Beauregard biographer called "unusual coloring for a Creole. [a racial] deviation from type." Villeré would bear Pierre three children before her untimely death nine years into the marriage. But despite Marie Antoinette's all-*Américain* features, the descendants took after Pierre. Late-nineteenth-century portraits of the Beauregard clan are dotted with racially unplaceable children—one could be, perhaps, a Gulf Arab, another a Central Asian. Ascending the ranks, Beauregard, with his bronzed skin and regal cheekbones, looked more like a general from a Mexican army than an American one.

As a Union resupply ship steamed towards Fort Sumter, Beauregard ordered his old professor to surrender. Anderson refused. Acting on direct orders from Jefferson Davis, at 4:30 a.m. on April 12, 1861, Beauregard had his men fire the first shot of the rebellion. Over the next thirty-three hours, Beauregard fixed his dark eyes on the redbrick speck out in the harbor and used the skills Anderson had taught him to send thousands of shells flying towards the fort. The elite of Charleston gathered on their Battery porches and out along the waterfront to cheer on what they regarded as little more than a charming antifederal fireworks display.

On April 14, Anderson surrendered. Confederate boats streamed out to secure the fort. Franklin J. Moses Jr., an ambitious young man who had studied at South Carolina College and now worked as a private secretary to the state's secessionist governor, bragged that he personally pulled down the American flag.

Moses was a rather typical Charlestonian but he made for a strange Confederate. His mother was of Scotch-Irish stock, the most common ethnicity among white Southerners, but his father came from a prominent Charleston Jewish family. Moses's father, a wealthy Charleston-born attorney and state senator, took pains to downplay his Jewish roots. He had changed his name from Franklin Israel Moses to Franklin J. Moses, and his son, Franklin J. Moses Jr., was raised in his mother's Methodist faith. Junior wanted desperately to be rid of his ethnic otherness but, with the last name Moses, his options were limited. Practicing Christianity changed little in the nineteenth century, when Jewish identity was largely seen in racial terms. As an 1860s Charleston *Courier* anthropological report on "The Hebrew Race" made plain, Jews were members of the "oriental races." Even when Junior married a Christian, in 1869, and adopted her Episcopalianism, his bigoted mother-in-law barred him from setting foot in her home.

During the sectional crisis, one of the best ways to dispel suspicions about one's racial otherness was to openly and loudly support the Confederate cause. In the antebellum period, Moses had been a rabid supporter of secession, a "fire-eater" in the terminology of the time. Moses would spend the war defending Charleston harbor from the Yankees as an artillery lieutenant.

Charleston's biracial elite, under tremendous pressure from their white neighbors and relatives, reacted similarly. Just three weeks after South Carolina's secession ordinance was issued, several dozen prominent free men of color signed a letter alerting the mayor of Charleston and governor of South Carolina that they, too, backed secession. "We are by birth," they wrote,

> citizens of South Carolina, in our veins is the blood of the white race in some half, in the others much more, our attachments are with you, our hopes of safety and protection is in South Carolina, our allegiance is due alone to her, in her defense we are willing to offer up our lives and all that is dear to us, we therefore take the liberty of asking the privilege of volunteering our services to the State at this time, where she needs the services of all her true and devoted citizens. We are willing to be assigned to any service where we can be made useful.

The open letter received no formal response. Undeterred, individual biracial Charlestonians served the Confederacy in an ad hoc manner; roughly 150 free men of color volunteered to buttress the coastal defenses and some continued to petition to enlist. Elite Charlestonians of color also donated from their considerable wealth to the Confederate cause. In the summer of 1861, as the war intensified, the Brown Fellowship Society called a special meeting where the membership voted to support the care of wounded Confederate soldiers through a donation to the Ladies' Relief Association. In the first year of the war, wealthy members of the community donated a sum of $450.

In keeping with the city's antebellum norms, those most closely related to elite whites were the most trusted, and only they were permitted to enlist. Among the mixed-race volunteers was Charleston tailor Henry E. Hayne, the son of a white father and his free black wife, who joined the Confederate forces in July 1861. As his surname implied, young Henry was a mixed-race member of one of Charleston's leading families. His uncle was the late Robert Y. Hayne, the Charleston mayor who had gone out of his way to shield the Brown Fellowship Society from racist state laws.

In New Orleans, when Louisiana first weighed secession following Lincoln's election, Creoles of color similarly made clear where they stood. In a public statement "the free colored population (native) of Louisiana," explained that they "love their home, their property, they own slaves, and they are dearly attached to their native land, and they recognize no other country than Louisiana, and care for no other than Louisiana, and they are ready to shed their blood for her defense. They have no sympathy for Abolitionism; no love for the North, but they have plenty for Louisiana; and let the hour come [and] they will fight for her in 1861 as they fought in [the War of 1812]." The over-the-top proslavery rhetoric was, in part, an effort to ingratiate themselves with powerful whites, but could there have been a group of Southerners more loyal to their state and less loyal to America than New Orleans's Creoles of color? All of the community's problems—its eroding rights, its suspected disloyalty to the slave regime, the revocation of its citizenship—sprang from their city's unfortunate annexation by the United States in 1803.

Following the Battle of Fort Sumter, the call went out in New Orleans for rebel volunteers, and on April 21 the city's elite free men of color answered with a public announcement published in the *Daily Picayune*. Entitled "Defenders of the Native Land," it read, "We, the undersigned, natives of Louisiana, assembled in committee, have unanimously adopted the following resolutions: Resolved, That the population to which we belong, as soon as a call is made to them by the Governor of this State, will be ready to take arms and form themselves into companies for the defense of their homes, together with the other inhabitants of this city, against any enemy who may come and disturb its tranquility." Using the self-description "natives of Louisiana" rather than any reference to their varying complexions, the Creoles of color were tacitly arguing that they, with their multiethnic backgrounds and roots on many continents, were the ultimate New World people. As the creations of the New World, they were more American than the *Américains*.

The following day, nearly two thousand prosperous free people of color met at the Couvent Institute, a private Catholic school in the Marigny neighborhood, where many of them had been educated. Fifteen hundred men pledged to fight for the Confederacy and organized themselves into a regiment dubbed the Native Guards to emphasize their autochthonous nature. A week later, the city's free African-American nurses pledged their services to the Confederacy. One wealthy Creole of color, Bernard Soulié, loaned the Confederate government thousands of dollars to help finance the war effort.

On May 12, the governor of Louisiana accepted the Native Guards regiment, excited by the public relations potential in people of African descent volunteering to preserve Southern slavery. Among the mixed-race officers commanding the Native Guards was Arnold Bertonneau, the fair-skinned wine merchant who three years later would find himself in the White House lobbying the Union commander-in-chief for African-American voting rights.

White New Orleanians were mustered into a separate fighting force, but the city's "white" regiment was nearly as racially anomalous as its African-American unit. The Thirteenth Louisiana Volunteer Infantry Regiment included men with roots clear across Eurasia from Ireland in the west to China in the east and south into Latin America as well. As an aide to the colonel of the unit remarked, the Thirteenth Louisiana was "as cosmopolitan a body of soldiers as there existed upon the face of God's earth. There were Frenchmen, Spaniards, Mexicans, Dagoes, Germans, Chinese, Irishmen, and, in fact, persons of every clime known to geographers." The unit was fully bilingual, responding competently to commands issued in either English or French.

Charleston would last almost the entire war as a Confederate city, falling only in 1865 after a record-setting 545-day siege, but New Orleans was retaken by federal forces shortly after it left the Union. Just a year into the war, Union naval vessels under the torpedo-damning commander, David Farragut, entered the Mississippi at the Gulf of Mexico. With the city's "white" unit off fighting in Tennessee—the cosmopolitan Thirteenth Louisiana had just sustained heavy casualties at the Battle of Shiloh—a meager clutch of three thousand militiamen defended New Orleans. They included the Native Guards whom John L. Lewis, a former Confederate general and now the mayor of New Orleans charged with safeguarding the city, dispatched to defend their own homes. Lewis ordered them to patrol Esplanade Avenue near the riverfront, where the French Quarter meets Faubourg Marigny.

After a week of battling at the mouth of the Mississippi, Farragut's ships fought their way up the river to New Orleans. The waterway was unusually high at the time and the famously low-lying Crescent City found itself cowering beneath Farragut's gunboats as they peered down on the rooftops from over the Mississippi River levee. With New Orleans's defenders hopelessly outgunned,

Farragut demanded surrender. Confederate authorities acceded but laid the groundwork for an insurgency, ordering all Confederate militia, including the Native Guards, to disband, destroy their uniforms, and hide their guns in their homes. The Creole of color unit assured the Confederate leadership it would comply, but its troops quietly weighed their loyalties.

On May 1, 1862, New Orleans was placed under the military administration of Major General Benjamin Franklin Butler, a New England native who had opposed Lincoln's election and had long supported the tortuous compromises between the slave states and the free states. In the crucible of the war, Butler's views on slavery and race were being transformed. At the outset of the conflict, Butler commanded a federal fort in Hampton Roads, Virginia. Though careful to avoid the issue of emancipation, the question was forced on him when three runaway slaves who had been hired out by their masters to build Confederate fortifications ran off to his base. Returning the men to their owners would undoubtedly aid the opposing army, so Butler declared the runaways "contraband of war" and put them to work on his own fortifications. Congress soon formalized this "contraband" policy as a strategy to strip the South of its labor force. As word spread that slaves who made it to Union lines would not be returned to their masters, runaways from plantations all over the Virginia Tidewater began to bolt for Butler's famed "Freedom Fort." In short order, Union installations all over the South were flooded with self-emancipated runaways. The contraband policy, envisioned as a temporary strategic war measure, would become the first crack in the war's shattering of American slavery.

In occupied New Orleans, unrepentant white Confederates reviled Butler over his infernal Freedom Fort and they mocked the obese general, with his crossed eyes and bald pate, as "The Beast." But to the Creoles of color, the new power in New Orleans offered cause for hope. The Native Guards had always been ill-fitting Confederates. Many powerful white Southerners, particularly those beyond New Orleans, had long been skeptical of their loyalty, even of their humanity. Earlier in the war, when white Union POWs were unloaded on the New Orleans docks for imprisonment, the Native Guards were barred from standing watch over them on racial grounds. A white Louisiana militia leader insisted it would be fine, given the unique racial traditions of the city, but out-of-state Confederates overruled him. They felt that publicly exalting African-American Southerners over white men—even Yankee enemies—could weaken the racist cornerstone upon which the Confederacy stood. Facing such disdain from their ostensible allies during the war, the Native Guards hoped this new general from Massachusetts would treat them more respectfully. As the white militiamen hid their guns in their homes and blended into the civilian population or fell back to continue the fight in the countryside, the Native Guards did neither.

Reading his intelligence reports drawn from Southern newspapers' propagandistic coverage of the Native Guards, General Butler initially assumed the troops would be rabid Confederates. But when he first met an officer from the unit, Charles St. Manat—by trade, a translator of French, English, Spanish, and German—Butler began to wonder. He called a meeting with the unit's officers where they inquired "what disposition they [should] make of their arms." They were offering to switch sides. Cognizant of Lincoln's delicate balancing act—the president's insistence that the war was being fought to put down the rebellion, not to abolish slavery, let alone bring equal rights to all Americans—Butler stalled for time.

The Union general still didn't know quite what to make of these men. Until the war, Butler's experience with African-Americans had been limited. Growing up in overwhelmingly white New England, race was largely an abstraction to him. In Virginia, the illiterate slaves fleeing to his fort played right into his preconceived notions of Yankee paternalism and noblesse oblige. In New Orleans, for the first time, he met African-Americans who could see and raise him in education, erudition, and wealth.

A few weeks into his rule over New Orleans, Butler began to take the measure of the city's unusual social landscape. Writing to his superior in Washington, Secretary of War Edwin Stanton, General Butler explained New Orleans's puzzling racial reality. "In color, nay, also in conduct," Butler wrote, "they [the Creoles of color] had much more the appearance of white gentlemen than some of those who have favored me with their presence claiming to be the 'chivalry' of the South."

Over the first long summer of occupation, the mixed-race population reached out to Butler while the white elite shunned him. Over a seven-course banquet served on silver, the Creole of color community gained the portly officer's ear. The wealthy host of the fête vowed to Butler that he would commit himself and all he had to the cause of equal rights: "I only wish to spend what I have, and fight as long as I can, if only my boy may stand in the street equal to a white boy when the war is over."

Impressed with the free people of color and disgusted by the intransigence of the city's revanchist whites, Butler wrote north in a letter to his wife, "I am changing my opinions. There is nothing of the [white] people worth saving. I am inclined to give it all up to the blacks."

In August, when the city was threatened with an imminent invasion from Confederate forces near Baton Rouge, Butler finally accepted the Native Guards' request to fight for the Union. Butler welcomed the unit with an order reading, "Appreciating their motives, relying upon their 'well-known loyalty and patriotism,' and with 'praise and respect' for these brave men, it is ordered that all the members of the Native Guards aforesaid and all other free colored citizens . . . who shall enlist in the volunteer service of the United States shall be duly organized by the appointment of proper officers, and accepted, paid, equipped, armed, and rationed as are other volunteer troops of the United States, subject to the approval of the President of the United States."

Seizing the opportunity afforded by Butler, the community found its voice in a way it hadn't since New Orleans's uncomfortable annexation to the United States six decades prior. The idea that their children might stand equal to white children when the war was over no longer seemed entirely quixotic. That September, three men with mixed-race Haitian roots launched *L'Union*, a biweekly French newspaper that proclaimed itself the *"progressiste"* (progressive) "organ of the free colored population." Paul Trévigne, a biracial language teacher at the Couvent Institute, who had been born to a Spanish father in 1825, was tapped to be its editor. Louis Charles Roudanez served as publisher. Like his older brother Jean Baptiste, who would go to Washington to lobby President Lincoln in 1864, Louis Charles was the Louisiana-born son of a wealthy French merchant and Aimée Potens, a free woman of color. For his education, Louis Charles had been dispatched to Paris in an era when virtually every institution of higher learning in America was either tacitly or explicitly for whites only. In France, Louis Charles earned a Bachelor of Arts in 1847, a Bachelor of Science in 1849, and a medical degree in 1853, training at the prestigious Faculté de Médecine de Paris, arguably the world's top medical school at the time.

Living in Paris was a liberating experience for Roudanez as it would be for future generations of African-American expatriates. In the French capital Roudanez was schooled not only in medicine but in politics. When a revolt broke out, in 1848, to restore democracy in France and make good on the much-neglected promises of *Liberté, Egalité, Fraternité!*, Roudanez had helped man the barricades.

Returning to the United States, Roudanez initially settled in liberal New England rather than the ever more reactionary South, earning a second medical degree at Dartmouth College in New Hampshire in 1857. But when his native New Orleans fell to the Union in 1862, Roudanez immediately saw the potential for a new birth of freedom. The physician returned promptly to assist with the delivery.

On New Year's Day, 1863, President Lincoln issued the Emancipation Proclamation. Because it applied only to slaves in Confederate areas still beyond federal control (i.e., the only slaves Lincoln lacked the power to actually free), the executive order literally did nothing. But figuratively, it changed everything. The Civil War had begun as a war of necessity to preserve the Union; now it was being transformed into a moral crusade to end slavery. Could it be expanded further, as Creoles of color in New Orleans hoped, into a war for equal rights?

To the elite Creoles' dismay, the white Yankees who occupied New Orleans treated all people of color as if they were somehow beneath them. While those who had been born free before the war had long been understood on the streets of New Orleans as a biracial middle class, to the rest of America, they were simply black people. That winter, when Lincoln replaced General Butler with the more conservative General Nathaniel Banks, a former governor of Massachusetts, even the limited progress made during the early occupation period was reversed.

Trenchant observers were beginning to see that after the war either all African-Americans would get equal rights or none would. That summer, the equal rights agitation of *L'Union* was joined by activism in the streets. Pro-Union citizens seized on the symbolism of the Fourth of July to publicly model the egalitarian society they hoped to build. New Orleans being New Orleans, the organizers of the Independence Day event planned a Saturday night to remember. The rally-cum-rolling-street-party was organized by the Loyal National League of Louisiana, a white-run group that had opposed secession and drew its membership from the city's mix of Northern-born migrants, international immigrants, and heterodox Southerners. The group erected a grandstand at the base of Canal Street, where the parallel Anglophone and Francophone cities met, designed by "the indefatigable J. R. Terry, [a] decorator [of] matchless taste and art." As night fell, a torchlight parade to Canal Street, complete with marching bands and an array of red, white, and blue banners, led to a feast of "twelve bacon hogsheads."

After several white speakers warmed up the crowd—including one German immigrant who addressed the audience in his native tongue—Reverend James Keelan, a local black preacher, took the podium. It was, according to the organizers, "the first time on any public occasion in the South, among white men, a colored man spoke to a public audience like a man."

Keelan opened his speech by noting that African-Americans had served in the military in every war going back to the Revolution, yet they had been denied equal rights. "Fellow citizens, this is the first time for eighty seven years that the son of Africa is permitted to join in a public celebration of the Fourth of July—yet he had the right, according to the Declaration of Independence," Keelan intoned, invoking Thomas Jefferson's treatise officially adopted that very day four score and seven years ago. As Keelan saw it, the nation had given African-Americans equality when it declared to the world the self-evident truth that all men are created equal. Now was the time to finally seize it. "Our country has given us our rights—we have now but to defend them," he proclaimed.

At the conclusion of the rally, one of the Loyal National League leaders requested three cheers for Abraham Lincoln. In response, "white men and women, and black men and women, shout[ed] aloud in concert, in recognition of the glorious patriot." But in Washington, even Lincoln was loath to grant African-Americans full and equal rights out of his own skepticism of racial equal-

ity and worries about white backlash in the North. Just a week
after the integrated rally in New Orleans, white rioters rampaged
through the North's largest city lynching random black men whom
they blamed for the war.

And backlash was building in New Orleans as well. Months
before, General Butler had ordered local streetcar lines to desegregate their trolleys, but the transit companies had gotten sympathetic local courts to overrule him. And when a Creole of
color mother demanded that Butler desegregate the city schools,
recalcitrant school board officials got him to back off. Now General Banks was forcing African-American officers in the Native
Guards to resign. And ominously, Banks would oversee the process of Louisiana rejoining the Union, beginning with an election
for delegates to write a new state constitution. Banks pointedly
ignored a request from the Creole of color community to permit
those who had been free before the war to vote. Hoping to have the
general overruled, community leaders resolved to lobby Banks's
commander in chief, Abraham Lincoln.

Activists Jean Baptiste Roudanez and Arnold Bertonneau drew
up their petition addressed "To His Excellency Abraham Lincoln
President of the United States and to the Honorable [members of]
the Senate and House of Representatives of the United States of
America" and circulated it for signatures among their fellow elite
Creoles of color. The petition emphasized the community's wealth
("a large portion of them [the signers] are owners of real-estate
and all of them are owners of personal property") as well as their
United States military service dating back to the War of 1812. Taking pains to gloss over the community's wavering in the current
conflict, the petition characterized its signers as unceasingly loyal
to the Union ("[we have] rall[ied] under the banner of union and
liberty . . . spilled [our] blood, and are still pouring it out for the
maintenance of the Constitution of the United States."). Despite
this vaunted loyalty, the petition noted, "[we] have . . . until the

era of the present rebellion been estranged and even, repulsed, excluded from all rights, from all franchises." Most crucially, the petition demanded voting rights only for "citizens of Louisiana of African descent, born free before the rebellion," pointedly excluding the newly emancipated.

The authors of the petition, Roudanez and Bertonneau, whose signatures appeared above the rest, resolved to personally deliver it to the president in Washington. At the send-off for the pair on January 19, 1864, a white abolitionist Union officer exhorted the crowd: "We are passing through a revolution" that would only be resolved with a firm, nationwide acceptance of "the principle that all men are born free and equal." Yet this radical position went beyond the more modest demand of the Creoles' petition. As America's most famous abolitionist, William Lloyd Garrison, lamented, the Crescent City's Creoles of color, "with all their admirable qualities, have not yet forgotten that they were, themselves, slaveholders [and they remain] hostile to the black, except as slaves." Arriving in Washington, Bertonneau and Roudanez were pressed by another leading white abolitionist, Massachusetts senator Charles Sumner, to go beyond the limited text of their petition and demand universal male suffrage regardless of race, color, or previous condition of servitude.

A bushy-haired, Harvard-educated Boston Brahmin, Sumner had long been committed to the cause of equal rights. It was the family tradition. His father, also a Harvard-educated attorney, had scandalized Boston society by opposing antimiscegenation laws. As a young lawyer himself, in 1845, Charles had taken up the case of Sarah Roberts, a five-year-old African-American girl. Sarah had tried to enroll at the closest elementary school to her Boston home but was turned away because it was for whites only. Sumner took her case to the Massachusetts Supreme Court and lost—but he continued the fight for equal rights in Congress, as a "Radical Republican," the most egalitarian wing of the party. If equal rights were unpopular in Boston, they were toxic in Washington. In 1856, South Carolina congressman Preston Brooks beat Sumner unconscious on the Senate floor in retaliation for a fierce antislavery speech. But when the Southern fire-eaters abandoned their seats in Congress through secession, radicals like Sumner attained more power than they had ever imagined possible.

Pressed by Sumner, Bertonneau and Roudanez agreed to ask Lincoln for universal male suffrage. In the White House, as Roudanez later reported, Lincoln was sympathetic to the request but informed the gentlemen that he could only make a decision based on military and political pragmatism, not the demands of morality. Lincoln's letter, sent the next day to Louisiana governor Michael Hahn, urging him to bestow the right to vote on "very intelligent . . . colored people" and Union veterans, did not sway the governor. When the election for delegates to the constitutional convention was held, only whites were permitted to cast ballots. Winning equal rights would take more than backroom negotiations in the White House.

Still, the encounter with Sumner had broadened the visitors' vision for postwar equality. Speaking at a dinner of abolitionists in Boston a few weeks after meeting with Lincoln, Bertonneau now demanded equal rights for all. To the applause of the crowd, Bertonneau offered, "We ask that, in the reconstruction of the State Government there [in Louisiana], the right to vote shall not depend on the color of the citizen; that the colored citizen shall have and enjoy every civil, political and religious right that white citizens enjoy; in a word, that every man shall stand equal before the law."

Back in New Orleans, the broadsheet *L'Union* made the same argument. Editor Paul Trévigne penned a column urging the abolition of slavery in Louisiana and, in the same breath, the enfranchisement of the newly freed alongside those born free. "United, we stand! Divided, we fall!," Trévigne intoned.

Events soon proved the editor right beyond his wildest imag-
ination. That summer, General Banks ordered a 7:30 p.m. curfew imposed on all African-Americans in the city, regardless of
whether they were enslaved or free. On a night in August, several
prominent Creoles of color, among them Jean Baptiste Roudanez
and Paul Trévigne, were detained for being out after curfew. The
humiliation was shocking and its message was clear: New Orleans
was becoming an ordinary American city in which race would be
black or white and would trump class every time.

In early activist gatherings in Louisiana, elite biracial individuals had been so overrepresented that the meetings were dubbed
"black and tan conventions." At the 1863 founding of the state's
Republican Party, not a single African-American delegate had
ever been a slave and all were, as W. E. B. Du Bois would later put
it, "nearly white." But even as antebellum free people of color continued to take the lead in politics, they began to fight for the rights
of all. It had become clear that split off from the freedmen, Creoles
of color would most certainly fall.

The successor paper to *L'Union*, the bilingual *New Orleans Tribune*, demanded voting rights for both the freemen and the freedmen. As it explained in an editorial late in the war, "[Just as] we
assert[ed] that the sons and grand sons of the colored men who
were recognized French citizens, under the French rule, and whose
rights were reserved in the treaty of cession—taken away from
them since 1803—are not savages and uncivilized inhabitants of
the wild swamps of Louisiana [so] we contend that the freedmen
who proved intelligent enough to shed their blood in defense of
freedom and the National Flag, are competent to cast their votes
in the ballot-box."

The demise of slavery necessitated an alliance, perhaps even a
merger, between the two communities despite their disparate histories and experiences. As the *Tribune* explained with more than

a pinch of paternalism, "These two populations equally rejected and deprived of their rights, cannot be well estranged from one another. The emancipated will find, in the old freemen, friends ready to guide them . . . and teach them their duties as well as their rights. . . . The freemen will find in the recently liberated slaves a mass to uphold them." The editorialists understood that the "very peculiar situation" in Louisiana created rare opportunities. "In every other State," they wrote, pointedly ignoring the parallel situation in South Carolina, "we find only friendless and guideless emancipated slaves, or—as in the Northern States— a handful of freemen, entirely isolated, and wanting in numerical force and power." This "idea of uniting in a single unity the whole colored population of this republic," the paper predicted, "is a grand conception, full of momentous results, which will only be justly appreciated in the future."

In Charleston, even unchallenged Confederate power couldn't stop mixed-race soldiers from switching sides in the war. Henry Hayne, who had joined the Confederate ranks just weeks after Fort Sumter, ran to Union lines in July 1862. He later claimed he had always planned to fight for the Union—that he had only enlisted with the Confederates in order to get to the front to defect. When the First South Carolina Volunteers was founded in the recaptured Sea Islands in 1863, Hayne joined this Union unit of African-American Southerners commanded by white abolitionist Colonel Thomas Wentworth Higginson. Hayne rose to the rank of commissary sergeant, a respected position reserved for literate soldiers.

The Union started shelling Charleston from the sea in August 1863, but it was not until February 17, 1865, in the waning days of the war, that Confederate forces finally abandoned the city. The first Union troops to enter Charleston were African-Americans— the 21st U.S. Colored Infantry—and on February 18 the mayor formally surrendered Charleston to the unit's white commander. Though the war would rage for two more months before General Lee's surrender at Appomattox, the fall of the city where the conflict had begun was of tremendous symbolic significance. That it fell to African-American troops, some of them singing the abolitionist anthem, "John Brown's Body," as they marched into town, only underscored its meaning. By this point, all understood that the war had become a crusade to end slavery.

The progression from celebrating emancipation to demanding full racial equality was swift in the occupied city, much to the dismay of Charleston's reactionary and embittered white elite. It was as if the slowly escalating activist demands of the past three years in New Orleans were telescoped into a few weeks in Charleston. Three days after the mayor's surrender, a black soldier rode a mule down Meeting Street proclaiming emancipation with a simple banner reading "Liberty." A month later, the city's African-American community marched en masse down a two-and-a-half-mile route, demanding far more. The procession, which included nearly two thousand schoolchildren, still included antislavery placards ("We know no masters but ourselves") but others went further. Some signs called for full equality ("Equal rights") and others for the end of racism, even of race itself ("We know no caste or color!"). On March 30, 1865, with the war still being fought, the leaders of the city's centuries-old free people of color community met and pledged their support for the Union, openly declaring their opposition to the Confederacy many of them had initially backed. The early reticence of antebellum free people of color to associate with those they dismissed as upstarts, the "parvenue free," quickly abated.

Outside observers immediately saw Charleston's astounding potential. As one New England abolitionist who moved to the city to aid the freedmen and would later serve as the city's first Republican mayor observed at this moment, "Charleston ha[s] the facilities for a better civilization than it knew, or practiced." An

African-American Bostonian traveling through the South after
the war similarly noted the unique possibilities for urban progress. "There is among our people that abiding faith in justice of
their cause which enables them to look to the future, not only with
confidence but with exultation. This is the feeling of our people
in the cities," he reported back to his Northern brethren. But his
optimism dimmed as he cast his gaze on the rural South. "With
the dwellers in the country, it is different," he lamented. "Away
from the cities the condition of the colored man is deplorable [and]
he is still almost completely at the mercy of his old master. . . .
The power of organized effort which may be available in the city
is denied to him." Unsurprisingly, many rural freedmen moved to
Southern cities after the war, hoping to begin a new life beyond the
gaze of their embittered former owners.

A week after Lee's surrender, the Union authorities in Charleston held a ceremony to formally rehoist the Stars and Stripes over
Fort Sumter. It was exactly four years to the day after Franklin J.
Moses Jr. pulled it down. The honor of raising the federal flag went
to Major Robert Anderson, the officer who had surrendered the
fort in 1861. As the Stars and Stripes went up the pole, one white
officer broke down, moved to tears that, as he put it, "now for the
first time [it] is the black man's as well as the white man's flag."
Soon all loyal Americans would be in tears. That night, President
Lincoln went to Ford's Theater, where John Wilkes Booth assassinated him in a violent bid to stop the president's plan for what
Booth derisively dubbed "nigger citizenship."

The next morning, Lincoln was dead and the meaning of the war
unresolved. Slavery was no more, but whether equality would
reign was in dispute. And if not, how would it work? Would a distinction remain between the freemen and the freedmen? Would
there be a continuum of power and prestige running from light
to dark as had been practiced in earlier times in Charleston and

New Orleans? Or would there be a strict color line drawn between the ostensibly "black" and the supposedly "white"?

As freedmen flocked to Charleston hoping to enjoy their new-found liberty and seek their fortunes, biracial elites initially hoped to preserve their mixed identities and social status above those of the former slaves. One white Northern woman who came to Charleston with the abolitionist American Missionary Association noted that "many of the 'brown people' here, think they are a great deal better than those who were slaves; and whenever you meet them, they are sure to tell you, that they were free." When African-American Charlestonians initially began to press for equal rights, mixed-race people of more modest means took the lead while the wealthiest and most established Browns stayed home. Not one of the fifteen richest African-Americans in Charleston showed up for any of the political gatherings held during the autumn of 1865. And the Brown Fellowship Society continued to meet, suggesting their biracial self-understanding had made it through the war intact. As one member wrote, the Fellowship's "foundation-stone [is] Charity and Benevolence [but] its capstone [is] Social Purity." By contrast, in the wake of emancipation a rival organization, the Society of Free Dark Men rebranded itself in universalist terms as the Humane Brotherhood.

In tandem with the influx of freedmen to the cities of the South came an influx of thousands of white Confederate veterans. The rural South's economy had been upended by war and emancipation; if there was any hope of economic growth it was in an industrialized, urbanized New South. The white veterans brought with them their dichotomous notions of whiteness and blackness, having no familiarity with the heterodox port city racial systems that had reigned before the war. Their outlook was echoed by the white Northern troops who arrived as an army of occupation. As one of Charleston's leading African-American preachers complained of the racist Union troops who were supposedly protecting his community, "It appears that all the jail birds of New York, and the inmates of [Philadelphia's] Moyamensing [prison] had been left in this State to guard the freedmen's interest. No southern white man in Charleston, has heaped as much insult upon colored females passing the streets, as those foul-throated scamps who guard this city." Postwar federal occupation would complete the long-delayed Americanization of Charleston and New Orleans.

The savviest among Charleston's Browns understood immediately that they stood to become the biggest losers of the Civil War if Confederate defeat left an unequal society based on a black/white binary. To prevent such a fate, the Charleston Brown community began to follow the same path New Orleans's Creoles of color had trod during the war and unambiguously demand equal rights for all. As a reporter for *The Nation* visiting South Carolina shortly after Appomattox noted, "The old jealousy between blacks and mulattoes is disappearing. [The] wealthy slaveholding mulatto families of Charleston are fully identified in interest with the mass of the colored people, and are becoming the leaders among them."

On a postwar fact-finding trip through the South with United States Supreme Court Chief Justice Salmon P. Chase, the budding journalist Whitelaw Reid reported that New Orleans's Creoles of color had fully made this transition. At a lavish dinner hosted in a New Orleans mansion, the youthful Yankee was taken by the grace and beauty of Creole women, noting that they could mix easily with European royalty even though their white neighbors wouldn't deign to dine with them. "These people were not always outcasts," Reid explained to his presumably ill-informed Northern readers:

Under the great Napoleon they were citizens of the French Empire. It was only when the flag of the free came to cover them that they were disenfranchised; only when they were transferred to a republic that they lost their political rights. Hitherto they have held themselves aloof from the slaves, and particularly from the plantation negroes; have plumed themselves upon their French descent, and thus isolated from both races, have transferred to Paris an allegiance that was rejected at Washington.

But now the community was embracing a new role as leaders of the freedmen. Over ice cream in the parlor, Reid recounted, wealthy Creoles bought raffle tickets to fund a school for children newly freed from slavery. As one of the guests "very frankly said during the evening, 'we see that our future is indissolubly bound up with that of the negro race in this country; and we have resolved to make common cause, and rise or fall with them. We have no rights which we can reckon safe while the same are denied to the fieldhands on the sugar plantations.'"

A broad coalition was forming but not without tensions. Former slaves yearned for economic change; most crucially, they sought land reform to give them ownership of the plots they had worked without pay all their lives. The biracial elite often owned land and many were wary of reparations through what they considered confiscation (though, to its credit, the *Tribune* editorialized for land redistribution). Most elites yearned for something less tangible: dignity. They wanted equal access to theaters, restaurants, and hotels—the finer things in life that few freedmen could afford. The freedmen vastly outnumbered the freemen in the state but not in the corridors of power. At the 1865 Louisiana Republican Party convention, only one of the twenty African-American delegates was a freedman. Still, there were issues all could agree on. All wanted access to schools and all needed the ballot. When the newly reconstituted legislature of Louisiana proposed a bill to enfranchise "quadroons"—biracial men with one African-American grandparent—even the Creole of color community opposed it.

If universal male suffrage were to follow the universal emancipation the war had brought, freedmen could be a powerful voting
bloc for equal rights. Louisiana and South Carolina had outright
African-American majorities, as did Mississippi. And in Louisiana
and South Carolina, this mass black constituency could be paired
with the advocacy of educated mixed-race elites in New Orleans
and Charleston to potentially win full equality. Those states would
have both the votes to pass civil rights legislation and the savvy,
prosperous people of color to enforce equality through the courts.

The demographics of the cities were only becoming more favor-
able for this type of coalition. During its long period under Union
control, wartime New Orleans attracted fifteen thousand African-
Americans running away to freedom. In the aftermath of the war,
a freedmen's influx from the plantations to Charleston returned
the city to its traditional black-majority status.

Sensing the opportunity, elite African-Americans who had
fled Charleston during its most reactionary antebellum incarna-
tion came home much as Louis Charles Roudanez had returned
to New Orleans after his years in France and New England. In
1865, Francis Lewis Cardozo, the mixed-race scion of a prominent
Charleston family, returned to his hometown to found a school for
African-American youth. Born in the late 1830s, the son of a Sephardic Jewish father and a free woman of color of mixed African-
American and Native American descent, Cardozo had begun his
education in Charleston's private academies for free children of
color and continued it in Europe. He earned a bachelor's degree
from the University of Glasgow and, having been raised Christian,
went on to attend a Protestant seminary in London. Returning
to the United States while the war raged, he settled first in New
Haven, Connecticut, where he preached at an abolitionist church
near Yale's campus. When Charleston fell to the Union, Cardozo
returned home and, with the backing of the abolitionist American Missionary Association and the newly created federal Bureau

of Refugees, Freedmen, and Abandoned Lands, helped found his Saxton School. Though Cardozo initially stocked the academy with students like himself, from what one Charleston newspaper called the city's "aristocracy of color," he was adamant that children born in slavery could achieve as much as those born free and he worked to reach them. Cardozo's ultimate goal was to create a school for teachers that would dispatch skilled instructors to the Southern countryside, bringing literacy to the emancipated masses.

Whatever the relative privilege and snobbery with which he was raised, Cardozo understood that in the new America where everyone was free, his tan skin and freeborn status would not protect him. Soon after the Saxton School opened, the old white elite made clear that they no longer distinguished between the aristocracy of color the school enrolled and ordinary freedmen. As Cardozo recounted in an 1866 letter, while teaching his elite students one day, "a prominent Rebel of the chivalrous aristocracy of South Carolina" dropped by to call the academy "a damned nuisance." Another day, "a woman, very finely dressed, and apparently quite ladylike, stopped at the door . . . while the children were singing . . . patriotic songs [like] 'rally round the flag' [and] 'John Brown's body lies a-mouldering in the grave,' . . . and said, 'Oh, I wish, I could put a torch to that building. The niggers!'"

Just as blackness expanded to fully encompass all people of traceable African descent regardless of skin color or antebellum status, whiteness too went into flux after the war—in no place more intensely than in New Orleans with its continuum of complexions from Irish to Andalusian. The Yankee soldiers stationed in New Orleans and the rural Confederate veterans who flocked there were unsure what to make of its ethnic Mediterraneans, the so-called white Creoles. As one Union soldier wrote home from the occupied city, "It is hard telling who is white here[,] the Creoles [of French and Spanish descent] are blacker than some of the mulattos." For the Mediterranean-Americans, the new instability in the racial order was ominous. If rights and status were to be doled out on a purely racial basis, even antebellum slaveholders would be at risk if they couldn't prove the purity of their bloodlines.

After the war, the most famous "white Creole" of all, Pierre Gustave Toutant Beauregard, returned to New Orleans for the first time in four years. When he arrived, it was early summer— the season when the geographic fact that New Orleans shares the 30th parallel with Cairo is at its most obvious—and the African-strength sun left its imprint on Beauregard's skin. A week into his return, the retired general went to visit his mother. He took a boat across the Mississippi River to the Algiers Point suburb and began the short walk to her home. En route, a disheveled man he didn't know, possibly a Confederate veteran and quite possibly drunk, stopped the old general in his tracks.

"Are you Beauregard?" he demanded.

Beauregard warily nodded his assent to the stranger.

"I believe you are a damn nigger," the man screamed. "I always did believe you were a nigger. Tell me if you are a nigger or not."

Beauregard did not answer.

Trailed by a hail of abuse, the man who had fired the first shot of the Civil War, a man who had once owned other men, staggered through this disconcerting new world to his mother.

3.

LEGALLY BLACK

Francis Lewis Cardozo of Charleston.

With the Holy City under Union military occupation, paranoid white Charlestonians braced for race war. Ominously, people of color were not showing deference to whites on the streets. "Insolent [African-Americans] never pretend to give place to you" one white society lady sniffed; another smarted at being "jostled by flaunting mulattos with their soldier beaux (sometimes white)." Could violent revenge for generations of humiliation be far behind?

In the absence of the intimidating plantation-pass checks of slavery times, Charleston's all-white municipal police force stepped up patrols in the blacker parts of town. Police brutality followed. African-American homes were ransacked, often at the behest of former masters who alleged that they had been robbed. With the *Dred Scott* decision still on the books, African-Americans had no rights white cops were bound to respect; these warrantless searches and seizures were perfectly legal. As for any potential race war, one African-American Charlestonian observed that it was the police who were the most likely aggressors: "They only required a little encouragement from the civil authorities to butcher us like sheep."

If the city's African-Americans were counting on the federal troops stationed in town to protect them, new developments suggested otherwise. In July 1865, white soldiers from New York sparred with their black comrades from Massachusetts in the Charleston city market.

Though the city never descended into uncontrollable violence, flare-ups were constant. One day, a groups of whites and blacks massed on the Battery waterfront like Civil War troops, "forming alignments and pelting each other with stones," as the *Charleston Daily Courier* reported. This tiny skirmish ended in a draw, but the real race war—the one in the legislature, fought with pens, not swords—would be a rout for white supremacists.

In September 1865, South Carolina held a constitutional convention to draft a post-slavery blueprint under which the state would rejoin the Union. Hewing to the precedent set by Louisiana and followed by all of the other states of the collapsed Confederacy, the delegates were chosen in a white-men-only election, and they themselves were all white men. James L. Orr, a judge who had opposed secession, openly convened the convention with a paean to "white man's government." The delegates proceeded to ignore a petition from 103 African-American Charlestonians requesting the right to vote even though the prosperous, educated petitioners were open to using literacy—just not race—as a qualification for enfranchisement. As the petition put it, "We ask not at this time that the ignorant shall be admitted to the exercises of a privilege which they might use to the injury of the State."

For the all-white convention delegates, in a new South Carolina without slaves, race would be the central social divider. The convention ordered a special committee to write laws ostensibly for the "protection and government of the colored population." When one of the committee leaders solicited advice from Edmund Rhett Jr., a Charleston newspaper editor and Confederate veteran, he advised him that "the general interest of both the white man and the negro requires that he should he kept as near to the condition of slavery as possible."

The result of the committee's work was a so-called Black Code, an entire separate legal code that would apply to African-Americans only. Modeled on legislation passed by Mississippi after the Confederate surrender, the legislature ordered the creation of two parallel judicial systems for people of different races with different rights, laws, and punishments. Separate black-people courts, overseen by whites, would adjudicate criminal cases with black defendants and civil disputes where one or more of the parties were African-American. Those convicted in these separate and unequal courts could be executed for crimes for which white convicts faced only prison time, including "stealing a horse, a mule, or baled cotton." The South Carolina Black Code deputized all whites to arrest African-Americans for any crime they allegedly witnessed and it created new blacks-only gun laws that prohibited African-Americans from keeping firearms without the written consent of a white judge.

The South Carolina Black Code also attempted to overturn the black-majority demographics of the state. New African-Americans were all but banned from migrating to the Palmetto State by a provision requiring them to secure a thousand-dollar bond within twenty days of arriving. And for the first time in its history, South Carolina banned interracial marriage. Consensual interracial sex outside of marriage was also barred under a law prohibiting African-American men from "impersonating [a white woman's] husband for carnal purposes." The penalty for such "impersonators" was death.

To the Brown community, the new laws felt like a targeted assault even if South Carolina's Black Code did not go out of its way, as Mississippi's did, in eliding the status of freemen and freedmen. (Mississippi's laws used the airtight phrasing "any freedman, free Negro, or mulatto" in its restrictions.) Though a proposal to bar people of color outright from all but manual labor was defeated, a measure requiring expensive licenses for any work besides farming or butlering passed. Under this law, African-Americans pursuing more exalted occupations had to obtain an annual license from a district court judge, at a cost ranging from $10 for mechanics to $100 for shopkeepers. The license could be revoked upon complaint; white competitors, obviously, had the clearest interest in lodging such objections. The prosperity of the biracial community in Charleston had grown out of its domination of trades like carpentry, barbering, and tailoring and the Black Code threatened their abilities to pursue those métiers. No doubt some framers of the Black Code could envision a scenario in which the antebellum free people of color became the political leaders of the state's black majority, so they treated the community as a threat.

Beyond erecting these demeaning and debilitating borders around African-American life in South Carolina, the Code explicitly defined the borders of blackness. For the first time in the history of South Carolina, blackness was given a biological definition and under it most Brown South Carolinians became officially black. According to the new race code, anyone with more than one-eighth African ancestry was legally black. This new law overrode the 1835 state supreme court decision that had treated whiteness in South Carolina as a fungible class status rather than a biological fact. Under that decision, a free, high-status Carolinian could be legally white no matter his or her complexion or ancestry. Now the antebellum free people of color, nearly all of whom had at least one great-grandparent of African descent, were legally black no matter how light their skin, how large their bank account, or how prominent their white relatives.

The assault from the all-white legislature prompted an equal and opposite reaction among Charleston's Browns. Now more than ever they united with the freedmen and threw themselves into the fight for equality. With the new constitution ratified and the Black Code taking shape in the legislature, in November 1865, African-American leaders joined together in Charleston for a statewide political convention presided over by Thomas M. Holmes, a Brown Fellowship Society member and antebellum slaveholder. Half of the delegates were Charleston locals and, of those, nineteen out of twenty-two had been free before the Civil War. Though mixed-race people who had been born free were overrepresented, there were also darker delegates present and a smattering of former slaves.

Noting the wide array of complexions, one delegate commented, "It is hard to tell where Africa ends and Caucasia commences." By the new definitions of the Black Code, however, there would be no such confusion and already at the convention the members were acting as if they had always regarded each other as one people. Even a proposal to acknowledge the tensions but blame the institution of slavery for "caus[ing] us to make distinctions among ourselves," was removed in a parliamentary maneuver by Robert Carlos DeLarge, a Brown Fellowship Society member. Like fellow convention delegate Francis Lewis Cardozo, DeLarge was the son of a mixed-race free woman of color and a Sephardic Jewish father. And like Cardozo, DeLarge's multifaceted, only-in-Charleston, Afro-Euro-Latino-Semitic identity was now being reduced in the eyes of South Carolina law to something much simpler: black.

The mixed-race elite who smarted against the economic restrictions taking shape in the Black Code dominated the convention. Being men of property, most sought a colorblind libertarian equality, not reparations and redistribution. Overruling the demands of the freedmen who were terribly underrepresented among the delegates, they buried a call for land reform. In the convention's collective public statement, a single voice came from the racial space the legislature had forced them all into: "We simply desire that we shall be recognized as men; that we have no special obstructions placed in our way; that the same laws which govern white men shall direct colored men."

Their statement positioned the demand for equal rights regardless of color as America's self-evident destiny and the nascent Black Code as the aberration. The nation had been founded on the Declaration of Independence's principle that "all men are created equal," it noted, and "that the phrase 'all men' includes the negro no one will attempt to deny." It called for the repeal of the "'negro code,' [and] any other class legislation by the State . . . that ha[s] been enacted, that apply to us on account of our color" and for its replacement by "a code of laws for the government of *all*, regardless of color." And the convention delegates now demanded universal male suffrage on the grounds that the nation's founding declaration had already set this course: "We ask that equal suffrage be conferred upon us, in common with the white men of this State . . . because 'all free governments derive their just powers from the consent of the governed.'" It was a clever retelling of American history, glossing over the inconvenient truth that the nation had spent the first half of the nineteenth century retreating from the egalitarian racial implications of its founding creed.

Two months after the convention, its leaders requested a meeting with James Orr, now the state's governor, to discuss voting rights. Only after the third request, a full year later, and after hundreds of South Carolina freedmen had sent a petition to Washington demanding equal citizenship, did the governor agree to meet his disenfranchised African-American constituents. At the Charleston gathering, Orr told them he supported a literacy test and demeaningly urged the men to educate their children so the next generation could be enfranchised. None of the petitioners could have possibly imagined how history would play out—that it would be they who would vote and their children who would not.

In New Orleans, events followed a similar script. Beyond outlawing slavery, Louisiana's new state constitution granted African-Americans no rights at all. The first loyal legislature of Louisiana, made up entirely of white Unionists, pointedly ignored a petition from five thousand African-Americans demanding the ballot. They also endeavored to halt Louisiana's centuries-old practice of race mixing by taking action to block marriage licenses from being issued to interracial couples.

The state's politics seemed to grow more reactionary by the day. In the first election after the war, the martyred president's Republican Party didn't field a single candidate, while the Democrats ran a slate of Confederate veterans who had only recently ended their

armed insurrection against the United States. The Louisiana Democrats' official platform demanded "a government of white people,
made and to be perpetuated for the exclusive political benefit of the
white race, and in accordance with the constant adjudication of the
United States Supreme Court, that the people of African descent
cannot be considered as citizens of the United States, and that
there can in no event nor under any circumstances be any equality between the whites and other races." Hoping to keep freedmen
tied to the land despite emancipation, the new legislature passed
a Black Code in all but name, which required plantation laborers
to sign year-long labor contracts each winter, presumably to farm
the same land they had worked as slaves for the very families that
had owned them. Those who remained unemployed after the con-
tracting period could be arrested for "vagrancy," whipped, and sold
into bonded labor when found in towns where they didn't live (i.e.,
conducting a job search). Not only were freedmen barred during
their one-year contracts from leaving their plantation without the
permission of their employer, they couldn't even quit for a higher-
paying job, the most basic right a worker has in a capitalist economy. Competing employers were similarly barred from offering
laborers better jobs under a newfangled crime called "enticement."

Even as freeborn mixed-race Louisianans escaped the harshest
legislation targeting their brethren in South Carolina, Louisiana
legislators' racist rhetoric and their crackdown on interracial marriage terrified them. Racial conceptions had been hardening for
decades and now mixedness in and of itself had come to be seen
as a threat. After the war, one South Carolina aristocrat blamed
the South's loss on the region's rampant antebellum race mixing:
"It does seem strange that so lovely a climate, and country, with a
people in every way superior to the Yankees, should be overrun and
destroyed by them," he mused. "I am firmly of the opinion . . . that
it is the judgment of the Almighty because the human and brute
blood have mingled to the degree it has in the slave states. Was it

not so in the French and British [Caribbean] Islands and see what
has become of them." This theory aside, most white supremacists
saw American racial purity as intact, but threatened by demands
for racial equality. As one Texas politician put it when faced with
calls for African-American enfranchisement, "If a republican form
of government is to be sustained, the white race must do it without any Negro alloy. A mongrel Mexico affords no fit example for
imitation. I desire the perpetuation of a white man's government."
Even the Great Emancipator himself seemed to share these fears.
Before his elevation to the presidency, Abraham Lincoln went on
record saying, "The separation of the races is the only perfect pre-
ventative of amalgamation." That amalgamation had already been
happening for centuries was something a politician in landlocked,
rural, slave-free Springfield, Illinois, could plausibly deny. In the
places where this reality couldn't be ignored a new racist strategy
arose after slavery: banning intermarriage, recategorizing mixed-
race people as black, and revoking their rights.

Given the mid-nineteenth-century racism that spanned both sides
of the Mason-Dixon Line, the defeated Confederates could have
sought a white man's truce. Slavery would be extinguished but
the types of restrictions that had long been imposed on free blacks
in the North—the denial of suffrage and the right to be served in
white-owned businesses—could be enforced nationwide.

Black suffrage was a nonstarter for most Northerners. Postwar
referenda on the question, held in Connecticut, Minnesota, Wis-
consin, Kansas, Nebraska, Ohio, and New York, all went down to
defeat. The extension of equal rights into public accommodations—
the demand, for example, that a private hotelier host anyone who
could pay the nightly rate regardless of color or creed—remained
controversial as well. Even in liberal Massachusetts, where the
state legislature had passed a school desegregation law in the wake
of Charles Sumner's unsuccessful Sarah Roberts suit, the state

supreme court ruled in 1866 that billiard parlors could restrict their clientele to whites only.

But when the white South reacted to the abolition of slavery by drawing up separate legal codes that attempted to keep former slaves in slavery by another name, Northern opinion grew inflamed. Winning the war had cost Northerners hundreds of thousands of lives, including that of their martyred president. Faced with the Black Codes, the *Chicago Tribune* vowed that the North would reduce Mississippi to "a frog pond before they will allow any such laws to touch one foot of soil in which the bones of our soldiers sleep."

The sticking point of the Black Codes for Northerners was not the restrictions on African-American professionals and business owners but the provisions that attempted to prevent the freedmen from participating in the labor market as white workers did. For many white Northerners, equal opportunity in a free labor market would have been a perfectly good substitute for equal political rights, but the white South would not even grant that. For the victorious Yankees, the Black Codes were an outrage.

Union military authorities remained in place in the Southern states, ostensibly to guide the South towards the resumption of civilian rule, so when South Carolina passed its draconian Black Code, the army stepped in. The general in charge was Daniel Sickles, a mustachioed upper-crust Manhattanite who had given his right leg for the Union, amputated without anesthetic at Gettysburg. With Lincoln now assassinated for his "new birth of freedom," Sickles would be damned if the South reversed the results of the war with cynical legalese. Using his military authority, in January 1866 Sickles nullified the state's Black Code mere months after it was passed.

But Lincoln's assassination had brought to power a man who would never see eye to eye with Sickles. A Southerner who had opposed secession, Andrew Johnson had initially been tapped by

Lincoln to serve as military governor of retaken portions of his native Tennessee during the war. In the 1864 election campaign, Johnson became Lincoln's running mate. After ascending to the presidency courtesy of John Wilkes Booth's crime, Johnson saw nothing objectionable in the Black Codes. A bundle of resentments barely held together by his trademark black bowties, the only people Johnson loathed more than white Southern aristocrats were their former slaves.

Born to illiterate parents so poor they sold him at age ten to a tailor for a decade-long term of indentured servitude, young Andrew grew up resentful of free white Southerners who had inherited land and slaves. All that separated him from those doomed to lifelong captivity was his white skin, and he grew proud of it. Even when Johnson became rich enough to purchase slaves himself—he ultimately owned eight people, including the three mulatto children of his first slave, Dolly, who were rumored to be his progeny—the class-born anger of his youth festered. For Johnson, the war had been fought to destroy the South's disloyal aristocracy, not to bring forth racial equality. As he declared during the conflict, "Damn the Negroes, I am fighting those traitorous aristocrats, their masters."

Johnson's racism was visceral and most sharply directed at African-Americans who had achieved greatness despite long odds. When President Lincoln pointed out Frederick Douglass to Johnson at their 1865 inauguration, the new vice president sneered at the famed African-American abolitionist. As Douglass later recounted, "The first expression which came to his face, and which I think was the true index of his heart, was one of bitter contempt and aversion. Seeing that I observed him, he tried to assume a more friendly appearance, but it was too late."

The Black Codes squared neatly with Johnson's views, and this set him on a collision course with Northern public opinion and with Congress. Despite Lee's surrender, Congress remained an all-

Northern institution. When elections had been held in the postwar South on a whites-only basis, voters had sent an array of Confederate veterans—including ten generals and the Confederate vice president Alexander Stevens—to Washington to represent them. The Constitution permits Congress to determine the qualifications for its own membership, so the Northern congressmen, loath to welcome representatives who months earlier had been fighting a war against the United States, refused to seat them. By excluding the Southerners, Congress gave itself carte blanche to pass any racially egalitarian law it committed itself to, over the veto of Andrew Johnson, if necessary.

In one of its first actions, the new Congress voted to extend the life of the federal Bureau of Refugees, Freedmen, and Abandoned Lands, which Lincoln had authorized for just a single year at the end of the war. Commonly known as the Freedmen's Bureau, the agency helped newly freed slaves obtain food, shelter, and clothing. It also provided education through a network of schools largely staffed by white abolitionists and freeborn people of color. To Johnson, the Bureau was a temporary wartime measure; he vetoed the bill, arguing that, in peacetime, the freedmen should be self-reliant rather than "fed, clothed, educated, and sheltered by the United States." Undaunted, Congress quickly drew up a new, nearly identical version of the bill.

Congress also nullified the Black Codes with the nation's first civil rights law. The measure granted retroactive birthright citizenship to everyone born on U.S. soil besides "Indians not taxed." Like all other citizens, it asserted, the newly freed would now have the right to make and enforce contracts, buy and sell property, sue and be sued, and testify in court. Striking at the heart of the Black Codes, it outlawed states from mandating "different punishment[s to people] who had been held in a condition of slavery." The bill dodged the controversial issue of African-American suffrage.

President Johnson vetoed the civil rights bill with an accompanying message to Congress that played on Northerners' fears of race mixing and immigration. The contracts provision, the president mused, could apply to marriage contracts, warning that laws that "no white person shall intermarry with a negro or mulatto" were squarely in the congressional crosshairs. To Johnson, perhaps hoping to stifle rumors about the nature of his relationship with Dolly through fulsome protest, this was a "revolting . . . offense against public decorum." The civil rights bill would also, Johnson noted, convey citizenship on "Gipsies" and on "the Chinese of the Pacific States," a nakedly racist way of referring to the American-born descendants of Chinese immigrants to the West Coast. Given such a radical bill, the president baited his audience, could the right to vote be far behind?

As Radical Republicans in Congress whipped the caucus to override Johnson's veto, much of the Northern press took the president's side. The *New York Herald*'s editorial on the bill bespoke a kind of institutional apoplexy. Interspersed at random throughout the newspaper's domestic coverage were rhetorical questions about a future dystopia should the civil rights bill become law.

"Shall Negroes intermingle with our refined ladies in steaming hot theaters, ball rooms and opera houses? The Civil Rights Bill declares that they must," the paper screeched.

> Shall the Negro intermarry with our daughters, and take an equal place in our households? The Civil Rights bill says that he shall. . . . Are we to have Negroes representing this government as United States ministers at the courts of England and France? The Civil Rights Bill says that we are. . . . Shall Negroes sit in Congress, in the Cabinet and other high stations side by side with white men? The Civil Rights bill says that he may. . . . Shall our children see a Negro in the

Presidential chair? The Civil Rights Bill provides for such a contingency. . . . Is this a white man's government for white men? The Civil Rights bill says that it is not.

Despite the opposition in the press, for the first time in American history Congress overrode a presidential veto on a major piece of legislation. On April 9, the Civil Rights Act of 1866 became law. In May, for good measure, Congress finished its amended Freedmen's Bureau bill and passed it over Johnson's veto. And that June, Congress drew up and quickly passed the Fourteenth Amendment that would, once ratified by three-fourths of the states, safeguard the equal-citizenship provisions of the new Civil Rights Act by enshrining them in the Constitution. The amendment would protect the Civil Rights Act from the Supreme Court by invalidating the *Dred Scott* ruling that African-Americans were not citizens. Since the Constitution assigns the president no role in the amendment process, a boxed-out Johnson could do nothing beyond publicly register his opposition.

On paper, the Black Codes had been overturned, but on the ground, equality remained elusive. In New Orleans, the *Tribune* lamented that despite the passage of the new Civil Rights Act, "Nothing has changed, no more regard is paid to-day to our rights than was before, and we have not met with a larger sense of justice than previously." In the countryside, it was even worse; white mob rule appeared intractable. In tiny Sumter, South Carolina, a black man who took a seat on the traditionally "white side" of the Spring Hall Methodist Church was assassinated. On the backwoods byways of Alabama, African-Americans who refused to halt at white men's commands were shot on sight. As one Northern-born federal official posted to Louisiana testified to Congress as it sparred with President Johnson, "The most odious features of slavery [a]re preserved [just] a hundred miles from New Orleans." Hundreds of white-on-black murders plagued the South with virtually no perpetrators ever brought to justice.

Even the cities were not immune from flare-ups of lawlessness. In May, just after the passage of the Civil Right Act, a race riot broke out in Memphis. Following a collision between two horse-drawn carriages—one driven by a white man, the other by a black man—a group of discharged African-American Union veterans, white Memphis policemen, and civilians of both races began to argue on the sidewalk. The row soon turned violent and then spread citywide. Over the next three days, Memphis erupted as white mobs, largely drawn from the city's all-white police and firefighting forces, ransacked African-American neighborhoods. Every black church in Memphis was torched and the city's small freeborn African-American elite were targeted for robbery as white muggers stole cash, watches, and jewelry. With the commander in chief indifferent to the violence gripping his home state's largest city, the federal military authorities stationed in Memphis sat on their hands. By the massacre's end, at least forty-eight African-American men, women, and children were dead and five black women raped; only two whites died. To Northerners reading the news from Tennessee, the riot made plain Johnson's complicity in the white South enforcing its own race-based mob rule.

Underscoring all that was at stake, in late July white vigilante violence broke out in New Orleans, the South's most promising candidate for racial progress. The spark was simply men of varied skin colors meeting to craft a democratic framework for governing their state. Louisiana's 1864 constitution, which barred African-Americans from voting, allowed for reconvening a constitutional convention, so activists did just that. On July 30, they opened a multiracial constitutional convention at the Mechanics Institute, the makeshift state capitol building on the *Américain* side of town.

The delegates placed African-American enfranchisement at the center of their agenda.

The forces of white supremacy seethed over the publicly announced interracial convention. One particularly reactionary outlet of the city's conservative white press threatened that the leaders of this convention of "niggers and half-niggers" would be hanged. The mayor of New Orleans, unrepentant Confederate John T. Monroe, vowed that the meeting would never take place, on the pretext that "all assemblies calculated to disturb the public peace and tranquility [are] unlawful." Monroe had first been elected in a whites-only election before the Civil War; he had been removed from office by Union authorities when they took the city in 1862 but then returned to office by the voters in the whites-only election of 1866. President Johnson let it be known that he backed Monroe in his bald-faced attempt to thwart the First Amendment speech and assembly rights of his citizenry, announcing that federal troops would "sustain the civil authority in suppressing all illegal or unlawful assemblies."

On the eve of the meeting, Mayor Monroe ordered his police force to sleep in their precinct houses. They were a battle-tested crew: over two-thirds of the all-white corps were Confederate veterans and their commander, police chief Thomas E. Adams, had served as a colonel. The local sheriff, Harry T. Hays, had been a general in Robert E. Lee's army. For the city police, the multiracial convention presented an opportunity to violently avenge their defeat on the battlefield.

As morning dawned on Monday, July 30, a rally of approximately two hundred veterans of color paraded through the French Quarter. Led by an African-American "Spirit of '76" tableau—a fife player, a drummer, and a flag bearer hoisting the banner of the Louisiana Native Guards—the marchers encountered only a few hecklers along the route; they were greatly outnumbered by supporters who cheered the parade and, in New Orleanian fashion, joined it. When the procession crossed Canal Street, the old dividing line between the Francophone, quasi-Latin American city and the more starkly racist metropole of the *Américains*, the mood turned. As the suffragists massed in front of the Mechanics Institute, inside the delegates worked on their first order of business—arranging bail bonds as a precaution should the mayor arrest them all for unlawful assembly.

Outside the hall, shortly after 10 a.m., a white mob of roughly fifteen hundred, a mix of civilians and policemen, assembled. It was virtually impossible to tell who was who. Many of the police had flipped around their hatbands, the era's version of police badges, and a sizable number of civilians had been temporarily deputized as officers for the day of the convention. One ex-Confederate colonel showed up for the confrontation in his battle grays, packing side arms.

The white mob unleashed a hail of bricks on the paraders. After initially reeling from the assault, the protesters grabbed the bricks and flung them back against the mob. A volley of gunfire erupted from the whites and the terrified marchers ran for cover inside the hall. Realizing that they now risked more than just arrest, the delegates began barricading the doors and ordered everyone to take cover under tables and desks until federal military authorities arrived. In short order, the mob broke through the doors. Delegates rushed the windows, jumping out only to be picked off by waiting snipers.

White delegates, seen as race traitors by the mob, were targeted for assassination. Michael Hahn, the Unionist Louisiana governor during the Civil War and now an active supporter of immediate African-American suffrage, sustained what a congressional report later termed an "incised wound of head." Universal suffrage advocate Anthony P. Dostie, a New York–born dentist who was among the vast cohort of white Northerners who moved to New Orleans during the boom years before the Civil War, was shot half a dozen times and then, for good measure, run through with a sword. Reverend Jotham Horton, a white man of the cloth who had given the invocation at the convention's opening that morning, was shot in cold blood while waving a white flag of surrender.

While whites were targeted for their political beliefs, African-Americans were executed solely on account of their color. Once the mob cleared the hall, vigilantes fanned out across the central business district attacking African-Americans at random on the streets, in shops, and on the city's streetcars.

It was 3 p.m. before federal military authorities showed up. By then, at least thirty-eight people had been killed—all but four of them African-American—and 184 wounded. When regional commander General Philip Sheridan returned to New Orleans from an assignment in Texas, he telegrammed his commander, General Ulysses S. Grant. "The more information I obtain . . . the more revolting it becomes," Sheridan opened, in what sounded like a dispatch from a war zone. "It was no riot; it was an absolute massacre . . . a murder which the mayor and police of this city perpetrated without the shadow of a necessity; furthermore, I believe it was premeditated."

Indeed, as one ex-Confederate rioter explained, "We have fought for four years these god-damned Yankees and sons of bitches in the field, and now we will fight them in the city." It was a textbook insurgency: an army that has surrendered on the battlefield returns home and secretly reconstitutes its units to continue the fight. Congressional investigators looking into the New Orleans Riot that winter found involvement by the Southern Cross, a secret society of Confederate veterans.

The possibility that the results of the war could be overturned through terrorism steeled Northern opinion much as the passage of the Black Codes had. *Harper's Weekly*, the New York–based periodical that had made its name with blanket coverage of the war, ran a lithograph of Reverend Horton's assassination on its August 25, 1866, cover. The portrait showed the preacher waving an

American flag with a white handkerchief tied to the pole as he is shot down in cold blood. Inside, *Harper's* editorialized that Mayor Monroe's order to ban a political gathering on the grounds that he disagreed with the opinions expressed there struck at the heart of Americans' First Amendment rights: "No meeting whatever, for the purpose of discussion or deliberation, assembled under any call whatever is illegal in this country. . . . A city of the United States is not his [Mayor Monroe's] slave plantation."

The martyrdom of white convention attendees gave Northern radicals a sympathetic cause to rally voters around. Delegate Dostie reportedly expired with the last words, "I die for the cause of Liberty. Let the good work go on." For African-American activists in New Orleans, the martyred people of color provided inspiration even in death. Victor Lacroix, a well-to-do biracial delegate who had been executed while offering his surrender—his corpse was subsequently stripped of its pocket watch and cash— reportedly spoke with Henry Rey, a famed spiritualist medium in the days and years after his death. In Rey's recounting of his séances, Lacroix's ghost told him that the blood of the martyrs which "water[ed] the bricks of the bloody city and mark[ed] the scene [of the riot] in infamy" would transmute itself into guideposts "chart[ing] a new route for new citizens, called to exercise all the rights and privileges that the Republic accords her children."

Whatever the veracity of the voodoo séance, in the cold hard world of American politics, the New Orleans Riot really did bring about African-American suffrage. Though no one was ever punished for the massacre—a local all-white grand jury blamed "political tricksters" inside the conventional hall for their own murders, a view echoed by President Johnson—Northern voters drew other conclusions. As Radical Republicans campaigned for seats in Congress "New Orleans!" became a campaign rallying cry akin to "Remember the Alamo!"

Sensing that the tide had turned, in the midst of the 1866 campaign a chastened all-white South Carolina state legislature repealed its own already nullified Black Code. The replacement law mandated that African-Americans "have full and equal benefit of the rights of personal security, personal liberty and private property, and of all remedies and proceedings for the enforcement and protection of the same as white persons now have, and shall not be subjected to any other or different punishment, pain or penalty, for the commission of any act or offence, than such as are prescribed for white persons committing like acts or offences." The only plank of the Black Code the legislature left on the books was the prohibition of interracial marriage.

In the November elections, the radical wing of the Republican Party gained veto-proof majorities in both houses of the still all-Northern Congress. The *New Orleans Tribune* hailed the vote tallies as "a revolution in the North." Emboldened by the election results, Radical Republicans in the outgoing Congress pressed forward on their equal rights agenda. In January 1867, over President Johnson's veto, Congress granted African-American men in the District of Columbia the right to vote, and in February it sent the first of what came to be known as Reconstruction Acts to Johnson's desk. A direct reaction to the New Orleans Riot, these laws divided the South into military districts and empowered federal authorities to hold trials when local courts ignored crimes against African-Americans. Most crucially, the legislation mandated that each secessionist state ratify the Fourteenth Amendment and again draw up a new constitution before being readmitted to the United States. This time around, the bill stated, delegates to these constitutional conventions would be elected by black men as well as white men and the constitutions themselves would be ratified through universal male suffrage. Radical Republicans saw African-American enfranchisement in the South as the only way to safeguard the Union victory in the war as well as the only way to make the Party of Lincoln competitive in the region. To this end, the bill mandated that "the male citizens of [each] State, twenty-one years old and upward, of whatever race, color, or previous condition, who have been resident in said State for one year . . . except such as may be disfranchised for participation in the rebellion or for felony at common law" be given the ballot. The idea of disenfranchising ex-Confederates sprang from the congressional committee investigating the New Orleans Riot, though its main electoral impact was in states with white majorities—not Louisiana, South Carolina, or Mississippi, where most citizens were African-American. In black-majority states, universal suffrage alone would ensure that white supremacists got outvoted. (Congress would only mandate universal male suffrage in the North two years later, when it passed the Fifteenth Amendment to the Constitution and sent it to the states for ratification.)

In his veto message for the first Reconstruction Act, President Johnson railed against African-American suffrage. "The negroes have not asked for the privilege of voting," he sneered. "The vast majority of them have no idea what it means." In a White House interview with the editor of the *New-York Evening Post*, the Tennessean who had, in his youth, smarted against the arrogant slaveholding aristocrats of the South, now seemed to be taking their side. "The old southern leaders," the president told the newspaperman, "must rule the South." But whatever his opinions, the president held few cards. He would spend most of the coming session of Congress preoccupied with escaping removal from office—after impeachment by the House, he would be spared by a single senator's vote in 1868. With Congress calling the shots, Reconstruction policy going forward became known by two names that were, essentially, synonymous: Congressional Reconstruction and Radical Reconstruction.

In the South, white supremacists braced for impact. North Carolina's all-white state legislature greeted the dawn of African-American suffrage that would wash them out of office by getting wasted. On March 1, 1867, with the veto override in the works in Washington, the legislators in Raleigh embarked on a bender of historic proportions. "Some of the rich old colts from the East," one reveler later recounted, "gave a general treat on the East Portico of the capital furnishing the very best liquor. . . . The whole Capitol was in an uproar." Three days later, when the hung-over legislators finally abandoned the statehouse, the override vote had gone through and North Carolina was legally part of the 2nd district of military Reconstruction, overseen by General Sickles, the New Yorker in Charleston.

Others vowed violent resistance. As dispossessed Charleston slave master Thomas Pinckney Lowndes later recounted of the period, "For us the war was not ended. We had met the enemy in the field and lost our fight, but now we were threatened with a [new] war in which the negro savage backed by the U.S. and the intelligent white scoundrel as his leader was our enemy."

Not all ex-Confederates greeted Radical Reconstruction with such panic. When the editor of the *New Orleans Times* solicited the opinion of retired general Pierre Gustave Toutant Beauregard, now the president of the New Orleans and Carrollton Railroad, the company that operated the St. Charles Avenue streetcar line, the Little Creole seemed firmly convinced that the sky was not falling. Perhaps because he had grown up in the Louisiana sugar plantation belt among its racially and ethnically diverse master class, he understood that African-Americans were not necessarily radicals. Rather than oppose African-American voters, he suggested that probusiness conservatives like himself attempt to co-opt them. "With regard to the suffrage of the freedmen, however objectionable it may be at present, it is an element of strength for the future," he advised. On the issues of importance to the New South, "protective tariffs, internal improvements, etc., the freedmen of the South will side with the whites of the South." Though Beauregard preferred African-American suffrage with "education and property qualifications," nonwhite voting in itself was not to be feared. A system of race-based rights and the strict delineation of whiteness such a regime would require scared him far more.

4.

FREEDOM RIDERS

A New Orleans "star car" in 1867, shortly before desegregation.

(bpk Bildagentur / Napoleon Museum, Arenenberg, Switzerland / Theodor Lilienthal /

Art Resource, NY)

Three weeks after Congress enfranchised the South's African-American men, a committee assembled in Charleston with an audacious mandate: to bring the Party of Lincoln to the cradle of secession. The task of crafting the platform for the new Republican Party of South Carolina fell to an elite crew of thirteen, which included both Francis Lewis Cardozo and Robert Carlos DeLarge. Twelve of the thirteen were men of color; historical records show that at most just one had ever been enslaved.

Continuing the strategy of presenting racial equality as the fulfillment of the American experiment in self-government, the party platform began with a nod to the Declaration of Independence. Opening *"Whereas*, the founders of this Republic based the same on the self-evident truths, 'that all men are created equal; that they are endowed by their Creator with certain inalienable rights; that among these are life, liberty, and the pursuit of happiness,'" the platform called for an array of progressive integrated institutions, most centrally "a uniform system of common schools, which shall be open to all, without distinction of race, color or previous condition."

Though launched by people of color who hadn't been enslaved, the party found a broad constituency among the freedmen. On the afternoon of March 26, 1867, a crowd of roughly two thousand African-Americans gathered on Citadel Green, the square in the heart of the Charleston peninsula, to ratify the platform the committee had written. With the coming of black male suffrage, the Republicans had, overnight, become the leading political party in the Holy City. Most Charlestonians, after all, were of African descent.

The reporters for the city's white newspapers took in the massive crowd and scratched their heads, seeing that most of the attendees were women and children, not potential voters. The city's African-Americans understood something the reporters and maybe even the party's elite founders did not—that empowerment would take community organizing in addition to procedural politics. How, for example, could a school be integrated without women and children at the center of the effort? Indeed, women of color would play a crucial, albeit largely unsung, role in the civil rights struggles of the era.

After speeches by Cardozo, other local African-American leaders, and a white Northern abolitionist who demanded "impartial laws, impartial justice, and impartial privileges to all men . . . of every race," the platform was overwhelmingly adopted by voice vote. But it wasn't the speakers who made the news that day; it was the crowd. As the meeting let out into a torchlight parade, something remarkable happened. Several African-American attendees decided to take the city's new streetcar system home. Up to that point, blacks had been officially barred from the cars.

When Charleston's horse-drawn streetcar system, long in the works but delayed by the war, finally opened in October 1866, the contentious decision about how it would handle African-American passengers had yet to be made. In a front-page story hailing the opening of the transit system, the *Charleston Daily Courier* noted that "proper arrangements will, in due time, be made to allow persons of color to avail themselves of the benefits of the railway, but it has not, as yet, been determined whether this will be accomplished by placing special cars upon the road for their accommodation, as is the case in New Orleans, or by assigning to them a portion of the ordinary cars, as is more usual in other cities." In practice, this nondecision meant that African-Americans were left to ride on the outside platform, precariously hanging on the cars as they rumbled down the city streets, paying full fare for the privilege of being publicly demeaned.

Half a year after the system opened, with the Black Codes repealed, people of color were no longer willing to wait for the "proper arrangements" to be made "in due time." When the Republican rally on Citadel Green let out, several attendees boarded the streetcar at the intersection of Calhoun and Meeting streets, paid their fare, and took seats like the other passengers. The boarders hoped that by pretending nothing was amiss, all would proceed without incident. But Mr. Faber, the conductor, told the group to leave immediately. If not, he warned, he would eject them.

Frightened and intimidated, the passengers complied. But when the humiliated riders rejoined the crowd that had taken in speech after speech exhorting them to demand equal rights, their fellow Republicans grew enraged. By the time Faber's streetcar returned to the corner of Calhoun and Meeting for its next run, word of the racist outrage had spread through the assembly. This time, a much larger group of African-Americans piled aboard and when Faber again issued his ultimatum, they mounted a sit-in, vowing not to budge from their seats. Faber flailed as his authority was undermined; in a panic, he ordered the driver to unhitch the horse to immobilize the car. In response, the crowd ran around back and began to physically push the car down the track while a stunned Faber yanked on the brake. Only with the arrival of the city's all-white police force were the activists extricated from the streetcar.

In its coverage the following day, the *Charleston Daily Courier* fretted over the "seemingly well-organized effort . . . to test their right to ride upon the street cars in violation of the rules of the Company." In reality, the post-rally protest was a wildcat action; only after it did the movement become well organized. Less than a week later, in a new, premeditated protest, a pair of African-Americans, Sydney Eckhard and Daniel McInnis, returned to the very same intersection where the initial incident had occurred and together boarded a streetcar. Little is known about the background of McInnis, but Eckhard appears in the last antebellum census's list of the "Free Inhabitants of Ward 3 City [of] Charleston." In the 1860 census rolls, Eckhard is listed as the eleven-year-old biracial son of a free black single mother, making him roughly eighteen at the time he mounted his protest.

Shortly after Eckhard and McInnis climbed aboard at Calhoun and Meeting streets, a policeman entered the car and placed them under arrest for disturbing the peace. The Charleston Guard House, a downtown police station, happened to sit along the streetcar line, so the officer directed the conductor to continue down the route to where he could take the two men in for booking. As the *Charleston Daily News* reported with disdain, "The news of the occurrence spread like wild fire, and the corners of Meeting and Broad streets [by the Guard House] were soon occupied by a[n] excited crowd of darkeys." The group that had massed a few days before to assert their rights now spontaneously rematerialized to fight for them. Soon Mr. Faber's streetcar rumbled down Meeting Street on its usual run; the crowd recognized the now-infamous conductor. The transit worker who had faced the initial revolt the week before now found his streetcar under attack in a hail of bricks. Later that night, two more streetcars had bricks thrown through their windows. A choice between justice or peace faced the city.

By coincidence, the technology of the horse-drawn streetcar arose in American cities in tandem with antebellum America's hardening of racial categories and transformation of suffrage into a universal white male privilege. Transit systems were built to serve the American public but, increasingly, the conception of the American public, both North and South, was bounded by the borders of whiteness. Unless a streetcar company made specific provisions for African-Americans, urban transit was implicitly for whites only.

Anyone who hoped to challenge this situation in court faced an exceptionally high legal threshold. In the nineteenth century, public transportation was operated by private companies. City governments would give transit companies regulated monopolies on different routes in exchange for their laying the track and operating the streetcars. Those who objected to discrimination faced the legal challenge of arguing not only that they deserved equal treatment by the state—a tough proposition in an America of legalized slavery and whites-only suffrage—but also that their rights before the state were relevant to their dispute with a private company, on the circuitous grounds that company had been granted a license by the state.

When New Orleans opened its first streetcar lines in the 1820s, the municipal government had been conspicuously mute on the issue of race, leaving it up to the various streetcar companies to create their own policies for serving—or not serving—African-American passengers. Some opted to ban people of color altogether, while others ran specially marked cars for nonwhites, the most popular marker being a black star painted on the outside of the vehicle. "Star car" became part of the city's lexicon and, in the local patois, the term "star" came to be used to describe anything segregated (e.g., "star schools").

New Orleanians of color resented the system from the start and occasionally frustrations would boil over. On a sweltering July day in 1833, when a group of free people of color heading to the beach at Lake Ponchartrain were denied the right to board a whites-only streetcar, they attacked it in retaliation. But despite such sporadic actions, until the Civil War activists made no systematic attempt to overturn segregated transit in the South.

In New York City, meanwhile, by the mid-1850s, an organized desegregation effort had been launched. In 1855, Elizabeth Jennings, the daughter of a prominent African-American abolitionist, got booted from a Third Avenue streetcar and won a $225 judgment from the company. But the court order applied only to the Third Avenue operator, and suits against other companies were not always successful, leaving a patchwork of policies. The result was a Kafkaesque city where an African-American could take any car up Third Avenue but, coming back down Sixth, would have to wait for one of the two cars an hour set aside for passengers of color.

Ultimately, even the New York activists' limited success was undermined by the United States Supreme Court's devastating 1857 *Dred Scott* decision. The following year, in the case of Maria Jenkins, an African-American hairdresser who had been thrown off a Sixth Avenue car, the white judge wrote that the *Dred Scott* precedent was "sound law" and therefore Jenkins had "no right to a seat [since blacks did] not possess the same rights and privileges as white[s]."

In the crucible of the Civil War, the streetcar issue was up for renegotiation. After Union forces retook New Orleans, in 1862, elite Creoles of color had gotten General Benjamin Butler to issue an order ending streetcar discrimination, but it was pared back by local courts. African-American Union troops were permitted to take the first car that arrived on account of military necessity, but black civilians remained barred from starless cars. Yet even this small break in the color line inspired hopes for full equality. As one white Southerner complained, "hundreds of idle negroes," seeing black soldiers boarding whites-only streetcars, "st[and] around, laughing and applauding."

The very fact of black soldiers fighting in Union blue gave African-Americans a new claim to Americanness that could not easily be ignored. With African-Americans joining up, in 1863 Massachusetts senator Charles Sumner passed a bill banning racial discrimination on the streetcars of Washington, D.C. But the senator's reach was limited. In 1864, Robert Smalls, a bona fide African-American Union war hero—as an enslaved seaman in Charleston, he had commandeered a Confederate steamer to

freedom—found himself booted off a whites-only streetcar in Philadelphia. Even the Quaker-led transit boycott that ensued was
not enough to desegregate the system. And in 1865 Sumner had
to push through an enforcement act to revoke the charters of the
recalcitrant D.C. streetcar companies that continued to discriminate. His return to the issue was forced by an incident in which an
African-American soldier in full uniform had been ejected from a
streetcar in the capital.

The outrage to American patriotism of a uniformed soldier suf-
fering such treatment was plain to see. But in defending his bill,
Sumner hinted at another argument against segregation that
would become central to Reconstruction-era civil rights efforts:
the nebulousness of race itself. Perhaps drawn to this rationale
by his 1864 meeting with Arnold Bertonneau and Jean Baptiste
Roudanez, the racially unplaceable New Orleanians, in his Senate floor speech, the gentleman from Massachusetts read into the
record newspaper coverage of a recent streetcar dispute:

> EJECTED FROM A STREET CAR—As car No. 1 was passing
> along the avenue yesterday morning, at about nine o'clock, a
> young woman of about eighteen summers called the conductor
> and asked him if he allowed colored people to ride in his car.
> He replied he did not, and said he did not know of any colored
> person being in the car. The young woman told him that the
> person sitting next to her was a colored woman; whereupon
> the conductor compelled her to leave the car, she, at the same
> time, being whiter and fairer than the person complaining of
> her presence in the car.

Moved by such a clear example of a system whose cruelty was
matched only by its absurdity, the all-Northern Congress passed
Sumner's enforcement legislation. But the real test would come
once the nation was reunified.

When the war was won in 1865, the right to ride that had been secured for African-American soldiers in New Orleans was demanded by all in the city. Civil rights advocates, grouped around the *New Orleans Tribune*, who had long wondered why, in the words of one editorial, "a colored soldier be received in the cars [but] his mother expelled," pressed to open seating for everyone. That summer, the Union authorities in the city ordered that "the attempt to enforce police laws or regulations that discriminate against negroes by reason of color, or their former condition of slavery . . . will not be permitted." The *Tribune* greeted the order with a joyous "remind[er to] our friends that the distinction between 'star cars' and 'no star' is no longer of any value." But the celebration was premature. Just two weeks later, a local court ruled that each streetcar company had the right to decide which customers to serve. Star cars kept on rolling, with only Union soldiers retaining the right to ride any car. According to a dubious report in a reactionary local newspaper, this prompted an epidemic of soldier impersonation: "Every negro who is able to sport a blue jacket or a soldier's cap, no matter how greasy, [can] thrust himself amongst ladies in a crowded car," the New Orleans *Daily True Delta* alleged.

With the passage of the federal Civil Rights Act of 1866, New Orleans activists regrouped and the *Tribune* editors took up the issue anew. They fulminated against star cars as incompatible with the new Civil Rights Act, appealed to federal authorities in the city to reissue their antidiscrimination order, and created a donation-based legal defense fund to mount test cases. But nothing worked. African-American civil rights, they realized, would never be enforced without African-American voting rights. Then, of course, through a surprising turn of events, the Northern reaction to the racist violence of that summer's New Orleans Riot dropped the ballot into their hands.

As Sydney Eckhard and Daniel McInnis went on trial in Charleston for their civil disobedience, the federal authorities struggled to keep the city calm. Instead of holding sit-ins or, worse yet, brick-batting streetcars, the federal authorities asked anyone who felt their rights had been violated to file a formal complaint. The assistant commissioner of the Freedmen's Bureau in Charleston, Robert Scott, issued a public announcement: "Attention . . . has been called to a late attempt by the colored people to obtain, through force, a recognition of certain rights which have hitherto been denied them. Such attempts will certainly not further the recognition of their rights, but will, on the contrary, retard their acknowledgement. Whenever the colored people think that any of their rights are withheld, they should appeal to such authorities as are constituted to decide upon the justness of their claims, who will undoubtedly secure to them all rights and privileges."

Just two weeks later, on April 17, a complaint to this effect materialized at the local Freedmen's Bureau office, filed by Mary P. Bowers, an African-American Charlestonian who had been forced off a streetcar. In an impeccably written statement, Bowers recounted the outrage. Though she had previously ridden the streetcar system without incident, she explained, this time, when she boarded, the conductor objected. Being "very unwell and much fatigued from a long walk," she nonetheless took a seat. Bowers found herself next to "Dr. North, one of our most respectable physicians," who had no objection to her presence. But the conductor refused to drive the car with her in it. As tensions rose, Dr. North suggested that Bowers debark since she was "too respectable a person to create an excitement on a streetcar." She replied, "the very fact of my being a respectable person [i]s a sufficient reason for my being allowed to ride." Eventually, tiring of the standoff in the airless, immobilized streetcar, Bowers decided to give up for now but vowed she would see the conductor in court. "As I am detaining those gentlemen from their business and the children [from their mealtime] I will leave the car, but for no other reason," she told him. "But if there is any way, I will make you pay dear for it."

Little is known of Bowers's biography but from her assertion that she had ridden the streetcars many times before without incident and the descriptions of her, even in the white press, as "respectable," it is likely that she was free before the Civil War and of such mixed African and European ancestry that her racial categorization under a white/black binary system was unclear. Bowers's erudite letter of complaint "respectfully apply[ing] for redress" strongly suggests that she was literate and educated. The perfect legalese of her account stands in stark contrast to most Freedmen's Bureau complaints, which recount heartbreaking tales of oppression in heartbreakingly broken English.

In a time when educational opportunities for women were limited and patriarchal family structures the norm, free biracial women in Charleston and New Orleans stood apart. Antebellum census forms show free "mulatresses," as they were known, vastly overrepresented in jobs requiring literacy and special training, including positions as schoolteachers and principals, boardinghouse operators, nurses, and midwives. The system of *plaçage* in New Orleans and its less formalized analogue in Charleston resulted in free women of color serving as the heads of their households in an era when female-headed households were rare.

That Bowers made for an exceptionally sympathetic complainant was almost certainly not a coincidence. Charleston activists wanted to bring a test case in the courts to force the hand of the federal Reconstruction authorities, and Bowers had likely been specifically chosen to bring it. In garnering public sympathy, Bowers's gender was an asset. Women made good test-case plaintiffs in part because the rationale for segregation was so often framed in terms of protecting white women from supposedly predatory black men. The *Charleston Daily News*, for example, editorialized against the streetcar integration movement on the grounds that if desegregation occurred, "it will not be safe for ladies to ride in the cars." The *New York Times*'s Charleston correspondent broadcast this to the North, writing, "If the negroes here, the large majority of whom are squalid and filthy, obtain the right to ride inside the cars, it is feared that the whites, especially ladies, will shun the line." Forcing segregationists to flail about explaining why African-American women should be excluded from streetcars gave the lie to their supposed Southern chivalry.

For these reasons, a disproportionate number of Reconstruction-era transportation civil rights cases were brought by women. In Louisiana, two days before Bowers's incident, a fair-skinned freed-woman, Lydia Wilkinson, had been thrown off a New Orleans–bound Mississippi riverboat and filed a suit under the federal Civil Rights Act of 1866. A few weeks later, in South Carolina, Frances Rollin, a woman born to one of antebellum Charleston's most prestigious free Brown families, filed a complaint against the captain of the steamship, *Pilot Boy*, that had transported her from Charleston to Beaufort in second-class accommodations despite her first-class ticket.

African-Americans who had been free before the war, like Rollin, were similarly overrepresented in the civil rights test cases of the era. Of course, they were more likely to have the resources to fight back in court than the newly freed. But they were also more likely to have experienced the war as a reduction in status. Frances Rollin's father, the lumberyard- and slave-owner William, a descendant of Haitian free people of color, had routinely traveled out of state on business despite regulations officially forbidding it on racial grounds. Now his daughter, Frances, couldn't even make the short jaunt to Beaufort without being demeaned. Similarly, Francis Cardozo, who had traveled extensively both North

and South before the Civil War observed in 1866 that segregation enforcement on interstate transportation "is worse now than
it was before the war." The following year, Cardozo, his wife, and
their young son found themselves booted from the first-class carriage on a train from Washington, D.C., to Richmond, Virginia.
Keen to win back what they had lost, this historically conservative
community embraced radical activism.

The Monday after the Freedmen's Bureau received Mary Bowers's letter, Assistant Commissioner Scott wrote to the president of
the Charleston City Railway Company sternly informing him that
"public carriers have no right to exclude individuals from their
conveyances on account of Color." And the company dare not delay,
Scott warned. "In consideration of the large number of Colored
citizens resident of this City," he wrote, "it seems both unwise and
unjust on the part of your company to deny them a privilege which
the laws of the United States will surely and eventually grant
them. I would therefore submit that it would be judicious for you,
without any unpleasant compromise, enforced by law to at once
conceed voluntarily, what will be eventually imposed upon you by
a resort to the Courts of Law."

Despite Scott's warning, the company stalled for time, citing
the judicial challenges to streetcar segregation currently working
their way through the courts in other Southern cities. In Mobile,
Alabama, federal authorities had asked African-American passengers denied seats on streetcars to peaceably disembark, note
the line and car number, and report it—a bureaucratic policy that
would delay progress in that city for months. In Richmond, Virginia, a test case was pending; ultimately, the courts ordered the
city's whites-only system to begin running star cars for African-
American passengers rather then forcing all streetcars open to all
passengers.

Such half-measures would be a nonstarter for the more popu-
lous, prosperous, and politicized African-American community of

Charleston. When the Charleston City Railway Company floated the ideas of running separate-but-equal star cars or adding partitions to existing cars and relegating African-Americans to the back of the omnibus, neither the activists nor the federal authorities deemed them acceptable.

Under pressure, the company's board of directors convened on May 3. Just five weeks after the initial wildcat action on Citadel Green and two weeks after Bowers filed her complaint, the company caved, passing a resolution that "the cars be thrown open to the public, and that instruction be given to the several conductors to recognize the right of all persons to ride therein." General Sickles, the top federal authority in the city, commended the company president on taking action voluntarily rather than dragging it out in the courts. This prompt solution, Sickles wrote, constituted "emphatic testimony of the disposition of the people of the South to accept in good faith the legitimate consequences of the enfranchisement of the colored race." Sickles saw presciently that it was voting rights that secured civil rights.

The day after the new company policy was announced—a Sunday—African-Americans rode Charleston's streetcars while, according to newspaper coverage, "the whites took it with good-humored resignation." A few recalcitrant white supremacists attempted to mount a streetcar boycott but most quickly gave up, "leg-weary and tired of the expense of paying for private conveyances." Almost overnight, the city accepted the new normal. People had places to go. Later that month, federal authorities in Charleston expanded their ban on discrimination "because of color or caste" to all public conveyances on "railroads, highway, streets, and navigable waters."

As they followed the news out of Charleston, activists in New Orleans grew frustrated. New Orleans had a rich history of fighting for the right to ride going back to the great streetcar pile-on of 1833, but now other cities were leaping ahead. It wasn't just Charleston; there were also the test cases underway in Mobile and Richmond. To New Orleans urbanites, the erstwhile capital of the Confederacy was hardly even a city. Richmond's streetcar system, such as it was, consisted of eight rolling cars while New Orleans boasted 225 cars traversing over a hundred miles of track.

As Mary Bowers fought for her rights in Charleston, the *New Orleans Tribune* editorialized against the stubborn persistence of the Crescent City star cars. "In every civilized country public conveyances are made for the people, and not the people for the public conveyances," the paper offered with bitter humor. Claims that civil rights activists had been "too hasty, too anxious to realize the progress that could only be brought up by a gradual change of opinion and the enlightenment of the people," were off base, the editorial argued. The war had changed everything. Now that African-American suffrage was a reality in Louisiana, it was high time to desegregate not just the streetcars but the New Orleans police force and the local public schools as well. "All these discriminations that had slavery at the bottom," the editorial concluded, "have become nonsense."

The following week, the organ of the city's white liberals, the *New Orleans Republican*, called for a new test case to enforce the federal Civil Rights Act on the city's transit system. "More than a year has elapsed since the Civil Rights Bill became the law of the land," it noted, "and yet we [still] see a discrimination practiced in New Orleans, by the city railroad companies." The only solution was for a "colored man [to] assert his legal rights by riding in any car. . . . If he is *put out by force*, let him offer no resistance . . . but go immediately to the Recorder of the district . . . and make affidavit against the party for assault and battery." If local authorities still ignored his claim, the *Republican* advised, he should take the case to federal court. After all, "the streets of the city of New Orleans belong to the people of New Orleans—*to all of the people*."

Just hours after the paper hit the streets, an African-American activist named William Nicholls answered the call. Perhaps Nicholls had read the paper and was inspired to act, but more likely the editors of the *Republican* had coordinated with him. Prior knowledge of Nicholls's plan would explain the paper's seemingly sexist assumption that the plaintiff would be a "colored man" in an era when it was women who were at the forefront of bringing transportation test cases. At roughly two o'clock that Sunday afternoon, Nicholls boarded a starless streetcar on Canal Street and, when the conductor asked him to leave and board the next star car, he refused to budge. A policeman was nearby and the conductor demanded that he make an arrest. The officer demurred, claiming there was no public disturbance. The conductor then proceeded to manufactured one: he forcibly ejected Nicholls and complained again to the officer when Nicholls attempted to reboard. At the close of this absurd ballet, the activist was duly booked.

When Nicholls appeared in court the following day, April 29, he posted bail immediately, showing access to resources far beyond the typical defendant's. He also brought excellent legal representation. His attorney was Henry Dibble, an Indiana abolitionist who had come to Louisiana as a Union soldier and gotten wounded in the war. After his left foot was amputated at the ankle, Dibble had moved to New Orleans to recuperate at his aunt's house and stayed on in the city to study law. A striking figure about town with his walrus mustache and his peg leg, as Radical Reconstruction dawned Dibble moved in Republican political circles. With Dibble at the defense table, it was clear that Nicholls was consciously bringing a precedent-setting test case to certify that streetcar segregation was illegal under the Civil Rights Act of 1866. The judge, either impressed with the defendant's polished demeanor or slyly trying to scuttle his test case, dismissed the charges on the grounds that there had been no breach of the peace. To salvage his legal challenge to segregation, Nicholls responded by pressing charges against the conductor for assault and battery.

As Nicholls's well-funded test case worked its way through the courts, Creole of color community leaders simultaneously worked a back channel towards the same end. Felix Cassanave and P. M. Tourne met privately with the president of the City Railroad Company, one of the leading streetcar operators in New Orleans, and demanded integration. In response, the company president, presumably worried about Nicholls's legal challenge and trying to meet activists halfway, issued a new policy: the star cars would remain but the company would not forcibly evict African-American riders who insisted on riding in nonstar cars. The corporate executive was gambling that only a small subset of the African-American community, presumably the freeborn Creoles, would insist on boarding the whites-only cars.

The visibility of Creoles of color at the helm of civil rights activism had led many elite whites to convince themselves that civil rights mattered only to the most privileged African-Americans. The week of the compromise proposal, the *Daily Picayune* fumed that social change was being pushed "not so much [by the] freed men or negroes, as [by the] ambitious mulattoes and others of lighter admixture of negro blood, free born, and in times of slavery the most exacting and frequently most cruel masters of slaves." It was they who "thrust themselves into dress circles in theatres [and] claim a vast number of 'rights.'" While there were civil rights issues where few beyond the wealthiest mixed-race people had a direct stake—for example, the right to buy the best tickets at the New Orleans Opera House, which Creole of color activists were demanding simultaneously—the streetcars were not one of them. Access to public transportation was a basic urban necessity for all.

The City Railroad Company president's compromise satisfied no one. For white supremacists, it went too far; for equal rights activists, not far enough. Racist rogue drivers decided that if they could no longer evict African-American riders, they would register their objections by refusing to drive their cars whenever people of color boarded. When this happened to one Mr. P. Ducloslange, a Creole of color, the *Tribune* fulminated not merely against the individual outrage but against the continued existence of star cars. "The victory is not yet won; the evil IS NOT corrected," the paper railed. "It will only disappear when the stars shall be erased from the colored cars."

As long as the star cars rolled, the specter of wildcat protests loomed over any whites-only car that dared traverse the downtown Creole wards. The Friday after the new policy was announced, a young Creole of color named Joseph Guillaume, a cigar maker by trade, boarded a whites-only City Railroad Company car on Love Street. When the conductor told him to leave, Guillaume seized the reins and drove the car down the street himself. A company official called in the incident to the Tremé police station, hyperbolically, as an "open riot." Rumors spread that such protests would jump Canal Street into the Anglophone side of the city. Even the St. Charles Avenue line, which ran through the most prestigious *Américain* neighborhoods and was run by P. G. T. Beauregard's New Orleans and Carrollton Railway Company, soon faced calls to desegregate.

That weekend, Beauregard's underling J. M. Reid dashed off a panicked letter to the newly installed mayor of New Orleans, Edward Heath, a New England native charged with bringing orderly racial progress to the Crescent City. Reid wrote,

> I have been informed this morning by the Superintendent of the Railroad Station on St. Charles Street . . . that threats have been made by coloured persons that they intended to force themselves onto the cars reserved for white persons, some time during to-day or tonight; and that should the driver resist or refuse them passage they would compel him to leave the car and take forcible possession themselves.
>
> Being desirous of avoiding any difficulty of the above

nature, and being satisfied that there is much danger of riotous conduct: I respectfully request that you will take such
action as may be necessary to ensure the preservation of the
public peace.

Whether Mayor Heath read Reid's letter before scrambling out
to the mass protest engulfing the city's main African-American
public space, Congo Square, is unclear. In any case, the urgency of
the situation was now obvious.

Every Sunday for over a century, African-American New Orleanians had been meeting on Congo Square, a small park abutting
the French Quarter. In colonial times, the Catholic observance
embedded in the prerevolutionary French legal code required slave
masters to give their slaves Sundays off, and each Sunday, *Place
Congo* would erupt with the music and dances of West Africa.
Even after New Orleans was annexed to the United States and
the international slave trade banned by Congress, the descendants
of these captured Africans kept the tradition alive. As a visitor
to the city in 1819 wrote, "On sabbath evening" in New Orleans,
"slaves meet on the green, by the swamp, and rock the city with
their Congo dances." Only in the 1840s, as slave-revolt paranoia
gripped the South, were the gatherings banned. Freedmen quickly
revived the tradition after emancipation. On Sunday, May 5, 1867,
the meeting became a protest of free citizens demanding the right
to move through their city unimpeded.

Massing on the southern edge of Congo Square, roughly five
hundred protesters took up positions on either side of Rampart
Street. As star cars came rumbling down the rails, the crowd
shouted to riders of color to disembark. Then, when whites-only
cars approached, African-American riders leapt aboard. As the
protest escalated, the police showed up and drew their weapons
to intimidate the crowd. This was the scene that greeted Mayor
Heath when he arrived.

Peaceful protest, the mayor explained paternalistically to the crowd, was the right of every American citizen but violence would not be tolerated. An African-American protester named Barjean responded angrily that he was ready to "spill the last drop of blood." At this, the calm New Englander put his hand on Barjean's shoulder and told him that he was not here to debate the merits of violent resistance. No doubt Barjean found this condescending but most protesters accepted that the Maine-born mayor was on their side and the crowd dispersed without violence.

After breaking up, scattered groups of protesters mounted wild-cat sit-ins on white-only streetcars all over New Orleans. The incidents went on well into the night. There were so many flare-ups that the *New Orleans Times* speculated that it "appeared to be the result of an understanding, a concert of action." Burying sporadic integration efforts going back decades, the paper fumed against this "systematic attempt . . . to enforce an equality to which they never previously set up a claim."

The following morning, fresh at the start of the new work week, the presidents of the various streetcar companies met to plot their next move. The federal official placed in charge of the city by Congress's Reconstruction Act, Major General Philip Sheridan, showed up at the meeting and gave the assembled executives an ultimatum: "Erase your stars and make all your buses open to all." After Sheridan left the room, the presidents mulled their options, but they didn't have many. Sheridan was still a military commander—his side had won the war—while Pierre Gustave Toutant Beauregard now attended the meeting as a civilian. With William Nicholls's test case set to be heard that Wednesday and the previous night's mass civil disobedience fresh in their minds, the presidents saw little alternative but to defuse the situation by caving. Beauregard's desire for a swift resolution carried the day.

Hours after the streetcar company presidents' meeting let out, official word went forth that the star cars would be eliminated and all streetcars would be open to all riders. That afternoon, Mayor Heath ordered New Orleans police chief Thomas Adams, the violent racist who had led the New Orleans Riot, to make an announcement that he surely hoped he would never have to make. "Have no interference with negroes riding in cars of any kind," Adams ordered. "No passenger has a right to eject any other passenger, no matter what his color. If he does so, he is liable to arrest for assault, or breach of the peace." Mayor Heath would soon integrate Adams's force as well, appointing the first police officers of color the city had seen since colonial times.

When Nicholls came to court that Wednesday, the defendant-turned-complainant arrived for a test case that had already been won. His attorney, Dibble, stated that by adopting an integration policy, the company had already conceded that it had been wrong to eject Nicholls from the streetcar, so there was no need to move forward. The judge asked Nicholls if he agreed to drop the charges. He did.

Within days, streetcar company employees had painted over all of the stars on the segregated cars. As in Charleston, the Crescent City's white residents accepted the change with remarkable speed. The *New Orleans Bee*, a newspaper with little sympathy for civil rights protesters, prefaced its printing of the police chief's desegregation order with the statement, "For the present . . . if not permanently, this vexed question can be considered settled." That Friday, Major General Sheridan wrote to his superiors in Washington, "The bitterness which has existed in this City for the last two weeks, about the Street Car question has subsided. I advised the Companies to make no distinction as there was no law, State or Municipal, to support them, and that ultimately the Colored people would be permitted to ride in any car. This view they cheerfully adopted; and the excitement died at once. There is no trouble now."

And that, it seemed, was that. As a radical Belgian émigré who worked for the *New Orleans Tribune* later wrote in his memoir, the very day after the desegregation orders came down, "Travel on the city buses had taken on an entirely new aspect. Whites and blacks could be found on each car, and this system seemed so natural that it appeared to have always been in force. [Y]ears of propaganda . . . had accomplished nothing against a prejudice which by the order of a military commander had fallen in one hour!"

P. G. T. Beauregard's stature as a Confederate war hero helped white New Orleanians quickly come to terms with desegregation. As New Orleans journalist and author George Washington Cable would recount decades later, "[White] Southerners recognized [equality] in the horsecars, when General Beauregard as a railway president had forced it upon them."

With the streetcars integrated so quickly and with overnight acceptance, civil rights activists expected other victories would come just as easily. When William Nicholls was pressing his case, the *Tribune* predicted that if he won, "It will settle all the other questions under the Civil Rights Bill. The right to have all children admitted into the public schools and the right of going into all public licensed establishments will be carried by a decision in conformity with that law of Congress." Now, with the streetcars desegregated, the *Tribune* predicted optimistically that the school district would be no harder to integrate: "We recollect the threats made . . . ONE DAY only before the cars were open to all. It turned out to be but wind. And so will it be with the schools."

5.

PROGRESS ON PARCHMENT

Robert Carlos DeLarge of Charleston.
(Brady-Handy Photograph Collection, Library of Congress, Prints &
Photographs Division [LC-DIG-cwpbh-00549])

In his purported ghostly return to the Crescent City after his murder in the New Orleans Riot, the spirit of Victor Lacroix had implored séance attendees not to despair over the bloodied bricks of the Mechanics Institute. In November 1867, the scene of that crime was inhabited by a new assembly, one the *New Orleans Tribune* hailed as "the first official body ever convened in the United States without distinction of race or color . . . the first mixed assemblage clothed with a public character." The task at hand was the same as in 1866—crafting a new egalitarian constitution for the State of Louisiana—but this convention had the full force of the federal government behind it. All understood its import; hundreds of citizens, most of them African-Americans, packed in to watch the proceedings.

The delegates convened on Saturday, November 23. Precisely half were white and half were men of color. The white delegates were a mix of Southerners who had pledged loyalty to the Union during the war and postbellum Northern transplants. It is an indication of how thoroughly slandered these progressive whites ultimately became in the Jim Crow era that American English has no names for them other than slurs. The reformist white Southerners are known to history as "scalawags" and the progressive Northern transplants as "carpetbaggers." Among the forty-nine African-Americans, fair-skinned Creoles of color were overrepresented, so much so that to the untrained eye, the assembly appeared to have a white majority. As the white liberal *New Orleans Republican* reported, "The white and colored races are about equally divided

[but] as the majority of the colored are but slightly so[,] the proportion appears to be different." Even those who were "black . . . as the darkest negro in the wilds of Africa," the paper insisted to a prejudiced public that conflated whiteness with self-rule, "know how to express their views as eloquently and stand by their rights as firmly as the fair-skinned Saxons who sit beside them."

Given their tremendous diversity of color, wealth, and status, the African-American delegates were hardly a unified block. Freedmen clamored for land reform while antebellum freemen were more concerned with equal access to public accommodations like theaters, restaurants, and riverboat cabins. As W. E. B. Du Bois would later explain, "Economic and social differences were, in Louisiana, more complicated than in any other American state. . . . [Its] colored leaders had a task of enormous difficulty [since] they differed in origin and education. Some looked white, some black, some born free and rich, the recipients of good education; some were ex-slaves, with no formal training."

There were also disagreements among the white delegates. Though all accepted African-American suffrage—indeed, they understood that it was the only hope for progressive reform and for the Republican Party in the South—they were divided on other questions. In the language of the time, all supported "political equality" (the right to vote, hold office, sign contracts, and testify in court) but not necessarily "social equality" (the right to freely mix in integrated schools, taverns, and railcars, and to intermarry).

Given the reticence of some white delegates, controversy greeted a comprehensive proposal by David Wilson, an African-American barber born free in Kentucky who had settled in New Orleans, to prohibit discrimination in "all conveyances by water or land [and] all amusements, drinking saloons, hotels, eating and lodging houses, billiard saloons, confectionaries, stores, shops, and all places where merchandise is sold." The sticking point was Wilson's strict penalties: revocation of the business's license, at least a year in jail for the proprietor, and payment of at least $1,000 in damages to each victim. His proposal was buried in committee. A replacement by Pinckney Benton Stewart (P. B. S.) Pinchback, the manumitted, educated son of a white Mississippi planter and an enslaved black woman, was adopted in a landslide vote, with nearly four-fifths of the delegates in support. It read, "All persons shall enjoy equal rights and privileges while traveling in this State upon any conveyance of a public character. . . . [A]ll business places . . . for which a license is required by either State, parish or municipal authority shall be deemed places of a public character, and shall be opened to the accommodation and patronage of all persons without distinction or discrimination on account of race or color." While it left penalties unspecified, it was the strongest antidiscrimination plank in any state constitution in America. Delegates hoped it would expand statewide the racial progress now evident on the New Orleans trolleys plying the streets outside the assembly hall.

The most contentious issue at the convention was the question of integrated schools. The lily-white Louisiana constitutional convention of 1864 had rejected school desegregation by a vote of sixty-six to fifteen. Perhaps hoping to illustrate how much had changed in three short years, it was a repentant white supremacist who now offered a school desegregation plank. Dr. George M. Wickliffe was a country dentist from Clinton, Louisiana, a tiny speck of a town not far from the Mississippi state line. In his youth, Wickliffe had been a true believer in slavery and had even edited an antiabolitionist journal. But after moving to New Orleans, he embraced racial egalitarianism. In Clinton, as in other backwoods Southern towns, the all-encompassing nature of African-American slavery had created a kind of tautological defense of the peculiar institution: virtually every African-American Wickliffe had encountered was enslaved and, by state mandate, illiterate. For a white man brought up in such a community, a stroll down

Esplanade Avenue in New Orleans was a revelation. If Americans of African descent were inherently inferior to Americans of European descent, how come African-Americans in New Orleans could do all the same things successful whites did—attain higher education, conduct business, even own slaves? Fittingly, Wickliffe represented New Orleans, not Clinton, at the convention.

Wickliffe proposed establishing Louisiana's first-ever statewide system of public schools and doing so on an integrated basis. His proposal read, "The Legislature shall establish free public schools throughout the state [to which] all children . . . shall be admitted . . . in common, without distinction of race, color, or previous condition. There shall be no separate schools established for any race." Wickliffe also proposed the creation of a new state university, in New Orleans, that would "be open in common to all students capable of matriculating, without distinction of race, color, or previous condition" and that "all [existing] colleges [and] seminaries . . . be open in common to all classes of students, without distinction of race, color or previous condition."

For many of Wickliffe's fellow white delegates, the mandate to desegregate higher education went too far and, under pressure, it was removed. The final text read, "The General Assembly shall establish at least one free public school in every parish throughout the State. . . . All children of this State, between the ages of six (6) and twenty-one (21) shall be admitted to the public schools or other institutions of learning sustained or established by the State, in common, without distinction of race, color or previous condition. There shall be no separate schools or institutions of learning established exclusively for any race by the State of Louisiana." It was adopted by a vote of sixty-one to twelve and became Article 135 of the new state constitution.

Only the most conservative whites voted "Nay," including two delegates from north Louisiana who refused to approve the final constitution largely over school desegregation. "Mixed schools," they warned in a joint written statement, "will not elevate the negroes, but will debase the whites." Another upstate white delegate backed the constitution but publicly warned that "the removal of deep-seated prejudices and time-honored civilized customs by mere acts of legislation, is not encouraged by the teachings of history."

The reactionary white press beyond New Orleans railed against the proposed constitution, the newspapers outdoing each other in assailing the document in terms slyly chosen to highlight the mixed-race backgrounds of its framers. The *South-Western* of Shreveport dubbed the constitution a "mongrel monstrosity," while in tiny St. Martinville, The *Courier of the Teche* called it a "wretched abortion." The *Bossier Banner* slammed the convention as a rogues' gallery of "bastards [and] slubberdegullions." But all they could do was rage. Given the nonwhite-majority demographics of the state, the constitution's ratification was never in doubt.

In South Carolina, the state constitutional convention opened on January 14, 1868, at the Charleston Club House, a stately Corinthian-columned social club on Meeting Street. Convening a short walk from the Battery, the heart of the city's revanchist white high society, the symbolism was unmistakable. The old establishment was being pushed aside by a new one dominated by freeborn, mixed-race Charlestonians, many quietly related to the aristocrats they were displacing.

The Charleston delegation to the convention consisted of three whites and five African-Americans, all born free before the war, four in the Holy City itself. Two months before the convention, Francis Lewis Cardozo had written north to his superiors in the American Missionary Association: "My friends here have requested me to become a candidate for the Constitutional Convention, and I have consented to do so, more, however, from a sense of duty, than from choice, for I have no desire for the turbulent political arena."

Joining Cardozo, the Charleston delegation included Robert Carlos DeLarge who echoed Cardozo's almost farcically mixed background, encompassing multiple categories Americans typically viewed as mutually exclusive—European and African, Anglo and Latino, Christian and Jewish. William J. McKinlay, a biracial real estate magnate who, on the eve of the Civil War, had holdings worth tens of thousands of dollars, which he rented to both black and white tenants, was the wealthiest member of the delegation; McKinlay had also owned slaves. Delegate Alonzo J. Ransier came from more modest stock. Born to free, mixed-race Charlestonians, possibly Haitian refugees, Ransier had worked as a shipping clerk before the war and a newspaper editor after it. Rounding out the delegation was Reverend Richard Harvey "Daddy" Cain, a preacher who had come down from Brooklyn after the war to reopen Charleston's famed "Mother Emanuel" African Methodist Episcopal Church, long shuttered from the crackdown on free people of color after the attempted 1822 slave revolt. The son of an African-born father and a Cherokee mother, Cain had been born free in Virginia and raised in Ohio, where he attended Wilberforce University, founded in 1856 as the nation's first college opened specifically for African-Americans.

The influence of Charleston's unique African-American community was further bolstered at the convention because many rural, overwhelmingly black districts, plagued by near-universal rates of poverty and illiteracy, sent Charleston transplants to represent them. Henry Hayne, the mixed-race Charlestonian and Civil War veteran, represented tiny Marion, South Carolina, at the convention.

Faced with this challenge to their traditional monopoly on power, the white elite of Charleston could do little more than take rhetorical stabs at the statesmen. Delegate by delegate, the *Charleston Mercury* demeaned the representatives in its coverage. To the paper, Cardozo was nothing but "a large portly mulatto . . .

very pompous [who] affects the manners of a man conscious of his wealth and good looks. Although, as has been often said of distinguished individuals of colour, he has neither abilities nor accomplishments that would distinguish him among white men, yet he appears to great advantage among the more ignorant people of his own race." DeLarge was dismissed as "the light colored delegate from Charleston, with conspicuous whiskers [who] might have lived and died without having his name appear in print . . . if it had not been for the great social revolution which, like boiling water, has thrown the scum on the surface." As for McKinlay, the paper reduced the real estate baron to "a respectable colored tailor [who] while few gentlemen would object to consulting him on a pattern of a coat or a pair of pants, none have the same confidence in his judgment as to the pattern of a State Constitution." Alonzo Ransier, the *Mercury* sneered, was a "light coloured . . . second rate or third rate negro delegate," while the university-educated Reverend Cain was a man of "little education" who managed to combine "a negro's complexion, with the features of a very ugly white man." As for Hayne, the paper described him as "a small, bright mulatto— the word 'bright' being used in regard to color, and not to intellect [who] is to all intents and purposes a foreigner to the people of the district which he represents. . . . He hails from the City of Charleston [but at] the close of the war was keen enough to see that if he returned home, he was sure to be [a] nobody."

The Northern press, by contrast, was floored by the erudition of the delegates. The *Atlantic Monthly* correspondent on the scene was impressed to find African-Americans serving in all capacities at the Charleston convention when, back home in Boston, Charles Sumner had been unable to convince legislators to permit a black man to serve as statehouse chaplain. A reporter from the *New York Herald* went even further, calling the Charleston convention "the most incredible, hopeful, and yet unbelievable experiment in the history of mankind."

The assembly in Charleston had a significant African-American majority. Between seventy and seventy-three of the delegates were men of color and between fifty-one and fifty-four were white. Historians have struggled to create a precise racial breakdown using one-drop-rule racial definitions. Those in the galleries at the time would have been at a similar loss since, as W. E. B. Du Bois would later put it, the delegates "were of various colors and mixtures."

Among the white delegates, more than two-thirds were native-born Southerners (scalawags) while the rest were Northern transplants (carpetbaggers). Several of the white Southerners had been secessionists before the war. One had made his living as a slave trader and another had taken up a collection to buy South Carolina congressman Preston Brooks a new cane after he had savagely beaten abolitionist Senator Sumner on the floor of Congress. And then there was Franklin J. Moses Jr., the half-Jewish fire-eater who bragged of lowering the American flag over Fort Sumter at the outset of the war. Simply participating in the convention as a white delegate was a statement of support; many white South Carolinians had boycotted the nominating election.

At the convention, the leading voice for equality belonged to Benjamin Franklin Randolph, who represented Orangeburg, a small town near the state capital of Columbia. Born to mixed-race free people of color in Kentucky, Randolph had been educated in Ohio at Oberlin, the radical liberal arts college founded in 1833 as both racially integrated and coeducational. An ordained Presbyterian minister, Randolph volunteered with the United States Colored Troops during the war, serving as a chaplain. After Appomattox, he settled in South Carolina and helped to found and edit a pair of African-American newspapers in Charleston.

Randolph proposed a plank reading, "Distinction on account of race or color in any case whatever shall be prohibited, and all classes of citizens, irrespective of race and color, shall enjoy equally all common, equal and political privileges." In arguing for

its adoption, Randolph shrewdly cast his text less as a repudia-
tion of the nation's racist, blood-stained history than as the fulfillment of the founding fathers' vision. "Our forefathers were no
doubt anti-slavery men, and they intended that slavery should die
out," he offered. In Randolph's clever rhetoric, the hypocrisies of
the founding fathers—men who generally opposed slavery in principle yet owned slaves themselves and offered no concrete plans
for abolition—were chalked up to a tragic misunderstanding. "The
word color," Randolph noted,

> is not to be found in the Constitution or Declaration of Inde-
> pendence. On the contrary, it is stated distinctly "all men
> are created free and [sic] equal." But that was too general,
> too comprehensive, and our forefathers made a mistake, the
> result of which was that the land has been drenched in blood
> to perpetuate slavery. The Constitution of the United States
> was too vague; it was misinterpreted. On the one hand, the
> ablest statesmen of . . . America had pronounced it anti-
> slavery; on the other, equally able minds regarded it as pro-
> slavery in its character.

Randolph's retelling of the nation's founding was less about historical accuracy than contemporary pragmatism. It provided a
path for former slave-owning—even slave-trading—delegates to
sanction equal rights clothed in the mantle of Washington, Jefferson, and Randolph's own namesake, Benjamin Franklin, who had
been nearly alone among the founders in manumitting all of his
slaves and becoming an abolitionist.

As in Louisiana, the most controversial application of Randolph's
integrationist proposal would be in the public schools. Before the
Civil War, there was no statewide system of public education in
South Carolina. Wealthy whites had relied on private schools and,
in the rural plantation belt, private tutors; free people of color ran

their own private academies under ever increasing pressure and surveillance from the state government; poor rural whites received no formal education whatsoever; and slaves were prohibited by law from learning to read and write. Only in Charleston had there been a system of "free schools" before the war, but the system was underfunded and explicitly for white children only.

Francis Cardozo chaired the Committee on Education, composed of three white delegates and five African-Americans, and took up the task of crafting a plank mandating integrated schools. The committee, which included Henry Hayne, reported out recommendations that school attendance be compulsory for children aged six to sixteen and that all educational facilities "be free and open to all the children and youths of the State, without regard to race or color." It also required that institutions of higher learning be desegregated—a principle that had proven too controversial for the convention in Louisiana.

Rather than oppose school desegregation openly in a majority-African-American forum, white delegates hostile to integration took aim at the mandatory attendance clause. One of the most conservative white delegates at the convention seized on the fact that one of the white members of Cardozo's education committee was a carpetbagger from Massachusetts. The Bay State was held in high regard by radicals as a beacon of free public education where the schools had been desegregated by law in 1855, but conservatives tarred Massachusetts as the birthplace of the puritan North's trademark rapaciousness clothed in sanctimony. "Did any South Carolinian vote for the [mandatory attendance] provision?" Charles P. Leslie of backwoods Barnwell asked rhetorically, insinuating a shadowy carpetbagger plot.

At this, Robert Brown Elliott, a dark-skinned delegate born to West Indian parents, who represented rural Edgefield but lived in Charleston, leapt to the defense of Massachusetts. Universal free public education with mandatory attendance, he intoned, was what "made New England great, and made her citizens, poor as well as rich, low as well as high, black as well as white, educated and intelligent." The mysterious Elliott, who had married into the Charleston's Brown elite Rollin family, claimed to have been born in Boston and educated in England at Eton, the traditional training ground of British royalty. Even the *Charleston Mercury* couldn't deny the "splendour of his elocution."

Scrambling to bridge the impasse, Cardozo explained that attendance would be mandatory but integration optional, in that the decision would be left up to each individual parent. "I want to divest [this issue] of the imaginary consequences that some gentlemen have illogically thought will result from the adoption of this section with the word compulsory," Cardozo offered.

> They affirm that it compels the attendance of both white and colored children in the same schools. There is nothing of the kind in the section. . . . It simply says all the children shall be educated; but how is left with the parents to decide. It is left to the parent to say whether the child shall be sent to a public or private school. [The proposal] does not say [that] there shall not be separate schools. There can be separate schools for white and colored. It is simply left so that if any colored child wishes to go to a white school, it shall have the privilege to do so. I have no doubt, in most localities, colored people would prefer separate schools, particularly until some of the present prejudice against their race is removed.

Cardozo ultimately defused the situation by agreeing to a compromise that would make school attendance compulsory only after the statewide system had been fully built out. Rather than foist integrated education on the state, Cardozo's strategy would be to desegregate those urban schools with the most potential for success—namely, those in Charleston and the state university in

Columbia—and hope their example would eventually shift opinion statewide. After all the back and forth, the constitution included a broad plank applying to primary, secondary, and higher education, reading, "All the public schools, colleges and universities of this State, supported in whole or in part by the public funds, shall be free and open to all the children and youths of the State, without regard to race or color."

Cardozo thought integration should begin with the youngest children. With them, he mused, bigotry could be more easily overcome. "To remove these prejudices," he offered, "the most natural method . . . would be to allow children[,] when five or six years of age, to mingle in school together, and associate generally. Under such training, prejudice must eventually die out; but if we postpone it until they become men and women, prejudice will be so established that no mortal can obliterate it."

Under the federal mandate of the Reconstruction Act, every Southern state wrote a new, egalitarian constitution. In Louisiana and South Carolina, with their African-American majorities, the constitutions went farther than the others both on paper and in the lived realities the documents created. In Mississippi, where an African-American majority also led to the drafting of an exceptionally progressive constitution, rampant voter intimidation resulted in the constitution initially getting voted down. In Alabama, merely voting for delegates to the state constitutional convention could endanger an African-American's life and livelihood. In Crenshaw County, in Alabama's Black Belt, local officials set up a rope line where blacks waited to cast their ballots as whites harassed them in a "gauntlet of . . . jeers and threats," their employers "watch[ing] to see whether their hands had voted." Georgia's constitutional convention was dominated by white conservatives who managed to remove a plank guaranteeing African-Americans the right to hold elective office by deploying the cynical claim that the clause was redundant. Just months later, all duly elected African-American legislators would be ejected from the Georgia House of Representatives in Atlanta on the grounds that the state constitution did not grant African-Americans the right to hold public office. Only four representatives, whose complexions were so light as to render it impossible to definitively determine their race, were permitted to serve out their terms.

It would fall to African-American elected officials—those brave enough to campaign and serve—to safeguard the rights written into the new state constitutions. The 1868 elections saw a wave of candidates of color. At the conclusion of the Charleston convention, Francis Cardozo, initially so reticent about "the turbulent political arena," was convinced to run for the statewide office of Secretary of State—a race he would win. In the election, fully thirteen of the eighteen candidates for state assembly from Charleston County were men of color.

In Louisiana, Francis E. Dumas, a patrician French-born "octoroon," who had been one of Louisiana's largest slaveholders before choosing to fight for the Union in the Civil War, offered his candidacy for governor. He was narrowly beaten by a white, Illinois-born carpetbagger at the state nominating convention. Oscar J. Dunn, born in slavery in New Orleans before being freed, joining the Union Army, and then rising in the activist circle around the *New Orleans Tribune*, became lieutenant governor—the highest-ranking African-American elected official up to that point in American history.

In South Carolina, fearing rural hostility and lawlessness, the state Republican Party largely limited its campaign activities to Charleston, the state's leading port, Columbia, the state capital, and Beaufort, the largest city on the black-majority Sea Islands. Elsewhere, the election campaign of 1868 was plagued by vigilante violence. In upstate South Carolina, largely devoid of federal troops and demographically more white than black, mobs ran rampant. White supremacist night riders shot up African-American homes and ritually reenacted the humiliations of slavery, whipping and raping blacks in revenge for their political activity. In Louisiana, a progressive former governor complained just weeks before the election that "murder and intimidation are the order of the day in this state." Even in New Orleans, there were instances of white toughs breaking up Republican Party meetings and racist street violence that was only halted by federal troops called in to back up the city's newly integrated police.

Much of the violence was targeted at political leaders. Stepping off a train at Hodges Depot for a campaign rally in rural Abbeville County, South Carolina, on October 16, 1868, Benjamin Franklin Randolph, the author of the state constitution's principal statement of racial equality and the chairman of the Republican State Central Committee, was shot dead. At the constitutional convention, Randolph had taken pains to absolve slaveholders of their past sins, but all for naught; local Democrats insisted that Randolph's "incendiary speeches" had made him fair game.

A new terrorist group claimed responsibility for the Randolph assassination. It called itself the Ku Klux Klan and its members dressed in white masks and robes, supposedly to appear as the vengeful ghosts of the Confederate war dead. Formed in Tennessee in 1866 by embittered slave-trader-turned-Confederate-general Nathan Bedford Forrest, it metastasized throughout the rural South during the election campaign of 1868.

In Charleston, a few days after learning of Randolph's assassination, Rev. Richard Cain wrote to Freedmen's Bureau veteran Robert Scott, now the state's governor, "I tremble for this city," he warned. "If any unwise Step be taken by the Democra[ts] to murder any prominent man in this Community, the people have sworne, to burn this city to ashes and have no mercy." In the end, Charleston remained calm and the Republicans were victorious in the November elections. When the first African-American aldermen took their seats in Charleston's city council, one white patrician seemed as much dazed as vengeant: "We actually have negroes in Council. It is the hardest thing we have yet had done to us. . . . It does not seem possible in the dispensation of Providence that the negro can rule over the white man."

Though not a single African-American yet dared run for Congress in Washington, at the national level the 1868 elections were a Republican rout. Even in the face of rural voter intimidation and an openly racist campaign—the Democratic presidential ticket ran on the official slogan "This Is a White Man's Country. Let White Men Rule"—the Party of Lincoln triumphed both North and South. Andrew Johnson, constantly fighting against Radical Republicans' Reconstruction policies, had failed to even garner a major-party nomination, and he was succeeded by Ulysses S. Grant, the retired Civil War general, who promised to take a hard line against racist vigilantism. Shortly after the violence-plagued election, the lame-duck Congress passed the Fifteenth Amendment guaranteeing universal male suffrage North and South regardless of "race, color, or previous condition of servitude" and sent it to the states for ratification.

As bloody and divisive as the 1868 campaign had been, it ended with the hopeful spectacle of America's first integrated inaugural ball. As one radical newspaper recorded, "In the grand procession . . . the advance the nation has made under the genius of liberty was epitomized. . . . All took part in a ceremony in which only a few short years ago none but white persons were allowed to participate. No organization military or civil withdrew from the line because colored citizens participated, no white person left the inaugural ball. . . . There seemed to be a general acquiescence to the new order of things."

6.

BROWNS VERSUS BOARD OF EDUCATION

A sketch for the chameleon costume mocking Creoles of color
at the Mistick Krewe of Comus Mardi Gras Parade of 1873.

(Carnival Collection, Louisiana Research Collection, Tulane University)

It took just a year from the passage of the first Reconstruction Act to the drafting of the new Louisiana state constitution mandating that "there shall be no separate schools or institutions of learning established exclusively for any race by the State." In Louisiana's largest city, however, school desegregation had been years in the making. Unlike streetcar integration, which became a reality in a matter of weeks and was widely accepted almost overnight, school desegregation proceeded in fits and starts over a decade and was fought relentlessly.

The first attempt at desegregation had taken place at the dawn of Union control, on the very first day of the school year in 1862. As the schools opened, rumors of integregation swept the city. One newspaper reported on "a story, actively circulated, that hereafter the public schools are opened to the black population, and that white children will receive instruction side by side with the dingy descendants from the sons of Africa."

The whites-only school district was taking no chances. In New Orleans, with its blurry color line, maintaining racial segregation required constant vigilance. The week before the schools opened, administrators ordered that "whenever the Principal of any schools of this District should have any doubt as to the color of a pupil applying to be admitted . . . said pupil shall be required to produce to the Principal of said school the certificate of his birth." In a city whose wide spectrum of complexions offered so many opportunities for racial passing, the color recorded on birth certificates, which listed the races of the mother, father, and child as black, white, or biracial, would be considered final.

A few brave souls among the city's Creole of color population tested the waters. When the public schools opened on September 15, a mysterious new teacher, one Miss Snyder, was presiding over a classroom at the Barracks School. Emboldened by her own hiring, Snyder, who was secretly biracial, encouraged her relatives to send their light-skinned free children of color to the school as well.

Sited in the French Quarter, the heart of the old Creole city, the Barracks School for girls was among the softest of racial targets. Even decades later, at the height of Jim Crow, the officially whites-only academy was Anglo-free, known as "being patronized solely by the French-speaking children and those of the other Latin races."

Soon after the 1862 school year began, gossip began to swirl about Miss Snyder's ancestry. By the end of the first week of classes, the city school board had convened a racial inquisition— a special three-member probe impaneled to get to the bottom of "rumors . . . spreading about this city that . . . Miss Snyder [i]s not of white origin." Embracing bureaucratic caution, the school board investigative committee ordered that Miss Snyder be fired but not informed of why she was being dismissed.

The investigative committee then turned its attention to the student body. Administrators ordered the principal of the Barracks School, Josephine Mettasca, hauled in for questioning. Under examination, Principal Mettasca copped to having accidentally enrolled three students of color, the Augustin sisters, aged seven, eight, and fourteen. The sisters, Mettasca conceded, "are very dark," but she maintained that "on admitting them I had no suspicion that they might be colored." It was all Miss Snyder's fault, Mettasca told the committee. The mendacious teacher had misled her by denying that she even knew the sisters let alone was related to them. It was only after realizing that the girls were "friends, even first cousins to Miss Snyder," Mettasca explained, that she decided to "make inquiry into what they might be." The principal scoured the neighborhood and interviewed a man named Leonville Pascal, who was rumored to be the father of the Augustin children. Though light-skinned, Mettasca explained, Pascal was "known . . . to be a colored man." Now suspicious that the children had falsified their surnames to obscure their racial background, Mettasca summarily dismissed them. When the board's investigators finally located the sisters' birth certificates, they found that, indeed, "their parents [we]re of color."

Outraged that this kind of racial witch-hunt could take place in a city ostensibly run by the Union Army, the mother of the girls fought back. First she marched to the Barracks School with her eldest daughter in tow and confronted Principal Mettasca using what the principal later described as "very insolent language." Then the outraged parent appealed to the highest-ranking Union official in the city—General Benjamin Butler himself. She had reason for hope; Butler hailed from Massachusetts which, in 1855, had become the first state in the Union to integrate its public schools. In response, Union authorities summoned Principal Mettasca to headquarters, ordered the girls reinstated, and impaneled a committee of the school board to reconsider its whites-only policy. But rather than appease the federal authorities, the committee members all resigned in protest. With Union victory in the war still unassured and integrated schools controversial even in the North, General Butler decided that school desegregation would not be his priority. Instead, in occupied New Orleans, the Union administration opened separate public schools for children of color. Though they were the first public schools in the South open to nonwhite children, this policy set a dangerous precedent: it blessed segregated schools with the imprimatur of the federal government.

When the Union won the war, prospects for integration looked, if anything, even bleaker. Unreconstructed Confederate veterans came marching home again and took up positions of power. In the whites-only election of 1865, archsegregationist Robert Mills Lusher, a founder of New Orleans's antebellum whites-only public school district, was elected state superintendent of education.

Looking out at the world through hooded, lupine eyes, Lusher had an unhealthy obsession with, what he termed in his handwritten 1889 autohagiography, "precious white children." For the Charleston-born, Georgetown-educated Lusher, the very purpose of public schools was to "vindicate the *honor and supremacy of the Caucasian race.*" Upon taking statewide office in 1865, Lusher tapped his white supremacist protégé William O. Rogers to serve as superintendent of the New Orleans schools. In his mission to stymie "the mental training of an inferior race," Lusher now had a loyal henchman in charge of the state's integrationist hotbed. Rogers ordered the local school board to take over the blacks-only public schools that had been set up under Butler in 1862 and run since the war by the Freedmen's Bureau. The board planned to use them as the nucleus for the black half of a segregated school system.

It was only the arrival of Radical Reconstruction in the spring of 1867 that put integrated public schools back onto the political agenda. Facing the daunting odds of a universal suffrage election in a black-majority state, Lusher opted not to run for reelection as state superintendent, begging off despite the Democratic Party's official nomination of him. In his last public statement before leaving office, Lusher went before the state legislature to protest plans for school desegregation.

The April 1868 election was a landslide for Louisiana's Republican Party, whose platform stated, "We . . . insist on perfect equality, without distinction of race or color . . . and will enforce the opening of all schools . . . to all children." The tallied votes showed the egalitarian constitution had been ratified, and Thomas Conway, an Irish immigrant and minister, who worked in New Orleans's Freedmen's Bureau schools for African-American youth, had been elected state superintendent. But Lusher hardly resigned himself to Republican rule. Instead, he worked as a private citizen to thwart integration—an effort he later called "[laboring for] the protection of white students and white children from the dreaded moral contamination portended by the . . . triumph of Radical Republicanism!" Lusher took charge of the Peabody Fund, an educational philanthropy founded by the late Massachusetts-born, London-based tycoon George Peabody, and hijacked it for the use of white children only. In an attempt to stymie the Republicans' integrationist plans, Lusher set up a parallel, privately funded, all-white school system in Louisiana's rural parishes "wholly apart from the offensive State System of Public Education." The schools became ideological training grounds where, as Lusher put it, "white children . . . would be properly prepared to maintain the supremacy of the white race in rural Louisiana."

Despite the Republican takeover, even in New Orleans integration came slowly. Backed by the city's white majority, segregationist William Rogers had been able to retain control of the Orleans Parish School Board in the 1868 election. In the very locale where the new constitution's mandate of integrated public schools stood its best chance of succeeding, the district was run by a Lusher protégé who pledged open defiance of the state constitution. Superintendent Conway was left scrambling to hatch bureaucratic schemes to oust Rogers.

On the ground, youth of color refused to wait. Days after the election, several mixed-race girls, including the daughter of activist Charles St. Albin Sauvinet, who would later be elected sheriff of Orleans Parish, enrolled in the Tremé district's Bayou Road School for girls. Almost immediately, white Bayou Road School parents, led by one Mr. Fremaux, grew suspicious and alerted the superintendent's office. William Rogers, who had never changed district policy to accord with the new state constitution, ordered an investigation. The probe began with a preliminary site visit. School board members visually examined "some 29 pupils . . . reported to be of color." One hotheaded board member immediately demanded the principal, Madame Bigot, be fired for "knowingly admitt[ing] into [her] school a number of colored children whose proper place is the Rampart St. School for colored girls, thereby violating a cardinal rule of this Board," but Rogers felt she deserved the presumption of innocence until the investigation took its course. Faced with New Orleans's confounding continuum of complexions, a simple classroom visit would never be sufficient for determining whether a school had been integrated or not. To carry out his racial inquest, Rogers demanded hard evidence, ideally full pedigrees of all twenty-nine students that could prove whether or not they were thoroughbred whites.

Seeking an orderly and methodical investigation, Rogers duly drew up a series of carefully edited letters of inquiry. He wrote Principal Bigot, "inform me if there are any children known, or generally reputed to be colored—who are now attending your school. If yes, how many, when & by what authority admitted." Rogers also sent a letter to Mr. Fremaux, the leader of the irate white parents, asking him to furnish "such evidence as may be in your possession and upon which your [allegations are] based." Finally, Rogers ordered his staff to have the city's recorder of births pull all of the students' birth certificates. By the rules of Rogers's racial inquisition, the children would not receive the presumption of innocence the superintendent had bestowed on their principal. The burden of proof lay firmly on the accused. If a child wished to continue attending the Bayou Road School, parents were informed, they would have to establish, as one newspaper put it, "the purity of their blood."

On May 23, the parents of the accused were sent a form letter from Superintendent Rogers:

Complaints have been made that certain pupils are attending the Bayou Road School in contravention to the Rules of the Board of School Directors, said pupils being of mixed race and this school having been designated as exclusively for white children.

The pupil _____ is named as belonging to this class.

I have been instructed . . . to request that you will send to the Superintendent's Office, 39 Burgundy Street, before 2 p.m. of Tuesday, 26 . . . such "<u>documentary evidence or testimony of sworn witnesses</u>" as will serve to establish the "<u>status, in point of color</u>" of said pupil.

I have been further instructed . . . to say, that, "<u>in the absence of such testimony, the said pupil will be dismissed</u>,'" from the Bayou Road School, "<u>by the Board of Directors</u>."

As the letters arrived, each family faced a crisis. Some parents were activists trying to enforce the egalitarian principles enshrined in the new state constitution. But others had children who were light enough to pass and simply wanted to enroll them in the best neighborhood school available. Others sincerely believed themselves to be of purely European descent either because they were—their dark features attributable to the combination of Mediterranean roots and New Orleans sun—or because the cover-up of their African ancestry had begun so many generations back and had been so successful that no living member of the family knew the truth.

Given their disparate agendas, each family responded to the racial inquisitors in its own way. Six of the families ignored the board's request for information presumably because they had no exculpatory racial evidence to present; their children were drummed out of the Bayou Road School a few weeks later. The evidence presented by twelve others, including two students who had been attending New Orleans public schools by passing for white since 1862, was deemed insufficient; they too were expelled. Nine of the twenty-nine children met the board's high bar, producing adequate genealogical evidence of their racial purity to remain enrolled.

Finally, two sets of parents informed the board that they were refusing to comply with the investigation on principle as a form of civil disobedience. In early June, the fathers received dismissal letters from Superintendent Rogers, written in an impeccably faux-polite bureaucratese. One of them read:

> Sir:
>
> Certain responsible and well known citizens have averred that the pupils Alie & Amais Meilleur are not of white parentage, and that, consequently, they are not entitled to attend those schools which have been established exclusively for white children.
>
> The Directors of the Public Schools, desirous only of discharging the duties entrusted to them in conformity to the best interests of the schools have studiously avoided any manifestation of ill will, haste, or injustice to the parties in question. You have declined to meet the reasonable requests of the Directors in the prosecution of a question, in which you are interested, and the evidence adduced from others has been deemed sufficient to require the withdrawal of the children named from the Bayou Road School. Instructions have been sent to the Principal not [to] regard these children as pupils of that school.
>
> By order of the Board of School Directors.
>
> Very respectfully,
>
> Wm. O. Rogers, Supt. P.S.

Having dealt with the students, the board turned its attention to Principal Bigot. Under interrogation, she pleaded ignorance.

One of the students the board had ruled colored, Bigot explained, had produced a birth certificate from France. And she herself had met people from the south of France who were as dark as that student. Another girl proven to be nonwhite had been enrolled by her white father and it never occurred to her, Bigot insisted, to inquire about the race of the mother.

Following her testimony, the school board debated Bigot's fate. A few members backed a hard line against the errant principal—firing her or, at least, demoting her to a school for colored girls—but most believed her alibi. After deliberations, the panel exonerated Bigot. Everyone understood how tricky race was in New Orleans—your school could be desegregated right under your nose without you even noticing. Two weeks later, the board sent Principal Bigot an official list of students who could no longer be admitted. As long as she faithfully enforced it, she could keep her job.

In response to the crisis, district officials tightened their policy of erring on the side of caution when it came to race. Principals were ordered to report every "case of grave doubt as to the [racial] status of any pupil," whereupon the board would conduct "an examination of the case" in secret. Rumors from those deemed "responsible and well known citizens" would be considered hard evidence; ignoring the school board's charges would be interpreted as an admission of guilt; and any students deemed "more or less colored" would be expelled from white schools. It was far better, administrators believed, to mistakenly expel a white student than to mistakenly enroll a child of color.

Frustration built among the city's civil rights supporters. The state constitution mandated school desegregation, the duly elected state superintendent backed it as well, and yet, on the ground, nothing changed. Reeling from their failures, activists launched a savvy, multipronged effort in the statehouse and the courts. The plan was to have the state legislature oust Rogers and his recalcitrant local school board and convince the courts to finally force school deseg-regation. It would be a slow-going, multiyear process and it would be led by Robert Isabelle, a brilliant civil rights leader who fought in three capacities: as a state legislator, as the father of a school-aged son, and as a test-case plaintiff.

Born free in provincial Opelousas, Louisiana, the light-skinned, mixed-race Isabelle had migrated to New Orleans in his youth and found work as a cotton processing plant clerk. When the war came, he joined up with the Native Guards and rose to the rank of second lieutenant only to face demotion in the mid-war backlash against African-American officers. Isabelle resigned in protest. "When I joined the United States army," he explained, "I did so with the sole object of laboring for the good of the Union supposing that all past prejudice would be suspended [but I found that] the same prejudice still exists." Like so many antebellum free people of color, Isabelle was in part radicalized by realizing that the nation beyond New Orleans's city limits made no distinction between peo-ple of his complexion and status and the masses of the freedmen.

With the arrival of Radical Reconstruction, Isabelle served as a police officer in the newly desegregated New Orleans force, a del-egate to the 1868 state constitutional convention, and a state leg-islator representing his Faubourg Marigny neighborhood. In the legislature, Isabelle authored an educational bureaucracy reor-ganization bill to replace the local Orleans Parish School Board with ward-based committees appointed by the state superinten-dent. Duly empowered, Superintendent Conway could pack these boards with integrationists who would carry out the mandates of the state constitution.

Defending the bill on the statehouse floor in February 1870, Isa-belle deemphasized its bureaucratic minutia and instead gave a rousing defense of school desegregation as the key to America's racial redemption. "I want the children of this State educated together," Isabelle began, his vision slowly unfurling. "I want to see them play together . . . to study together, to eat their lunch together; and when they grow up to be men they will love each other, and be ready, if any force comes against the flag of the United States, they will take up arms and defend it together." It was an inspiring dream but it was undercut by the mockery of a legislative peer who, when Isabelle began, "I want to see them," yelled out "amalgamated." The outburst suggested that the nefarious purpose of school desegregation was to merge the races through interracial coupling and simultaneously mocked Isabelle's own mixed background. Even worse, a major New Orleans newspaper published a transcript of the speech in which it appeared Isabelle himself had proposed mass miscegenation only to be laughed down by his colleagues. "Now, I want the children of this State educated together," it quoted Isabelle as saying. "I want to see them play together; to be amalgamated. [Laughter.]" Isabelle's bill was passed into law but the recalcitrant local school board refused to disband.

The humiliation Isabelle felt being mocked in the press echoed the humiliation felt by his son, William. The Isabelle family lived on Franklin Street, a short walk from the whites-only Fisk School, but William was forbidden to enroll. On a daily basis, William was denied the opportunity to get the best education his neighborhood offered. Now a plan was hatched: the Isabelle family would do it all. William Isabelle could be the lead plaintiff in a lawsuit that would enforce his father's new law; with the ward boards recognized as the legitimate district administrators, the schools could be integrated.

Robert Isabelle organized a Marigny neighborhood committee with other parents of African-American children. On May 16, 1870, he and William, along with two other boys and their parents, marched up Franklin Street to the Fisk School. The principal, Thomas W. Dyer, came out to meet the group, and refused to enroll them. If the new ward board wanted to desegregate his school, Dyer told the group, it would have to force him.

Cognizant that this could be the test case they needed, Robert Isabelle contacted a lawyer, John Howard, and went to court to vindicate his son's right to attend his local public school. In a petition filed on June 25, the Isabelles' attorney cited the law Robert himself had passed, "An Act to regulate Public Education in the State of Louisiana and city of New Orleans," and argued that the integrationist ward-based school boards it mandated were "vested with the sole and exclusive control and direction of all public schools within the city of New Orleans." Howard also took pains to emphasize young William's respectability, as was typical for test-case plaintiffs: "William R. Isabelle, is of good moral character and intelligence; quiet, peaceable and inoffensive in disposition [he] will be greatly improved by a regular system of instruction and education in the public schools provided by law. [It is only the] failure on the part of the said youth, William R. Isabelle, to receive such instruction and discipline as the public schools should afford, and to grow up deprived of education [that] would work irreparable injury to [him]. . . . Against [his] admission there is no lawful objection." The attorney's petition concluded by exhorting the court to empower the new ward boards and thereby enforce "the admission of all youths, between the ages of six and twenty-one years, to the public schools of the wards or school districts wherein they reside, and especially of William R. Isabelle to the aforesaid Fisk School."

The Isabelles' case ended up in the courtroom of Henry Dibble, the attorney who had represented William Nicholls in the 1867 streetcar desegregation case when the companies caved. Dibble had subsequently been appointed to the bench by Louisiana's Republican governor. The plaintiffs could not have hoped for a more sympathetic magistrate.

In November 1870, Judge Dibble issued his ruling. Seeing that the heart of the issue was the bureaucratic question of which school board—Rogers's or Conway's—was legitimate, Dibble found that

Conway's integrationist ward boards had been duly empowered by the new state law. Rather than give voice to the soaring egalitarian rhetoric in which he no doubt believed, Dibble decided the matter on narrow legal grounds. "It [i]s said that such a decision will prove disastrous to the beautiful and uniform system of education which has been the pride of New Orleans," Dibble wrote. "If such a result follows, I should feel deep regret as a citizen. As a judge, however, I cannot decide which is best law; I can only endeavor to determine which is the law upon the statute book." And the law upon the statute book was Isabelle's.

With Dibble's decision in hand, Conway at long last ordered the New Orleans public schools open to all. "The Ward District Boards will now take charge of the public schools," Conway wrote in a public announcement, "[and] the public schools of New Orleans . . . shall be open to all children residing in the district [with none] excluded because of race or color."

Pursuing a moderate course, the district enacted a policy of citywide school choice. Rather than assign African-American children to formerly whites-only schools and white children to formerly colored-only institutions, parents were empowered to enroll their child in any school regardless of whether it had formerly been reserved for whites or for nonwhites. Since whites-only schools were generally of better quality and sometimes located closer to the homes of children of color than the nearest nonwhite schools, hundreds of ambitious African-American parents took the opportunity to enroll their children in formerly whites-only schools.

After nearly a decade of fits and starts, large-scale desegregation began after Christmas break. Many integration pioneers came from the families of African-American politicians, like Isabelle. In the wake of Judge Dibble's decision, the wife of Oscar Dunn, Louisiana's African-American lieutenant-governor, arrived at the Madison Girls School with her three daughters, Fanny, Emma, and Charlotte, and successfully enrolled them.

Some children still found themselves turned away by racist principals, including several boys who tried to matriculate at the St. Phillip Boys School in the French Quarter, but now district administrators were on their side. When the boys returned with written orders signed by state superintendent Conway himself, the principal gave in.

Progress was swift. Shortly after winter break, a conservative newspaper lamented that "there is not a single white school in the city, we would venture to say, that does not contain at least one colored child." This was almost certainly hyperbole designed to rile up white readers—and it worked. At the Madison Girls School, two white students withdrew to protest the enrollment of the Dunn sisters. At the Bienville School, nearly half the student body—an estimated 175 white students—walked out after several African-American boys were admitted.

But as the months passed, it became clear that sporadic walk-outs could not overturn district policy and most whites acquiesced just as they had on the streetcars. At the close of the school year, a local African-American newspaper celebrated that integrated schools were "accomplished facts, which in their very nature are irreversible."

Whatever their personal feelings about race, teachers and administrators stopped resisting Conway's policy. A year into the integration experiment, Judge Dibble, who had since become a school board member, wrote that "no case has come to the [board's] knowledge of the exclusion of a pupil on account of race, color or previous condition [of servitude]." As tensions eased, one integrationist administrator quipped that there was little reason for resistance: after all, the schools had always been integrated on account of the common practice of prominent white fathers enrolling the children of their African-American mistresses in whites-only schools.

In the 1872 election, Conway bowed out, setting up a showdown. Lusher, who hoped to reclaim his old job, squared off against

William G. Brown, a mixed-race teacher and newspaper editor who had been born in New Jersey and educated in the Caribbean before arriving in New Orleans after the Civil War. Running on an openly white supremacist platform in a black-majority state, Lusher lost. But unable to accept the reality that he had been beaten by an African-American, for the rest of his life Lusher maintained that the election had been stolen by voter fraud and other "Radical rascalities."

Sworn in as the state's first African-American superintendent of education, Brown took stock. In a message to the legislature, he explained, "I am aware that the old leaven of prejudice because of race, etc., has not entirely disappeared." But he was heartened that the process was underway. If a single generation could be raised in integrated schools, Brown believed, the cycle of hatred, mistrust, and violence could be broken forever. "[My] officers are not influenced by the smiles or frowns of the narrow-minded and prejudiced," Brown intoned. "Would that we had more of them— and we soon will have, for it needs but five or six years more of labor like that performed in this State during the past three years; then our own schools will have developed them."

As evidence mounted that integration in the local schools was working as smoothly as integration on the city's streetcars, even members of the New Orleans *Américain* community, long steeped in prejudice, began to reevaluate. The most famous among them was journalist and author George Washington Cable. Born in 1844 to a wealthy New Orleans slaveholding family, Cable had served the Confederate cause as a clerk for Lieutenant General Nathan Bedford Forrest during the war. But after Appomattox, the two men's paths diverged. While Forrest busied himself organizing the Ku Klux Klan, Cable became one of the South's most eloquent and unlikely champions of civil rights.

Cable began his writing career as a cub reporter for the New

Orleans *Daily Picayune*, the mouthpiece of the conservative white elite from which he sprang. The first summer after the schools were integrated, Cable was assigned to report on the Teachers' Institute, a multiday professional-development course for New Orleans schoolteachers. Anything district progressives proposed, the reactionary *Picayune* pushed back against; Cable surely understood that his editors expected a hatchet job.

At the conference, the keynote speaker made for an obvious target. Cable tarred the lecturer, a young woman from New York, as a carpetbagging neophyte gorging on taxpayer funds. Cable sneered that "Miss Morris . . . the lady graduate from a New York training school . . . naturally requires of this business that it be, to her, a paying thing. It must pay her passage from place to place, and her board, and her lodging, and—her." The young reporter huffed that the conference was racially integrated, hardly shocking since attendance was compulsory for all New Orleans teachers in a district where African-Americans constituted a tenth of the faculty. The superintendent "call[ed] together his corps of teachers, male and female, *white and black*, into one hot room to listen to Miss Morris' lecture," Cable fumed in his dispatch. "The hall was nearly filled with female teachers, every here and there appearing among them some . . . mulatto appointee of the board." A precociously skilled wielder of the pen, Cable knew precisely what he was doing, conjuring for his readers a steamy chamber filled with young white women and old African-American men in a famously louche metropolis. His screed railed against this "mingling of races in [a] public assemblage" and was salaciously headlined "The 'Teachers' Institute' Trick."

But, in hindsight, this assignment was the beginning of Cable's civil rights conversion. Looking back nearly two decades later, the now-famous author recalled, "[I] was the first to notice and publish in resentful terms the fact that . . . compulsory attendance of all teachers . . . compelled whites and blacks to sit together under one roof, in one room, on terms of equality. . . . The other papers joined the hue and cry and I—suddenly weakened, slackened, ceased. I did not see that I was wrong. I only saw that there were two sides to the question and much doubted which side was least right."

Cable's editor, still oblivious to his underling's misgivings, and eager for another scandalous scoop, assigned him to spend several days reporting from inside the integrated schools. But this only made Cable more skeptical of white supremacism. "I saw, to my great and rapid edification," Cable later recounted, "colored women showing the graces and dignity of mental and moral refinement, ladies in everything save society's credentials; children and youth of both races standing in the same classes and giving each other peaceable, friendly, effective competition; and black classes, with black teachers, pushing intelligently up into the intricacies of high-school mathematics." Cable left the *Daily Picayune* soon afterwards. "By and by I lost my place," he phrased it, referring literally to his job but also to his place in society.

Through his work as an education reporter, he wrote, "I saw [that] the day must come when the Negro must share and enjoy in common with the white race the whole scale of *public* rights and advantages provided under American government; that *public* society must be reconstructed on this basis; that the Negro . . . has the ambitions and capacity to rise . . . and that reconstruction on this basis was the only way to come once more into harmony with those great first principles of government on which the nation has been founded." Turning scalawag in the midst of Reconstruction, Cable quit the "so-called Democratic party" and joined the Republican Party "rightly enough called radical since it alone went to the root of the difficulty."

But for many of his peers among the Uptown *Américains*, the defection of members in good standing only redoubled their sense of rage at a world upended. While much of the white population had quietly acquiesced to integrated schools and streetcars, to

African-American policemen and legislators, others smarted over their lost privilege. A small crew resolved to vent their dismay at New Orleans's defining public event: Mardi Gras.

A ribald rite celebrated since French colonial times, the pre-Lenten fête had begun as a downtown bacchanal of drunkenness, cross-dressing, and interracial debauchery. As one visitor to the city recorded of the 1835 celebration, "Men and boys, women and girls, bond and free, white and black, yellow and brown, exert themselves to invent and appear in grotesque, quizzical, dia-bolical, horrible, humorous, strange masks and disguises [and then] parade and march on foot, on horseback, in wagons, carts, coaches, cars &c, in rich confusion up and down the street, wildly shouting, singing, laughing, drumming, fiddling [and] fifing." To the *Américains*, this chaotic display was a civic embarrassment; shortly before the Civil War, they had hatched a plot to hijack Fat Tuesday. Improbably enough, they resolved to convert the bawdy feast day into a celebration of order and chastity.

Dubbing themselves the Mistick Krewe of Comus, a secret society of uptight Uptown Anglophones reoriented Mardi Gras celebrations around their own formal parade, which would run punctiliously on time along a fixed route and culminate in a debutante ball cele-brating their daughters' ostensible virginity. Rather than the free-wheeling party in the old Creole city that blurred the lines between male and female, white and black, slave and free, and spectator and participant, their parade, which first rolled in 1857, sharpened these lines. Enforcing rather than subverting social hierarchies, an all-white, all-male group of revelers placed themselves high on floats above their social inferiors and tossed them worthless coins. At the height of the city's integration, in 1873, the Mistick Krewe of Comus chose their most famous and controversial parade theme: "The Missing Links to Darwin's Origin of Species."

It was a timely choice. The theories of English biologist Charles Darwin had just crossed the Atlantic and were being hotly debated.

While backwoods fundamentalists fretted that men evolving from monkeys challenged the veracity of the Bible, better-educated Americans worried about the racial implications of Darwin's ideas. Before *The Origin of Species* was published, the theory of "polygenesis"—that each racial group had originated independently from "a different Adam"—had been popular. Its allure was obvious: if the various races of human beings did not spring from a common ancestor and, thus, were not interrelated, one race could be superior to another. To the dispossessed slave masters of Comus, the allure of the polygenesis theory was personal as well. To them, the idea that they were related to African-Americans was not some abstract possibility from prehistoric times; in many cases, it was the biological truth. The white elite of New Orleans and the mixed-race people across town were frequently different branches of the same family trees, sharing common white ancestors from the bygone era of slavery, quadroon balls, and *plaçage*. What in antebellum times had been an open secret was now something to be denied at all costs. For many of the members of Comus, eager to disown their African-American relatives, Darwin's attack on polygenesis felt like a personal affront.

On Mardi Gras night, 1873, the masked men of Comus rolled through town with a menagerie of "missing links"—grotesque part-animal, part-human figures—that mocked the civil rights activists of Reconstruction. Members of the city's biracial community were portrayed as humanoid chameleons, deviously changing their color to match their present company. Full-blooded blacks were represented by a tambourine-tapping monkey-man in a jockey outfit and a "Banjoist Orang[utang]," whom *The Daily Picayune* called, a "specimen . . . so amazingly like the broader-mouthed varieties of our own citizens, so Ethiopian in his exuberant glee, so fixedly at home in his pink shirt collar, so enraptured with himself and so fond of his banjo."

While some costumes lampooned social groups in general, others targeted specific individuals. General Benjamin Butler, the war-time Union administrator of the city, was portrayed as a carrion-eating hyena picking over a human skull. The chief of the city's integrated Metropolitan Police, Algernon Badger, was cast as a dopey bloodhound in a cop uniform. President Ulysses S. Grant, disdained by krewe members over his support for civil rights and his hard line against white supremacist terrorist groups, was presented as a cigar-smoking tobacco grub. Brazenly, the Mistick Krewe of Comus invited President Grant to their parade, hoping to mock the commander in chief to his face. The president demurred, writing that "it will be impossible for me to absent myself from the Capitol for so long a time during a session of Congress." Had he attended, Grant might have glimpsed the tableau at the postparade debutante ball, where a gorilla, flanked by the banjo-toting orangutang, wore a royal crown before being ousted by the white king of the krewe.

For all their self-regarding pomp, the reactionaries of Comus appeared to be out of step with their city. Rather than stew in racial resentment, growing numbers of New Orleanians were ready to accept equality. Shortly after the infamous parade, a diverse group of businessmen calling themselves the Committee of One Hundred began meeting in private to draw up a platform for racial reconciliation. If the city could unite behind an agreement recognizing equal rights for all, they ventured, it could emerge from a decade of federal oversight. Divided evenly between whites and people of color, the Committee drew heavily from the racially diverse downtown wards. Both "white Creoles" of ostensibly pure French and Spanish descent and openly mixed Creoles of color were well represented. It was a uniquely New Orleanian collection of American misfits—people who, not fitting neatly into America's black and white racial boxes, saw a brighter future in discarding the boxes altogether. Appropriately, they called their campaign the Unification Movement.

The leader of the African-American contingent was the state's new lieutenant-governor Caesar C. Antoine, elected in 1872. He was joined by forty-nine others, including Louis Charles Roudanez, the physician and businessman who had founded the *New Orleans Tribune*, and Aristide Mary, a biracial, Paris-educated attorney and philanthropist whose white father had left him a New Orleans real estate empire that included a full block of Canal Street, the city's main commercial thoroughfare.

While working on the platform, Roudanez gave an interview to the *New Orleans Times* in an attempt to put a human face on the campaign for civil rights. Aside from some familial roots on the African continent, there was little to distinguish the wealthy doctor from those in the highest echelons of New Orleans's white society. "I was educated at one of the most prominent universities in Paris," Roudanez noted, referring rather modestly to the Sorbonne. "I am better informed and better mannered than the average white man. I read, write and speak three languages fluently, and am a fair classical scholar. I am well off, have cultivated tastes, and, as you see, dress like a gentleman." And yet, on account of his background alone, he was often treated like a second-class citizen in his hometown. "When I visit a place of amusement," he told the paper, "the polite gentleman in attendance shows me to a cock-loft against the ceiling and into company I am not accustomed to. . . . I have often seen from my dizzy perch at the theatre, white men led out and ejected for misdemeanors that I never would think of committing. . . . Our principal wish is to see that, because of our skin we are not debarred from any public place to which we may choose to go."

The Committee of One Hundred was chaired by Isaac Newton Marks, a businessman and the city's fire chief. Originally from Charleston, Marx had moved to the Crescent City in his teen years and grown rich running the New Orleans, Florida, & Havana Steamship Company. Though Marks had supported the Confederacy during the Civil War—he had even signed the Louisiana secession ordinance, in 1861—he was by the 1870s a racial egalitarian. To win over conservatives, he argued as a realist that white supremacism in a black-majority state was a "suicidal course," but he also argued as a humanist. In a letter to the editor of the *New Orleans Times*, he swore, "It is my determination to continue to battle against these abstract, absurd and stupid prejudices, and to bring to bear the whole force of my character . . . to break them down. They must disappear; *they will disappear.* It is only a question of time." Marks's passion for destroying "stupid prejudices" was almost certainly related to his own experience dealing with them. Despite his having converted to Christianity, Marks was still widely regarded as belonging "as his name indicates [to the] ancient [Hebrew] race." This racial categorization, from an 1874 guidebook to the city and its powerbrokers, was a stunning testament to the entrenchment of late-nineteenth-century race theory, considering that Marks was the father of one of the city's most prominent Episcopal priests. If Marks's Judaism was an unalterable racial characteristic, he and his Christian children would surely be safer under a system of universal human rights rather than one of race-based legal codes.

To chair its committee on resolutions and, more crucially, serve as a celebrity endorser, the Unification Movement recruited the most prestigious misfit of them all: P. G. T. Beauregard. With his noble bearing and copper complexion, the old general already looked, even in life, like a venerated statue. The symbolism of having the man who had literally started the Civil War publicly back civil rights was stunning.

In a widely published speech, Beauregard laid out his pragmatic case for Unification. The state constitution already recognized equality in public accommodations and schools, so it was nothing but "obstinate denial" to still oppose it. For any doubters, his own decision to integrate his streetcar line vindicated such pragmatism. "It is manifest that nothing but the forbearance of the colored people prevents them from subjecting common carriers, and all keepers of places of public resort, to such losses and annoyances as would speedily compel the practical acknowledgments of their rights or the abandonment of business," the retired general explained. Further resistance would simply result in "a multiplicity of suits, the result of which . . . could not be doubtful [and] would soon exhaust the endurance of the most violent prejudice." More crucially, Beauregard argued, the whole notion that the color of one's skin trumped the content of one's character was absurd. After all, "in travelling, and at places of public resort, we often share these privileges in common with thieves, prostitutes, gamblers, and others who have worse sins to answer for than the accident of color." No doubt "the accident of color" that had rendered the general darker-skinned than many of the city's Afro-Creoles was a factor in his support for equal rights. The 1868 Louisiana constitution which, as Beauregard put it, mandated that "no preference is given on account of complexion," constituted the ultimate protection from those who questioned his whiteness.

Following the path cleared by Beauregard, the city's political, religious, and business establishments united behind the committee's platform. Two antebellum governors of the state endorsed the Unification Movement as did major corporate executives and bank presidents. The Catholic archbishop urged his multiracial flock to back Unification as well.

At a public meeting held in the largest venue in the city, Exposition Hall, on July 15, 1873, the Committee of One Hundred unveiled its platform. Hung around the long, detailed document was a banner that distilled its message into a simple statement: "Equal Rights, One Flag, One Country, One People." The platform mandated equality in all spheres of life—not only in politics but in employment, in investment, in "all places of licensed public resort [and] on all vehicles of public conveyance [and] in any of our public schools." To change hearts and minds, the white members of the movement publicly pledged "to exercise our moral influence, through personal advice and personal example, to bring about the rapid removal of all prejudices heretofore existing against the colored citizens." Befitting a city where assessing the racial breakdown of the crowd would have required pulling every attendee's birth certificate, the *Daily Picayune* described the gathering as majority white while the *New Orleans Times* reported it to be majority African-American.

After being formally installed as chairman, Isaac Newton Marks convened the meeting: "We come here to-night, I hope and trust in God, to lay upon the altar of our country all the prejudices of the past, to recognize all citizens of the United States as equals before the law." Following several speeches, the platform was adopted by voice vote. To Marks, the South's largest city embracing civil rights would "inaugurate . . . a new era, not only in our own State, but through the length and breadth of our entire land."

But even on this night of triumph, resistance to integrated schools simmered barely below the surface. When Marks brought up the schools in his speech, a heckler called out from the gallery: "Mr. President, I want to know whether you will be willing to send your children to the [integrated] public schools?" Marks responded weakly that those who disagreed with the platform were free to vote against it or to leave; but those who chose to stay must be respectful of the speakers.

It was an ominous interruption. The Committee of One Hundred's upper-crust membership left it vulnerable to populist attack. White corporate executives and government officials integrated the streetcars and public schools that neither they nor their children ever set foot in; elite people of color hoped to desegregate theaters most freedmen could never afford to attend. Isaac Newton Marks might ask rhetorically in his open letter to the *New Orleans Times*, "What is the state of things now, and what has it been since the 'star cars' were abolished? The white man, and the negro, ride together in them, without comment, notice, or contamination. . . . Prejudice . . . gave way to enlightened reason and convenience." And yet, how often was someone like Marks, the head of a multi-national corporation, taking the streetcar to work? Similarly, General Beauregard ran the transit company, but he wasn't packed into its vehicles twice a day on a sweaty commute.

And where was Beauregard? Despite his fulsome public endorsement, he was conspicuously absent from the mass meeting at Exposition Hall. Beyond New Orleans, the old general's support for Unification had been intensely controversial. Some conservative whites defended his endorsement of civil rights, if only as a reasonable concession to postbellum realities. Given "the encroachments of the combined carpet-bag and negro rule," the *Daily Phoenix* of Columbia, South Carolina, explained, "it is no disgrace to Gen. Beauregard, that he has excogitated and submitted for judgment an extraordinary remedy." But the rural South Carolina *Sumter News* tarred Beauregard as a "renegade" and a "traitor" and edged perilously close to issuing a death threat: "It is indeed a great pity that he was not killed by a stray [Union] shell . . . at the siege of Charleston, that he might have bequeathed an unsullied name to his children."

Most worrisome in New Orleans was the resistance brewing among Beauregard's fellow French Creoles. At the very height of the Unification campaign, the community's newspaper, *Le Carillon*, endorsed the adoption of the *Américains'* binary racial system, urging Louisianans to retroactively claim a mythical racial purity. In an editorial entitled, *"D'un coté ou de l'autre"* (To one side or the other), *Le Carillon* implored citizens to choose definitively whether they were white or black. "It's time to say it plain," the paper declared, "One must be either WHITE OR BLACK, let each man decide. There are two races here, one of them superior and the other inferior. . . . Their separation is *absolutely* necessary. Let's split, from now on, into two clearly delineated Parties: the WHITE PARTY and the BLACK PARTY. That way, the choice will be clear: white Louisiana or black Louisiana. Le Carillon raises the flag of the whites, in the firm conviction that it's only from within its fold that Louisiana can be saved."

At the very moment when New Orleans looked to move forward as one, enshrining a system of universal human rights befitting a place where the racial lines were hopelessly blurred, opponents vied to bisect the technicolor city into black and white.

7.

RADICAL UNIVERSITY

Henry E. Hayne of Charleston.

(Boston Public Library)

For years after the war, South Carolina was a state without a statehouse. As the damaged capitol building languished, the Reconstruction legislature met on the nearby campus of the state's flagship public university. Following the universal suffrage election of 1868, nearly equal numbers of white and African-American lawmakers arrived each day at the university chapel for their legislative sessions.

Union general William Tecumseh Sherman's wartime march had famously spared Charleston's historic heart, but the war left Columbia in ruins. General P. G. T. Beauregard had been charged with defending the South Carolina capital, and he had ordered its valuable cotton bales taken out of the city and burned rather than surrendered to the approaching army. But there was simply too much cotton in the city to evacuate and some got burned in the streets. These smoldering cotton bales sent featherweight wisps of embers far and wide, starting fires that incinerated the city. By the end of the conflagration, the statehouse was uninhabitable. One of the few sections of the capital to escape the inferno was The Horseshoe, the gracious U-shaped University of South Carolina campus. Closed during the war when its students found themselves drafted, and used as a military hospital, the college was saved from the fires by its brick perimeter wall.

The postwar legislative sessions in the campus chapel brought a daily reminder of all that had changed in South Carolina—and all that had not. Inside the chapel, legislators of all colors worked together as equals but outside, the state university remained whites-only. Students would sometimes visit to watch the proceedings of the legislature, many surely steaming that the body now accurately reflected the racial demographics of their state. Meanwhile the legislators, many of whom had personally enshrined the plank explicitly barring school segregation in the state constitution—"All the public schools, colleges and universities of this State, supported in whole or in part by the public funds, shall be free and open to all the children and youths of the State, without regard to race or color"—fumed that the university remained segregated.

Despite the broad guarantees of their state constitution, even in Charleston African-American parents felt too besieged by their white neighbors to dare desegregate the local schools. While Charleston had several excellent academies for African-Americans, including the Avery Institute, founded by Francis Lewis Cardozo as the successor to his Saxton School, it didn't have a single integrated public school.

Perhaps it was the physical proximity to a glaring contradiction that led South Carolina's leaders to a goal that would stun the nation: desegregating the University of South Carolina. Founded as South Carolina College in 1801, the school had traditionally educated the white male scions of the state's major slaveholding families. Prying open The Horseshoe for African-Americans would be a powerful symbol that even the most cloistered bastions of white privilege would be made accessible to the state's black majority.

Shortly after the integrated legislature first convened on campus, Radical Republicans called for desegregating the college. The state's white elite recoiled. A white legislator from Columbia proposed creating an all-black college at the Citadel in Charleston rather than risk the integration of the state's leading public university. Even the *New York Times* correspondent covering the proceedings dismissed university desegregation as a bridge too far. "Everybody, white and black, who is not a monomaniac," he wrote "sees that to force mixing of the youth of the two races in the same colleges upon the people of the State, would be to inaugurate a struggle, out of which the white would come very much worsted, and in which the negro would be annihilated."

Disregarding these predictions of race war, South Carolina legislators moved forward. As in New Orleans, a key barrier to change was bureaucratic—conservative school administrators who ignored their mandates and would have to be replaced. In 1869, under the leadership of Franklin J. Moses Jr., the fire-eater turned radical from Charleston, the legislature gave itself the power to appoint university board members. Moses had been elevated to house speaker with the support of the Brown Fellowship Society, which opted to back him over black South Carolina transplant Robert Brown Elliott. On the seven-member university board, Moses and four other progressive whites were joined by two African-Americans. Both were men of learning: Francis Lewis Cardozo and Dr. Benjamin Boseman, a New York–born free man of color who had earned a medical degree from Bowdoin College in Maine and had come to Charleston as a military doctor with the United States Colored Troops. The legislature also revised the articles of incorporation for the university to specify that "neither the . . . Board of Trustees, nor the Faculty of the University, shall make any distinction in admission of students or the management of the University on account of race, color or creed."

But outside the chapel, on campus, nothing changed. University applications dropped as white students grew apprehensive about attending a college that might be desegregated even as admissions officials continued to refuse applications from African-Americans. In the meantime, the integrated legislature found itself on the hook to support an all-white state university. With only the most radical of Republicans willing to force integration, it was not until a progressive sweep in the election of 1872 that the process moved forward. In the radical triumph, Moses was elected governor and Cardozo state treasurer; the new legislature appointed an African-

American majority to the university board, with Moses serving as a hands-on board chairman *ex officio*. In the wake of the election, the *Fairfield Herald* newspaper, published in the backwoods region north of the state capital, warned readers to brace themselves for "the hell-born policy which has trampled the fairest and noblest States of our great sisterhood beneath the unholy hoofs of African savages and shoulder-strapped brigands . . . the rule of gibbering, louse-eaten, devil-worshiping barbarians, from the jungles of Dahomy [modern-day Benin], and peripatetic buccaneers from Cape Cod, Memphremagog, Hell, and Boston."

With the zeal of the convert to the cause of equality, Moses, whom one Jim Crow—era historian would dub "the most perfect scalawag, perhaps, in all the South," prioritized desegregating the university, where he himself had been a student in the 1850s. Cardozo, who had had to leave South Carolina for Europe to get a university education, hoped to right this wrong for future generations. In his first annual message to the legislature, Governor Moses scolded legislators for dragging their feet. The Charlestonian misfits, Moses and Cardozo, just needed a spark to force integration.

The fuse would be lit on the evening of April 2, 1873. As part of its effort to transform from a training ground for South Carolina's elite to a font of general enlightenment, the university had begun offering public lectures. While no African-American had yet enrolled as a student or been hired as a faculty member, the lectures were explicitly open to all and were widely attended by Carolinians of all colors. After a long day of work at the state supreme court, Justice Jonathan Jasper ("J. J.") Wright decided to take in that evening's presentation on the principles of electricity.

Born free in New York State, Wright had been the first black man admitted to the Pennsylvania bar. He moved South after the war to work at American Missionary Association freedmen schools and became active in politics, serving as a delegate to the South Carolina constitutional convention of 1868 and then as a state senator from a black-majority district in coastal Beaufort. In 1870, Wright had been appointed to the South Carolina Supreme Court, becoming the only African-American to serve on a state supreme court in the nineteenth century.

Around 7:30 on the evening of the lecture, Wright entered the university-chapel-cum-statehouse through its right-hand door, whereupon he was immediately directed to leave, reenter through the left-hand door, and sit on the left side of the chapel. Wright, who was middle-aged and well known in Columbia, initially assumed that the right side had been set aside for university students and the left for public visitors. But as the hall filled up, the attorney realized that the faculty members who had organized the lecture were seating whites in the center and people of color to the left. His anger rising, Wright stormed out.

Over the next few days, Wright drew up a calculated but impassioned open letter and sent it to the capital's progressive newspaper, the Columbia *Daily Union-Herald*. The incident at the university lecture, Wright offered in his succinct legal prose, "is worthy of the highest and most profound consideration of every . . . well meaning citizen of our State, no matter of what complexion he may be, because the time has fully arrived when all distinctions in that direction should not be permitted to enter the sacred precincts of our . . . institutions of learning."

In careful rhetoric, Wright acknowledged that a distinction could still be made between the public and private spheres. "I do not ask or contend for social equality," he wrote. "I do not regard it as my right or privilege to demand of my neighbor, that I should be invited to his parlor to mingle with him and those of his choice. . . . But I do ask, and demand as a matter of right and justice, not only for myself, but of the people of this State and of the United States, of every or any complexion or political creed, that so far as public accommodations are concerned that no distinction be made on account of race or color. We, of all classes, have had enough of that."

Facing this savvy opponent, the lecture's organizers offered the far-fetched excuse that it was all a misunderstanding. Seating was not by race, they claimed, but by affiliation, with students seated in the center and state officials, like Wright, on the left. Wright countered that a white state official and his wife had also attended the lecture and they had been seated in the center, and an African-American private citizen had been seated on the left. The university board backed Wright and made clear to the faculty that their time for foot-dragging had run out. The university would be desegregated imminently.

The most hostile professors, including Robert W. Barnwell, a history teacher who had served as university president in the antebellum era, and J. L. Reynolds, a veteran philosophy professor, were forced out. Reynolds later sniffed that desegregation was "pretensive only—the purpose being to show the white people of South Carolina that the negroes intended to dominate in the State university and there enforce the social equality of the black with the white race." But even as the conservative Columbia *Daily Phoenix* lamented that "the axe continues to descend upon the necks of the unreconstructed . . . professors," not everyone quit in protest. Cyrus D. Melton, a university alumnus and Confederate veteran, continued to run the law school after integration until his death in 1875.

With integration looming, most white students transferred out rather than stay for the coming school year. In an ominous show of white supremacist solidarity on both sides of the Mason-Dixon line, Union College in upstate New York and Washington and Lee University in Virginia created bespoke scholarships for white South Carolina students who refused to remain enrolled with African-American classmates.

Cognizant that the nation was watching, South Carolina integrationists were keen to tap a model student to desegregate the university. As with the test-case plaintiffs in civil rights litigation, it was crucial to find someone broadly considered "respectable," so they chose a man of impeccable credentials: Henry Hayne, the biracial freeman and military veteran descended from one of the state's leading white political families. After fighting (on both sides) in the Civil War, serving as a delegate at the 1868 state constitutional convention, a representative in the statehouse, and a state land commissioner, in 1872 Hayne had been elected South Carolina's secretary of state. Having received a fine private education in his antebellum Charleston youth, there was no question Hayne was qualified for higher education. To break the color line, Hayne would enroll at the university's medical school.

On October 7, 1873, Hayne, with the proud bearing of an elite Brown Charlestonian, entered the university library. It was a space of supreme dignity, its light-filled, columned interior a model of Palladian proportion. A bust of Robert Y. Hayne, the now-deceased former Charleston mayor, South Carolina governor, and U.S. senator—and Henry's white uncle—silently looked down on the proceedings as his biracial nephew signed his name to the ledger of enrolled medical students. In response, a white medical student from Columbia, R. Gourdin Sloan, marched to the ledger and ostentatiously struck out his own name from the registration book, defacing the volume in the process. Several other white students followed suit, vehemently crossing out their names, thereby dropping out of the school.

When *Scribner's Monthly* correspondent Edward King arrived in Columbia later that week, he noted the jarring contrast between the college's placid, arboreal campus and the events that were rocking it. "The venerable University . . . nestle[d] charmingly in the midst of a grand tree-clotted park . . . give[s] the casual visitor the impression that he is visiting a 'grove of Academe,' rather than a perturbed . . . capital," King wrote. Remarkably, the Northern correspondent noted the bust of Robert Y. Hayne in the library, but failed to make the connection between the Hayne statue and the

Hayne student, noting "the busts of [John C.] Calhoun and [Robert Y.] Hayne seemed to look down from their niches with astonishment upon the changed order of things," and leaving it at that. Many Northerners, King apparently included, assumed that when African-Americans shared the last names of leading white Southern families, it was because they or their ancestors had been owned by those families as slaves, not because they were biologically part of those families (or both). White Southerners did little to disabuse clueless Yankees of this notion and sometimes actively dissembled. The Columbia *Daily Phoenix* greeted Hayne's enrollment with the Freudian slip that "the races can no more agree in the same classes in school or college, than they can in churches or in the family."

Robert Y. Hayne had died a year before his mixed-race nephew was born, so there is no telling how he would have greeted his matriculation, either publicly or privately. But for Henry Hayne's white cousin, noted poet Paul Hamilton Hayne, the mythic bonds of whiteness that connected him to complete strangers among the state's Caucasian minority outweighed his actual blood ties to Henry. Not long after his biracial cousin had been elected secretary of state in the Radical Republican sweep of 1872, Paul railed in a letter over "*rogues & negroes* . . . in political power."

In the wake of Henry Hayne's enrollment, two medical professors tendered their resignations in protest, threatening the viability of the university's modest medicine department. In response, the Board of Trustees put out a public statement:

> This Board accepts the resignations [but] deems it due to the public, to place upon record their conviction that the resignations of these gentlemen were caused by the admission, as a student of the Medical department of the University, of Hon. Henry E. Hayne, Secretary of State, a gentleman of irreproachable character, against whom the said Professors can suggest no objection except,—in their opinion,—his race;

and recognizing this as the cause of these resignations, this
Board cannot regret that a spirit so hostile to the welfare
of our State, as well as to the dictates of justice and claims
of our common humanity, will no longer be represented in a
University which is the common property of all our citizens
without distinction of race.

The statement went out of its way to flag the absurdity of the
faculty members' objection to "in their opinion,—his race." After
all, Henry Hayne was described in the press as being "as white as
any of his ancestors." In a state filled with people of such mixed
backgrounds, drawing hard-and-fast racial lines was folly. But as
resignations swept the faculty at the beginning of the fall semes-
ter, the integrationist board was left with the daunting practical
problem of simply keeping the university running.

The stakes were high. Successfully integrating the flagship university of the state that had started the Civil War would be a powerful symbol that Reconstruction could succeed—especially since
prior efforts elsewhere in the Deep South had all faltered. In Mississippi, a radical board failed in its attempt to desegregate Ole
Miss. Faculty vows to bar any African-American who dared enroll,
combined with an ever-present threat of white supremacist terrorism from the hinterlands surrounding the Oxford campus, resulted
in not a single student of color applying for admission. Giving up,
the radicals created Alcorn University, an all-black institution, in
1871. Even in Louisiana, for all the success in the New Orleans
public schools, higher education remained almost completely segregated. An effort by the state legislature to force Louisiana State
University to integrate was staved off in 1873 when the university president opted to forfeit state funding rather than obey the
mandate. Integration occurred only at Straight University, an
institution founded in 1869 to educate African-Americans, when a
handful of white students enrolled in its law school.

To keep the University of South Carolina running, the trustees recruited Fisk P. Brewer, a classics professor who had graduated with honors from Yale, to lead the faculty. The scion of a prominent New England abolitionist family, Brewer had briefly taught at the University of North Carolina before reactionaries retook the state. Beginning work in Columbia in October 1873, the same month Hayne enrolled, Brewer replaced William J. Rivers, a classicist who had walked out in July to protest plans for integration.

With the eyes of the nation on South Carolina's educational experiment, the faculty pulled off a hiring coup, snagging the man who had desegregated America's most prestigious university. In 1870, Richard Theodore Greener had become the first African-American to graduate from Harvard in its nearly two-and-a-half-century-long existence. With Greener's hiring as a philosophy professor, Governor Franklin Moses boasted to the legislature that "for the first time in the history of South Carolina one of the literary chairs in her highest institution of learning is worthily and acceptably filled by a colored Professor—a gentleman of varied attainments, cultivated and refined, and an honored graduate of grand old Harvard."

Greener had been born free in Philadelphia in 1844, and moved with his family to Boston nine years later. They arrived in the city after abolitionist attorney Charles Sumner had lost his test case to desegregate the local public schools but before the Massachusetts legislature overruled the state supreme court to integrate them, so young Theodore was sent to a progressive private school open to what it termed the "four different races . . . the Anglo Saxon, Teutonic, Celtic, and African." For higher education, the young scholar went to Oberlin, America's first college open to students of all races and genders, where he studied for two years. Returning to Boston, Greener enrolled at Harvard in 1865. In a fit of idealism spurred by the Union's war victory, Harvard opened its gates to an African-American for the first time, though it insisted on enrolling the twenty-one-year-old Greener as a freshman.

Being the only African-American student on campus, Greener later wrote, he felt "isolated from the race." Though widely known on Harvard Yard as a walking, talking integration experiment, Greener always insisted that, despite the awkwardness, he was treated well by fellow students and by the faculty. With greater anonymity off campus, Greener, who was light-skinned—an inheritance he attributed to his maternal grandfather, a Spaniard born in Puerto Rico, and possibly other European ancestors—sometimes passed for white. The 1870 census listed him as a white man. The confusion might have arisen from the census taker's evaluation of his light complexion but, more likely, the canvasser falsely assumed that since Greener's occupation was "Harvard student," he must be white. After all, until Greener's enrollment, Harvard students were, by definition, young white men; all of the school's thousands of alumni had been white men. Down South, with his mixed-race coloring and Harvard-bred accent, Greener referred to himself with self-deprecation as "a smoked Yankee."

After graduating from Harvard, Greener began his slow journey southward. He first worked as an English teacher at the Quaker-run Institute for Colored Youth in his native Philadelphia. In 1872 he moved to Washington, D.C., to become the principal of the Preparatory School, the top African-American academy in the capital's segregated public school system. While in D.C., Greener contributed articles to Frederick Douglass's *New National Era* newspaper and clerked for the district attorney in preparation for law school. He also began courting a mixed-race member of Georgetown's well-established antebellum free people of color community named Genevieve "Genie" Fleet, who worked as a music teacher in the city's all-black schools. Within two weeks of their marriage, the couple moved to Columbia, South Carolina, to begin Greener's new job as a university professor.

In addition to teaching students and giving open lectures as part of the university's enlarged mission to educate the general public, Greener also studied law, earning a degree in 1876, and ran the university library. When Greener took over, the facility was in shambles from vandalism. It had been ransacked, presumably by white supremacists registering their rage on the site where Henry Hayne had formally enrolled, but no one was ever arrested or charged with the crime. (The collection was also in disarray because Greener's white predecessor couldn't read Greek, Latin, or French and had made numerous cataloging mistakes.) By all accounts, Greener whipped the library into stellar shape.

With the faculty coming together, attention turned to student recruitment. Integrationists hoped to enlist African-American students on par with Hayne and Greener, whose qualifications were beyond question. Only by offering education at or above antebellum standards, could the university avoid the dangerous charge of dumbing down the curriculum for less qualified students of color. Enrolling youths born to Charleston's antebellum free aristocracy of color was the easiest way to vindicate the experiment.

Francis Lewis Cardozo threw himself into recruitment. Having been forced to travel to Scotland for higher education, he had always resented the racial rejection of his homeland. Now, in the aftermath of the Civil War, all-black colleges were springing up across America and scooping up the most talented students. Many of the rising generation of Charleston Browns had enrolled at the newly founded Howard University in Washington, D.C. Desperately wanting to bring them back to South Carolina, Cardozo went up to woo them home.

Convincing Charleston-born Howard University students to return to South Carolina proved rather easy. Charleston Browns had left town for higher education more out of necessity than desire. Cornelius Chapman Scott, a mixed-race Charlestonian born to a successful feather-fan maker and his wife, had studied at Cardozo's Avery Institute before leaving for Howard in 1872. His letters home from Washington paint a picture of acute homesickness.

Writing his father soon after leaving, he vowed, "I am going home as soon as I can make it convenient." Then, following his visit, on the return trip by boat, he fell ill from a mixture of homesickness and seasickness. "I began to feel sick just after we got past Fort Sumter," he recounted, "and emptied all my dinner into the waters of the wide Atlantic." Like every Southerner who has ever gone North, Scott complained about the weather, insisting that his particular dorm room was one of the coldest in the whole building.

As Scott later recalled,

> When the University of South Carolina threw open its doors to colored students, I was a freshman at Howard University, and learned of the changed conditions from Prof. F. L. Cardozo who had come to Washington . . . to acquaint [me and] other college students from South Carolina of the change and to say to them he advised our returning to the State immediately and entering the university. He gave me $100 to defray the traveling and incidental expenses . . . and we obtained honorable dismissal from Howard and left almost immediately. Each of us subsequently repaid Mr. Cardozo this loan. . . . All of us were colored Charlestonians and all of us were in the college department at Howard University. Other South Carolina students from Howard followed and, I think, some from Lincoln [University in Pennsylvania] and other Northern colleges.

Among Cardozo's protégés was Thomas McCants Stewart, also a transfer student from Howard who, in 1875, would become the University of South Carolina's first African-American graduate and his class's valedictorian. Stewart had been born free in Charleston in the early 1850s and raised in Charleston's Fifth Ward, a hub of the city's free, mixed-race community. Little is known about Stewart's parents—his mother was reputed to be related to a prominent white New York political family—but they were well educated and they enrolled Thomas in private school at age four. In 1865, when Charleston fell to Union forces, Stewart was the perfect age to embrace the new opportunities. He studied at a series of schools run by the Freedmen's Bureau and the American Missionary Association, where Cardozo spotted his potential. In his search for students, Cardozo swept Stewart up in what *Scribner's* correspondent Edward King called "the grand onward movement" of African-Americans into the formerly segregated university.

This movement actually began rather slowly. Opting for quality over quantity, in the first year of integration the University of South Carolina enrolled just twelve undergraduates—five whites and seven African-Americans. Of the five white students, three had been enrolled before Hayne broke the color line but had refused to follow their classmates out to protest integration. All of the African-American students were native Charlestonians. Six had transferred from Howard and one from Amherst College in Massachusetts. The faculty considered those who had studied under Cardozo at the Avery Institute to be the best prepared for college work. As Cardozo himself had written to his Northern patrons shortly after the war, "Again you are aware that in Charleston, and other similar Southern cities there has always been a large number of colored people who have *always been free*, and who were therefore allowed to educate themselves. One fourth of my [Avery Institute] school is composed of such, and they are advancing towards the higher branches, and are anxious to be prepared for Teachers."

With some of the best-prepared African-Americans in the state now enrolled at the university, administrators turned to the task of educating black students from the almost unfathomably underprivileged background of having been born enslaved. Up to that point, the only freedman enrolled in the university was James J.

Durham, the biracial son of a slave master and one of his slaves, who could enroll in the university because his white father paid his tuition bill. To make the university accessible to ordinary freedmen, in 1874 the legislature created a system of scholarships designed to support one gifted student from each county in the state. Administrators organized competitive exams in the county seats with the top performer awarded a full scholarship, free campus housing, and a $200 living-expense stipend, all renewable with passing grades. But even with this generous offer, administrators scrambled to recruit qualified candidates, and many of the scholarship seats went unfilled. To fill the spots, administrators sometimes tapped elite Charlestonians with only the most tenuous connections to the rural counties they purported to represent. It was a redux of the situation at the state constitutional convention of 1868, where representatives of rural areas, including Henry Hayne himself, were often ringers from Charleston. Cornelius Chapman Scott won the scholarship from rural Marion County presumably because his father, who owned several farms, had land holdings there. But Scott was a Charlestonian through and through.

In a further attempt to bring in students from more humble backgrounds, the legislature authorized a preparatory school on campus where students could complete remedial coursework to prepare them for university-level studies. The trustees defended these remedial courses taken by what the faculty termed the "sub-freshman" class, as the only way to "meet . . . the educational wants of the people of this State."

Conservative Carolinians seized on these new outlays as a way to oppose racial equality on fiscal grounds rather than for openly racist reasons. The Columbia *Daily Phoenix* derided the scholarship program as "a scheme to buy students," though progressives retorted that, by that logic, the tuition-free military academies at Annapolis and West Point would be guilty of the same offense. The hosting of a teachers' college on campus, founded in September 1874, similarly irked conservatives. The teacher's academy not only enrolled students of all colors but both genders. Overwhelmingly female—fully twenty-five of the thirty-one students enrolled in its first class were women—for the university's reactionary alumni, a nostalgic visit to The Horseshoe, now trod by African-American female students, had become a shocking experience. As before, white supremacists largely hid their racist agenda behind public laments of declining academic standards.

Yielding to constant pressure from conservative attacks, in April 1875 the board of trustees abolished the subfreshman class over Professor Greener's bitter opposition. Greener slammed the volte-face as tantamount to destroying the youths' life chances by "dismiss[ing] them to the several Counties where absolutely no opportunity for higher instruction lay open to them."

Despite this setback, the university grew rapidly and diversified geographically. In 1876 every member of the the tiny senior class hailed from Charleston, but the junior and sophomore classes were a mix of Charlestonians and natives of Columbia, the state capital, and the freshman class, boasted over sixty students, coming from all across the state, including such tiny hamlets as Dry Creek and Dorn's Mills.

The Radical politicians who had pioneered the integration experiment were quick to declare it a success. Governor Moses crowed to the legislature that the university was "flourishing." Even cautious observers, watching the university's development over several years, concluded that integration had become the new normal on The Horseshoe.

For faculty chairman Fisk Brewer, the university's grand experiment had done nothing less than validate the principles of the Enlightenment—that all were equal and that people of any background or color could be elevated by education. Initially, he conceded, "the Freshman Class [was] of a very elementary character [but] these belong to the time before the class entered upon their quadrennial college course." They quickly caught up, Brewer happily reported in an 1875 letter to a colleague, and they embarked upon the type of classical education required of any educated person in the nineteenth century. "The Class of 1878 (or Freshman Class)," Brewer bragged, "has recited, in Latin . . . Caesar, Cicero and Livy, . . . in Greek, the whole of Harkness' First Greek Book, in Xenophon's Expedition of Cyrus, and eight hundred lines in the Iliad. They have recited also in Hadley's Greek, and Harkness's Latin Grammar."

To racists' claims that African-Americans were uneducable, Brewer now had an airtight retort:

> Some, even [among the University's] graduates, may say in their bitterness, Would that it had been utterly destroyed before its halls were polluted by the admission of a negro! But . . . [e]ducation makes a gentleman. The black boy who has solved all the knotty problems in arithmetic, who can explain the cube root and complete the value of partial payments, who has learned the long paradigms of Greek and Latin, and read in the original of Caesar's wars and of Xenophon's march, Cicero's patriotic orations and the poetry of Virgil and Homer—is no longer a cornfield negro. He has a platform of common knowledge and sentiment with his white classmate. . . . It may seem strange to those who have never seen such a sight, but it is true that most of the advanced students of color now in the University to-day are gentlemen, and deserve to be treated as such.

Reports varied on the extent to which student life was integrated on campus. Brewer, perhaps honestly describing social realities or perhaps hoping to allay conservative fears, maintained that

it is an insult to both colored and white to stigmatize the institution as a "miscegenation university." Young men here have
the same feelings as young men elsewhere. The white neither
occupy the same bed-room, nor eat at the same table with the
colored. But they do not see why, if a black man and a white
man can ride on the same seat in the market wagon or in the
railroad car for the sake of convenience or economy without
any impropriety, why they may not sit on the same seat to
hear about medicine and law and science and literature.

By contrast, student Thomas McCants Stewart described a
much more integrated social environment in his 1874 dispatches
to Frederick Douglass's Washington-based *New National Era.*
"The University now numbers one hundred and ten students [and]
I want it distinctly understood that the University of South Carolina is not in possession of any one race," Stewart wrote in a letter to the editor. "The two races study together, visit each other's
rooms, play ball together, walk into the city together, without the
blacks feeling honored or the whites disgraced." To the future valedictorian, the university was a new society in embryo that only
needed to be nurtured. "If the time ever comes when the descendants of the [white slaveholders] shall believe in the unlimited
brotherhood of man," he wrote, "the University of South Carolina
will have a dwelling place in the breast of every Africo-American."
    The stormy days of walk-outs and vandalism now seemed dis-
tant. As the liberal Columbia *Daily Union-Herald* recounted in
1875, "It was prophesied that the admission of colored students
would never be endured—that it would break up the university;
but white and colored students are now pursuing their studies
amicably together, and there is no war of races." The *New York
Times,* which had once predicted black Carolinians would be "annihilated" through race war should the university be desegregated,
now informed its readers that, according to the university presi-

dent, "there was absolutely nothing in the color of a man's skin as indicating his mental capabilities, but everything depended upon his opportunities." The *Times* correspondent noted that the "President of the University . . . had taken special pains to test this question by a comparison not only of the blacks with the whites, but also with the partly colored or mulattoes, and . . . as a matter of fact, the black students were a little ahead, on their average marks, of both the whites and mulattoes, which he attributed to their closer application to study, arising perhaps, from their anxiety to maintain their standing and not fall behind." The reporter quoted one graduation attendee's claim that the speech given by an African-American graduate "was quite equal to anything . . . heard at a Harvard University Commencement." With the evident success in South Carolina, the president of Louisiana State University, David F. Boyd, decided he could no longer resist calls for integration. He grudgingly drew up a secret plan to desegregate Louisiana State.

For all its successes, the integration of the University of South Carolina continued to be regarded as an experiment, not a fait accompli. African-American students still faced harassment from white townies. In one incident, street toughs pelted the campus with stones; in another, they breached the gates of The Horseshoe in the middle of the night and were turned back only after an exchange of gunfire. Integration remained controversial politically as well, supported only by Radical Republicans. For Franklin J. Moses Jr., desegregating the university was his proudest achievement as governor. He bragged, "[When] the reconstructed administration of government in South Carolina . . . came into power it was a statutory offense against the law of the land to impart even the rudiments of a common school education to a South Carolinian, because, forsooth, he was black, while the reconstructed government has made it a statutory offense to hinder or prevent any child in the State, of whatever color, from obtaining a[n] education." But the Democrats continued to call the campus "Radical University"—and they didn't mean it as a compliment. What if they took over?

In the Southern states with white majorities, voters had already ousted Republicans from power, often with an assist from terrorist violence at election time. Giving their reconquest religious over-tones, the leaders of these campaigns—often suited politicians by day and hooded Klansmen by night—dubbed themselves "Redeem-ers" and their seizures of state governments "Redemption." Once in power in these "redeemed" states, legislators overturned or ceased to enforce whatever civil rights laws they found on the books and assiduously suppressed black voting. When white supremacist Democrats retook power in Tennessee, for example, they repealed the state law mandating nondiscrimination on railway cars and passed a new state constitution requiring segregated schools. In Georgia, Democrats enacted a poll tax to winnow down African-American voting rolls and, in the state capital, switched from dis-trict elections to citywide seats to purge nonwhites from the Atlanta city council. (Early-twentieth-century history books would christen the entire post-Reconstruction period the "Redemption era.")

In the fall of 1876, an African-American University of South Carolina student inquired of his professor, "what you think will be the result to us if the other party gains the election." There is no record of the professor's response. Undoubtedly, it was a fate almost too dispiriting to imagine.

8.

LAWS AND OUTLAWS

Alonzo J. Ransier of Charleston.

(Brady-Handy Photograph Collection, Library of Congress,

Prints & Photographs Division [LC-DIG-cwpbh-00613])

With civil rights progress varying state by state, even county by county, activists aimed to safeguard their achievements and spread them nationwide by passing federal civil rights legislation. In the state legislatures, breaking the memberships' color line had been crucial in passing equal rights laws, so as Radical Reconstruction took hold, activists set their sights on a momentous goal: integrating the national legislature in Washington. It began in New Orleans in 1869 when local voters sent a mixed-race man, John Willis Menard, to represent them in Congress. Born free, the grandson of a prominent French-Canadian politician from Illinois, Menard was elected to the House of Representatives in a special election to fill a vacant seat. All sides alleged fraud at the ballot box and both Menard and his white Democratic opponent, Caleb Hunt, went to Washington demanding to be sworn in. Faced with the prospect of seating its first ever African-American, Congress used its broad constitutional powers to determine qualifications for its own membership to duck the controversy. The House declared itself unable to adjudicate the dispute and opted not to seat either candidate.

The following year, with the ink hardly dry on the Fifteenth Amendment, ratified February 3, 1870—"The right of citizens of the United States to vote shall not be denied or abridged by the United States or by any State on account of race, color, or previous condition of servitude"—a Mississippian arrived to integrate the United States Senate. The multiracial Reconstruction legislature of the Magnolia State had chosen Hiram Rhodes Revels, a mixed-race educator and minister, to fill the vacant Senate seat abandoned by Jefferson Davis himself when he walked out of Congress, in 1861, to become the president of the Confederacy. How would Congress deal with a man whom one white civil rights advocate dubbed a "Fifteenth Amendment in flesh and blood."

Revels arrived at the Capitol Building and strode through its halls in a long black coat, a walking stick in his white-gloved hand. Born free in North Carolina and educated at a Quaker seminary in Indiana and an abolitionist college in Illinois, Revels had returned to the South to staff a Freedmen's Bureau school. With his mixed background—part African, part European, part Native American—there were undoubtedly slaves somewhere in his family tree, but their identities had been lost to history. As Revels wrote in his autobiography, all of his ancestors "as far back as my knowledge extends, were free."

Faced with a man of manifest dignity and impeccable educational credentials, Democrats scrambled for a way to disqualify him. In a heated debate on the Senate floor, Maryland senator George Vickers, the man whose vote had spared Andrew Johnson at his impeachment trial, seized on a legalistic reading of the Constitution's qualification for senators—that candidates must have been U.S. citizens for at least nine years before being elected. Like all free men of color, Vickers argued, Revels had had his citizenship revoked by the Supreme Court's *Dred Scott* decision in 1857 and only had it reinstated by the Civil Rights Act of 1866. Thus, in the reading of his Democratic opponents, the American-born Revels was only four years into his current American citizenship— five years shy of the minimum nine required for senators by the Constitution.

In their lawyerly defense of the Mississippian, Republicans noted that Revels's mixed ancestry left open the question of whether the *Dred Scott* decision even applied to him. After all, it had never been adjudicated by a court whether Revels was an

African-American, an American Indian, or a white man. "What is the evidence of his being a negro?" demanded Nevada Republican William Morris Stewart.

Civil rights stalwart Massachusetts senator Charles Sumner opted to defend Revels not with legalistic nitpicking but with soaring oratory. Taking the floor of the chamber where he had been physically beaten by South Carolina fire-eater Preston Brooks before the Civil War, Sumner reminded his colleagues that at the founding of the nation, free people of color were considered citizens by nearly all of the original thirteen states. *Dred Scott* was an aberration that was immediately overruled by both war and law. "All men are created equal, says the great Declaration [and] to-day we make the Declaration a reality. For a long time a word only, it now becomes a deed. For a long time a promise only, it now becomes a consummated achievement. The Declaration was only half established by Independence. The greater duty remained behind. In assuring the Equal Rights of all we completed the work," Sumner intoned. "Colored persons must be Senators."

And so it was. Revels was accepted with an overwhelming vote from his new colleagues. As one observer wrote, the dignified new senator, "who had been sitting all day on a sofa in the rear of Mr. Sumner's seat, advanced toward the clerk's desk with a modest yet firm step. . . . He was in no way embarrassed [but] swallowed the iron-clad oath without wincing, and bowed his head quite reverently when the words 'so help you God' were rendered."

The scene was repeated later that year across the rotunda when Joseph Hayne Rainey, a mixed-race barber from Charleston, arrived to represent the Holy City in the House of Representatives. Revels having set the precedent, Rainey was sworn in as the first nonwhite member of the House without a single objection from the nearly three hundred congressmen in the body.

By the time of his election, Rainey was a successful Charleston businessman who had blended seamlessly into the city's Brown elite, but he had more humble beginnings. Born sixty miles up the coast in Georgetown, South Carolina, he had spent his childhood in slavery. His mother was of mixed French and African descent, possibly part of the diaspora of Haitian slaves brought by their masters to America in the wake of the revolution there. His enslaved father, Edward, was a trained barber who was hired out by his master. Slowly building up a nest egg, Edward eventually purchased his family's freedom and two slaves of his own. After his liberation, Joseph went north to Philadelphia, where he met and married his wife, Susan, a Caribbean-born woman who, like his mother, was of mixed French and African lineage. The couple returned to Charleston before the Civil War, with Joseph plying the family barbering trade at the luxurious Mills House hotel and prospering in the city.

With war on the horizon, Rainey found himself conscripted into service for the Confederacy digging trenches. When the shooting began, Rainey was sent to work as a cook on a blockade-runner. As a married man in his thirties given servile roles solely on account of his ancestry, Rainey soon soured on the Confederate cause. In 1862, he and his wife left for Bermuda to wait out the war. When peace came, the Raineys returned to Charleston and Joseph became active in Republican politics. He represented his native Georgetown at the 1868 constitutional convention and, in 1870, was nominated to finish out the term of a congressman who had resigned in a corruption scandal. That November, Rainey won an overwhelming victory to retain the seat, cementing his stunning rise from slave to congressman.

With the congressional color line broken in Washington, civil rights advocates pushed to lock in gains, like streetcar desegregation, and enshrine others, like integrated schools, in federal law. Just weeks after Revels's seating, Senator Sumner introduced a new bill entitled "An act to protect citizens of the United States in their civil rights, and to furnish the means for their vindication." Sumner's far-reaching proposal required nationwide desegregation of public transportation ("railroads, steamboats, public conveyances"), lodging ("hotels"), entertainment venues ("licensed theaters, houses of public entertainment"), and public education ("common schools"). Treading on constitutionally shaky ground, it also mandated the desegregation of religious institutions ("church[es] and cemeter[ies]"). Sumner viewed his new bill as the capstone of a lifelong crusade for equal rights, begun decades earlier representing Sarah Roberts, the five-year-old black Bostonian who wanted to go to her neighborhood public school. If passed, this measure would bring recalcitrant states that had failed to enact civil rights legislation—a long list ranging from Arkansas to New York—up to the same standards that had been set by progressive legislatures in states like Massachusetts, South Carolina, and Louisiana. Beyond passing this bill, Sumner said, "I know nothing further to be done in the way of legislation for the security of equal rights in this Republic." But only the congressmen of color and the most radical of white Republicans lined up with Sumner. His bill stalled.

Nonwhite congressmen had more to fear than cynical legislative maneuvers on Capitol Hill. Back home in Georgetown, Rainey, just five months into his term, received a death threat from the Ku Klux Klan written in what appeared to be blood. "K.K.K. *Beware! Beware! Beware!*" the letter read, "Your doom is sealed in blood. . . . At a regular meeting of this [Klan] Post on Saturday night, 12:30 o'clock, it was unanimously resolved that due and timely notice be given to J. H. Rainey . . . to prepare to meet [his] God. . . . Take heed, stay not. Here the climate is too hot for you. . . . leave [at] once forever. We warn you to flee."

Unintimidated, Rainey would continue to serve in Congress for nearly a decade. But vigilante violence threatened to nullify anything he and his colleagues enshrined in legislation.

As Sumner's bill languished in Washington, D.C., the civil rights laws on the books in the Southern states needed to be enforced.

Activists realized early on that no matter what the lawbooks said, only integrated police forces could ensure they were carried out. In New Orleans and Charleston, the police departments were integrated quickly and thoroughly, while many other jurisdictions lagged behind. Even when Tennessee still had its law on the books prohibiting segregation on railroad cars, there wasn't a single African-American policeman in Nashville or Memphis to enforce it.

The creation of New Orleans's Metropolitan Police was a tribute to activist pressure. The week after the city's streetcars were desegregated, *New Orleans Tribune* publisher Louis Charles Roudanez wrote an open letter all but issuing an order to Mayor Heath: "Let him appoint colored police officers." The paper's editors made the tendentious argument that African-American police officers were required in New Orleans because, by the one-drop rule (if not by the official census figures), New Orleans was a majority-African-American city. Despite the vociferous protests of inhabitants proclaiming their pristine whiteness, "everybody knows that one-half at least of the inhabitants of the Crescent City have more or less of African blood in their veins," the newspaper reminded a populace in denial.

Reconstruction's supporters were sympathetic to integrating police forces out of simple pragmatism. After all, the murderous rampages that had brought on Radical Reconstruction had been led by all-white police forces in Memphis and New Orleans. On May 28, 1867, the Louisiana governor announced the appointment of what he dubbed a "newly enfranchised" citizen, Charles J. Courcelle, to the state's Board of Police Commissioners. That June, over a dozen African-Americans joined the force. And in 1868, the state legislature created the state-run Metropolitan Police to patrol the city and its neighboring parishes. Three of the five commissioners appointed to run the Metropolitan Police were men of color and the rank and file was majority African-American. In the wake of white complaints, the percentage dropped to just over a quarter, roughly in line with percentage of the city that self-identified as African-American (albeit a far cry from the *Tribune*'s one-drop-rule population count). Among the white officers, most were international immigrants, largely from Ireland and Germany. Of the American-born whites, two-thirds were native-born Southerners and one-third Yankees. Creoles of color were spectacularly over-represented among the police; fully 80 percent of the African-American officers came from the biracial Francophone community.

In Charleston, the police force was integrated in 1868 with the appointment of Richard Holloway, a member of one of the city's leading Brown families. African-Americans, most of them ante-bellum freemen, flocked to join the ranks and by 1870 over 40 percent of the Charleston police were men of color. When *Scribner's* correspondent Edward King visited Charleston in 1873, he informed his readers that "the present police force of the city is about equally divided into black and white [and] at the Guard-House one may note white and black policemen on terms of amity." It was a remarkable scene considering that six years earlier white officers were booking African-Americans in the Guard House for simply riding the city's streetcars.

By 1870, African-American police officers had become a common sight on the streets of New Orleans and Charleston as well as Mobile, Montgomery, and Vicksburg, but there was not a single black officer in Atlanta, Savannah, Louisville, or Richmond. Even in Louisiana and South Carolina outside of New Orleans and Charleston, local law enforcement remained all white. In rural counties and parishes, African-Americans had little hope of enjoying the rights they had won on paper, even as civil rights victories piled up in the cities.

With an integrated officer corps ready to enforce the law, Charleston activists selected a prominent desegregation target: the Academy of Music. When the venue was under construction, in 1869, the blueprints specified segregated seating for African-

Americans in the balconies and upper tiers, far from the coveted orchestra section. Shunting well-to-do African-Americans to the worst seats in the house at the city's leading performing arts center was an affront to the Brown elite. As a letter to the city's white liberal newspaper, the *Charleston Daily Republican*, signed with the pseudonym "Justice" put it, "The seats arranged for the colored people are decidedly insignificant [and] are distasteful to the majority of respectable ones of that class." Others argued, according to another local paper, that the "black as well as white 'aristocracy' should be provided for."

To bring the Academy to heel, activists used a two-pronged strategy of fighting in the courts and in the legislature. Shortly after the hall opened, in January 1870, African-Americans who were refused seats filed charges, landing the theater owner, John T. Ford, under arrest. When the state passed a new civil rights law in March, specifically barring segregation in theaters, the Academy agreed to seat patrons without regard to color and the case was dropped. The author of the state's new "Act to Secure Equal Civil Rights" was Alonzo Ransier, who had been among the mixed-race freeborn Charlestonians at the state's 1868 constitutional convention.

Just as Robert Isabelle, the New Orleans legislator, used the strategy of first passing and then personally testing and enforcing his school desegregation law, so Alonzo Ransier led a band of African-American politicians through the taverns of Charleston to test and enforce his new public accommodations law. The group's pub crawl met with mixed results. Some formerly whites-only establishments warmly accepted the newcomers and, in some cases, even comped their drinks. But several saloon and restaurant owners refused to serve the legislators and vowed to see them in court. They did. The activists pressed charges and, with the new civil rights law on their side, they won. In time, the businesses gave in; even their own attorneys ultimately conceded that "persons [shall be] admitted to all public places without discrimination." What began in high-society institutions like the Academy of Music quickly trickled down to humbler establishments. Soon, the stands at the city's horseracing track were integrated, as were the Holy City's brothels, both their patrons and their employees.

In New Orleans, it was a schizophrenic era. In the makeshift state capital building, the St. Louis Exchange Hotel in the French Quarter, which in antebellum times had hosted slave auctions, ever more far-reaching civil rights bills became law. But out on the streets of the city, the Anglo-American binary racial system was, if anything, gaining strength as New Orleans continued to Americanize. In the downtown Creole wards, English was heard more often than ever before and with it came the Anglo-American notion of race. As Robert Isabelle complained in a speech on the statehouse floor, there were Portuguese café owners in New Orleans with skin the same color as his own who refused to serve African-Americans a cup of coffee. "What right have they putting on such airs?" he asked rhetorically. "Why does not darkness of skin make a difference in their case?" Similarly, Mexicans with his complexion would come to town and "run no risk of being turned out of doors." By what logic were Latinos afforded the privileges of whiteness while Creoles of color were doomed to the infamy of blackness? Why were rights and privileges being doled out on the murky grounds of "race" at all?

In the face of sharpening racial lines, it often fell to African-American law enforcement officials themselves to have the state's civil rights laws enforced. A Louisiana law required that all places of "business or public resort shall be open to the accommodation and patronage of all persons without distinction or discrimination on account of race or color" and it permitted those who still faced discrimination to sue for damages. In January 1871, the newly elected Orleans Parish Sheriff, Charles St. Albin Sauvinet, did just that after being refused a drink in an upscale French Quarter boîte. A freeborn Creole with a French immigrant father and a mother of racially ambiguous Haitian descent, Sauvinet had entered The Bank, a posh coffeehouse and bar, with two white business associates named Finnegan and Conklin. Sauvinet had patronized the bar many times before, presumably passing for white. But now that he was a public figure, it was widely believed that, despite his fair complexion, he was of partial African descent. This time when Sauvinet walked in, the bar owner, Joseph A. Walker, requested that he stop visiting The Bank as personal "favor," since it was bad for business.

"I have always drunk in all houses," Sauvinet replied, "and it is too late now for me to go back."

Six days later, Sauvinet filed a suit "for the purpose of vindicating his civil rights." He demanded a crippling settlement: $10,000 and the revocation of the café's business license.

The case unfolded in a curious way. According to the Louisiana civil rights law, Sauvinet's race, whatever it might be, was irrelevant to whether he could be served. Indeed, that was the whole point of the public accommodations law. Yet much of the courtroom testimony was dedicated to figuring out his race. In court, Walker's lawyers began this line of inquiry as a way of attacking Sauvinet's credibility. They insinuated that he had long passed for white and only began identifying himself as biracial to win African-American votes in the recent election. In fact, in a city like New Orleans, where most residents identified as white, it would have been a wiser electoral strategy to continue passing. It had been Sauvinet's political opponents who had insisted that he was a man of color. On the witness stand, Sauvinet quipped, "I am very much astonished that I should be wanted to be proven a white man, when a few months ago [during the campaign], I was called a negro."

Contrary to the defense counsel's insinuations, for his entire life, Sauvinet explained, "my general reputation in the community was that I was a person of color" even though "whether I am a colored man or not is a matter that I do not know myself." His parents, he explained, had both been born abroad in societies where humans were not sorted into binary racial categories. In New Orleans, he had long been considered a Creole of color and was an active member of that community. "Prior to the war," he told the court, the government had clearly considered him nonwhite since "you had always refused me, though born and raised here, the rights of citizenship." But in his social life, neither had he tried to pass for white nor had he had been treated as a second-class citizen. "It was my habit before the war to go into different saloons and barrooms and drink as white men did," he explained. Only now was he being denied service.

As the case unfolded, Sauvinet didn't resist the adjudication of his race with a simple insistence on equal rights for all; instead, he focused his case on it. Sauvinet actively called into question the entire edifice of race. He volunteered that "Finnegan and Conklin who were with me are said to be white men. I do not know. To all external appearances, they are." But, of course, as Sauvinet himself proved, you couldn't necessarily ascertain people's races by looking at them. The ineffability of race was reiterated when Finnegan took the stand and told the court that "I did not know that Sauvinet was a colored man by his appearance." If race could exist independent of physical appearance, by what metric could it be adjudicated?

Before the war, as free people of color lost suffrage rights and other formerly class-based rights became race-based, a tautology of race had formed. Once all native-born free white men were given the right to vote, then any native-born, free men who were denied the right to vote must be, by definition, people of color regardless of their skin tone. But with the collapse of the race-based rights regime, what was left of race itself? When Walker's attorney grew frustrated with Sauvinet's circular definition—clearly I must be a person of color because before the Civil War I was not permitted to vote—he asked him point blank: "Have you not stated that you are as much a white man and of white blood as any man in the community?" Sauvinet answered him with a quip, "I have stated so.—ain't I?" Asserting that racism creates race, not vice versa, Sauvinet's curious courtroom performance suggests he saw more hope in undermining the concept of race than in accepting it and calling for equal treatment regardless.

Fortuitously, Sauvinet's case ended up in front of the judge who months before had ordered the desegregation of the New Orleans public schools, Henry Dibble. As the father of a mixed-race daughter, Sauvinet himself had been among the activist parents attempting to enroll children in the Bayou Road School, and had been vindicated by Dibble's decision in the Isabelle case.

Now, unsurprisingly, Dibble found in Sauvinet's favor. But the Indiana-born Dibble did not follow Sauvinet down the path of questioning race itself. Instead, Dibble personally adjudicated Sauvinet's race, finding in his decision that "the Plaintiff is reputed to be and is a colored man." Given his racial identity, his demand for justice was "in full consonance . . . with the thirteenth, fourteenth and fifteenth Amendments to the national constitution abolishing slavery and extending to men of African descent, whether they have been slaves or not, the rights of citizenship in the republic and in the States in which they reside." As for punishment, Dibble opted to leave the business open but teach the proprietor a lesson to "deter others from inflicting the same injury." Walker was permitted to keep his liquor license but ordered to pay Sauvinet $1,000 because "the plaintiff show[ed] an infringement of . . . civil rights [and that] his citizenship has been degraded." Dibble's decision was a victory over racism but it was not the victory over race that Sauvinet had sought.

Sauvinet was hardly alone in pressing charges to enforce Louisiana's civil rights statute. Sauvinet's case against The Bank was one of over a dozen lawsuits brought by New Orleanians against bars, soda shops, theaters, and opera houses that were slow to integrate.

Nor was Sauvinet the only civil rights plaintiff to question the reality of race in court. In 1872, Josephine DeCuir, a member of a prominent antebellum free people of color family, was blocked from riding in the "ladies' cabin" of a steamship and filed suit. DeCuir had hoped to travel in the luxury to which she was accustomed aboard the *Governor Allen* en route from New Orleans to Hermitage, a landing 160 miles upriver near her husband's family's ancestral home in Pointe Coupée Parish. Shortly after boarding and taking a seat in the ladies' cabin, a member of the ship's staff handed DeCuir a note asking her to move to the colored section. Never having encountered such treatment in her life—she had ridden without incident on steamboats in the United States and Europe countless times—she broke down in tears. Pulling herself together, she confronted the captain. Unmoved, he told her he was duty-bound to enforce company segregation rules. With DeCuir refusing to move to the inferior "colored cabin," the crew directed her to a small compartment at the back of the boat for the seventeen-hour overnight trip, all while she held a first-class ticket. They had picked a fight with the wrong woman.

Josephine DeCuir hailed from what had been one of the wealthiest nonwhite families in America. Before the Civil War, her family's sugar plantation had been worked by over a hundred slaves and in 1868, her brother, Antoine Dubuclet, had been elected Louisiana's state treasurer. But the postwar collapse of sugar cane production—a form of agriculture so brutal it proved unworkable with free labor—ruined many in the planter class. In 1871, DeCuir's husband's family had been forced to sell their plantation, Riverlake. Josephine DeCuir was now traveling home to deal with the financial wreckage left behind by her husband's death. With her pampered past and humiliating present, the treatment onboard caused Josephine, as she later told the court, "mental pain, shame, and mortification." The crew even mockingly referred to the ship's colored cabin as the "Freedmen's Bureau," a clear indication that African lineage was becoming synonymous with servitude, even for former slave owners of color like DeCuir.

In court, DeCuir and her attorneys purposefully highlighted the ambiguity of race. DeCuir herself was dark enough to generally be recognized on sight as a person of color—her copper complexion was compared at trial to the color of a "law book"—but her attorneys also called a white-looking French Quarter resident of Haitian descent, one Mr. Duconge, to problematize race for the court. In New Orleans, Duconge was widely understood to be a person of color but, on steamships outside the city, he was routinely directed to whites-only compartments. In his testimony, Duconge gave the statement, absurd in all but the American context, that "the difference between a white man and a colored man is that the colored man has a darker face than the white man, but you can find a quantity of colored men reputed to be colored men who have white faces." In further testimony, the clerk on the *Governor Allen*, J. H. Mossof, whose duties included enforcing segregation onboard, admitted that he may have, at times, accidentally permitted such people of color with white faces to sit and eat in whites-only sections, but "if I did [it was only because] I didn't know them to be colored."

Pressing her case in the sympathetic courts of Reconstruction Louisiana, DeCuir initially won. The verdict awarded her $1,000 in damages to be paid by the captain and owner of the *Governor Allen*, John G. Benson. But whether hers was a victory over race-based rights was unclear. The judge's decision foregrounded DeCuir's elite status. "The plaintiff in this case," the judge wrote, "is a lady of color, genteel in her manners, modest in her deportment, neat in her appearance and quite fair for one of mixed blood. Her features are rather delicate with a nose which indicates a decided preponderance of the Caucasian and Indian blood. The blackness and length of the hair, which is straight, confirm this idea. She was never a slave, nor is she the descendant of a slave. Her ancestors were always as free as herself."

While the judge ruled that the Louisiana constitution did not permit racial discrimination, his obsession with DeCuir's physical appearance called into question how firmly civil rights laws' protections on the basis of "race, color, or previous condition of servitude" really went in practice. Was the judge trying to enforce true equality or trying to preserve the anomalous middle-class status that free, mixed-race Louisianans had enjoyed before the Civil War? If DeCuir's attorney had called racially ambiguous witnesses in the hopes of problematizing the entire concept of race, the strategy appeared to have backfired. To Mr. Duconge's statement that some colored men have white faces, the judge appeared to have concluded that, well, if that is the case, then those individuals ought to enjoy all the rights and privileges of whiteness—not that there ought not be any rights accorded on the amorphous basis of race. On appeal, the decision was upheld by the state supreme court, but the riverboat company vowed to take their case to the United States Supreme Court.

Even though the courts never took DeCuir's and Sauvinet's bait to question the reality of race, the punishing monetary judgments against the offending companies changed Southern life. When *Scribner's* correspondent Edward King rode a Mississippi River steamship through the state the year after DeCuir's victory was upheld by the Louisiana supreme court, he noted rampant integration. "You come to some landing where a smart-looking young negro man comes on board with a quadroon wife," King wrote, "and you notice a hurried look of surprise on some of the old [white] men's faces as the couple are shown a state-room, or as they promenade unconcernedly."

King's experience echoed that of a white Northern teacher who rode a steamship out of Charleston and wrote:

here we found a decided change. . . . [Before] no colored person was allowed on the upper deck, now there were no restrictions,—there could be none, for a law had been passed in favor of the negroes. They were everywhere, choosing the best staterooms and best seats at the table. Two prominent colored members of the State Legislature were on board with their families. There were also several well-known [white] Southerners, still uncompromising rebels. It was a curious scene and full of significance. An interesting study to watch the exultant faces of the negroes, and the scowling faces of the rebels.

With activists making significant if incomplete progress in the Deep South in the early 1870s, Senator Sumner redoubled his efforts to push through his federal civil rights bill in Washington. If his bill passed, anyone who faced discrimination in places where the police and local courts still refused to enforce antidiscrimination laws could seek justice through the federal courts. This would end the patchwork civil rights system and its cruel absurdities. After South Carolina relegalized interracial marriage in 1868, for example, many North Carolina couples had crossed over the state line to get married. But when they returned home, North Carolina refused to recognize the validity of their unions.

In Congress, Sumner faced an uphill climb. Many white Northerners were souring on civil rights. Fearing political backlash, Illinois senator Lyman Trumbull, who had coauthored the Thirteenth Amendment abolishing slavery and penned the Civil Rights Act of 1866, kept Sumner's controversial bill bottled up in committee. Northern support buckled further when a financial crisis struck the nation in the fall of 1873. After a Philadelphia investment bank, Jay Cooke and Company, collapsed under the weight of unsalable railroad bonds, panic swept Wall Street. The New York Stock Exchange suspended trading for the first time in its history and the downturn rippled through the American economy, causing thousands of businesses to fail and millions of workers to lose their jobs. Preoccupied with survival and eager for scapegoats, white Northern voters' sympathy for black Southerners waned. Many guilelessly consumed racist propaganda, like journalist James Pike's 1874 bestseller, *The Prostrate State: South Carolina Under Negro Government.* In it, the onetime abolitionist author slammed the Palmetto State's "Africanization." Pike tarred South Carolina's integrated legislature as "the most ignorant democracy that mankind ever saw," playing on stereotypes of illiterate freedmen and burying the reality that Charleston had long hosted one of the best-educated African-American communities in the country, from which it sent myriad erudite representatives to Columbia. Pike slandered desegregation as a twisted effort at racial revenge rather than an honest effort at human equality. In the book's section on what Pike termed the "Destruction of the South Carolina University," the reporter explained to a credulous, far-flung readership that the college's "capture by the blacks is a useless humiliation to the whites [and springs] from no other motive than desire of domination." Ironically, for a man so incensed at the prospect of racial equality, Pike was honest with his Northern readers about his inability to ascertain his subjects' races. "There is really no way of knowing whether any given individual in South Carolina has black blood in his veins," Pike confessed, "except by tracing his descent."

The diversification of the antebellum free states through mass immigration—the Germans and Irish flocking to the East Coast; the Chinese to California—thrust vexing questions of multicultural democracy on voters who had never before grappled with them. As times got tough, the struggling native-born working class edged away from the expansive view of citizenship many had embraced in the wake of the Civil War and once-liberal elites went into full retreat. When the state legislatures were debating whether to ratify the Fifteenth Amendment, guaranteeing African-American men the right to vote while still withholding it from white women, suffragist leader Elizabeth Cady Stanton denounced it in the crudest possible terms. "Think of Patrick and Sambo and Hans and Yung Tung, who do not know the difference between a monarchy and a republic, who cannot read the Declaration of Independence or Webster's spelling book, making laws for . . . the daughters of Adams and Jefferson . . . women of wealth and education," she wrote, openly stereotyping Americans of Irish, African, German, and Chinese descent, not to mention assuming—incorrectly—that all of Thomas Jefferson's daughters were white women. "Shall American statesmen, claiming to be liberal, so amend their constitutions as to make their wives and mothers the political inferiors of unlettered and unwashed ditch-diggers, bootblacks, butchers and barbers, fresh from the slave plantations of the South?"

Facing this ominous political climate, in late 1873 Senator Sumner agreed to drop the most controversial—and, likely, unconstitutional—part of his bill: the clause requiring that churches and cemeteries not discriminate. He then moved to push the remains of his proposal through Congress. Benjamin Butler, the general who had run occupied wartime New Orleans and was now a Massachusetts congressman, introduced the House version of Sumner's bill. The man who had backed off on school desegregation in New Orleans in 1862 was trying to set things right at long last. But the most powerful advocates for the civil rights bill were the African-American members of Congress who defended the legislation through multiple sessions. In the pre–Civil War Congress, where every member was a white man, legislation was made for African-Americans, not by them. Now an array of nonwhite congressmen rose to defend the civil rights progress they'd seen in their home states and urge it be replicated nationwide.

The protracted debate in Congress became a national referendum on the changes pioneered in South Carolina and Louisiana. Opponents set their sights on discrediting the far-reaching
changes underway in the urban Deep South. Since school desegregation was the most controversial part of Sumner's civil rights
bill, the integration experiment at the University of South Carolina naturally became fodder for debate on the floor of Congress.
The university was first raised by Congressman Robert B. Vance
of North Carolina, who began his speech with a paternalistic homage to his grandfather who, he said, had "enjoined it upon his children and grandchildren to treat kindly the colored people upon the
plantation." In Vance's twisted opinion, civil rights would advance
most if activists stopped agitating for them. "If the [white] people
are let alone in the South," he advised, "they will adjust." By contrast, forcing integration would bring ruin. "In what condition is
the University of South Carolina?" the Southern patrician thundered rhetorically. At the college in Columbia, which once "turned
out some of the most eminent men of this country," he said, Henry
Hayne's enrollment had sparked a crippling white walkout. "In
passing bills of this kind and having mixed schools you destroy the
school system of the South," Vance warned.

When the North Carolinian took his seat, a South Carolina congressman rose to defend the experiment. Rev. Richard Cain, the
half African-American, half Native American leader of Charleston's "Mother Emanuel" Church, who had won a term in Congress
in the 1872 election, insisted that the university—which stood in
his state, not Vance's—was thriving. "[Congressman Vance] cited,
on the school question, the evidence of South Carolina, and says
the . . . University has been destroyed by virtue of bringing into
contact the white students with the colored," Cain offered. "I think
not." Correcting Congressman Vance's assertion, Representative
Cain explained that "there is a mixture of students now [with] colored and white students of law and medicine sitting side by side;

it is true, sir, that the prejudice of some of the professors was so strong that it drove them out of the institution; but the philanthropy and good sense of others were such that they remained; and thus we have still the institution."

The strongest arguments for Sumner's bill were the personal testimonies of discrimination from African-American members of Congress. When South Carolina congressman Joseph Hayne Rainey took the floor, he explained, "I cannot view [this bill] through the same optics" as its white opponents. Even as the first African-American seated in the House of Representatives in the nation's history, he was not accorded equal rights on the streets of the capital. "Why is it that colored members of Congress cannot enjoy the same immunities that are accorded to white members?" Rainey asked his colleagues. "Why cannot we stop at hotels here without meeting objection? Why cannot we go into restaurants without being insulted? We are here enacting laws for the country and casting votes upon important questions; we have been sent here by the suffrages of the people, and why cannot we enjoy the same benefits that are accorded to our white colleagues on this floor." Traveling to work from Charleston to Washington, Rainey saw firsthand how spotty state civil rights laws and enforcement were. In Charleston, as a mere barber, he had ridden integrated streetcars for years, but working in Washington as a duly elected member of Congress, Rainey found himself booted from a streetcar in neighboring Virginia. In Charleston, he could sit in the best seats at the Academy of Music, yet on a boat between Norfolk and Washington he was asked to dine with the waitstaff—and pay full price for the privilege.

This personal testimony was echoed by other congressmen of color such as Representative John R. Lynch of Mississippi, born in bondage in Louisiana in 1847, the son of a plantation slave and an Irish immigrant plantation manager. Lynch's father's plan to free him and his mother was upended by the Irishman's untimely death. John was not emancipated until 1864, when the Union army liberated the forced labor camp where he lived. Educated after the war in schools run by Northern veterans of the abolitionist movement, Lynch set himself up running a photography studio in Natchez, Mississippi, just over the river from the Louisiana plantation where he was born. A Republican Party activist, Lynch was elected to Congress in 1872. At twenty-five years old, he was the body's youngest member. Describing his prosperous and diverse district to his colleagues in Washington, Lynch explained, "[It is] one of the largest and wealthiest districts in the State of Mississippi, and possibly in the South [and it is] composed of persons of different races, religions, and nationalities." For such a district could there be a more fitting representative than Lynch, a self-made entrepreneur who was of mixed background in race (black and white), religion (Catholic and Protestant), and nationality (Irish and American)?

The disconnect between all he had achieved and his routine mistreatment traveling to and from the capital shook Lynch. He hoped it would shake his white colleagues as well. Speaking in favor of Sumner's bill, Lynch attempted to put his fellow congressmen in his shoes. "Think of it for a moment," the Afro-Irish congressman beseeched them:

> Here I am, a member of your honorable body . . . and yet, when I leave my home to come to the capital of the nation, to take part in the deliberations of the House and to participate with you in making laws for the government of this great Republic, in coming through the God-forsaken States of Kentucky and Tennessee, if I come by the way of Louisville or Chattanooga, I am treated, not as an American citizen, but as a brute. Forced to occupy a filthy smoking-car both night and

day, with drunkards, gamblers, and criminals: and for what? Not that I am unable or unwilling to pay my way; not that I am obnoxious in my personal appearance or disrespectful in my conduct; but simply because I happen to be of a darker complexion.

Only nationwide civil rights legislation could set this right, Lynch concluded. In its absence, enforcing equal rights in the "God-forsaken" white-majority states of the South would be hopeless. "You may ask why we do not institute civil suits in the State courts," Lynch offered. "What a farce! Talk about instituting a civil-rights suit in the State courts of Kentucky, for instance, where the decision of the judge is virtually rendered before he enters the court-house, and the verdict of the jury substantially rendered before it is impaneled."

To bolster the testimony of Representatives Rainey and Lynch, Congressman James Rapier of Alabama, a freeborn, mixed-race man, also elected to the House in 1872, described his degradation traveling to and from the capital. "There is not an inn between Washington and Montgomery, a distance of more than a thousand miles, that will accommodate me to a bed or meal," he told his colleagues. Then, with his words, he led them on the road to Alabama with a hypothetical "white ex-con" traveling companion: "All the way down he will be treated as a gentleman, while I will be treated as the convict. He will be allowed a berth in a sleeping-car with all its comforts, while I will be forced into a dirty, rough box with the drunkards, apple-sellers, railroad hands, and next to any dead that may be in transit, regardless of how far decomposition may have progressed. . . . Here I am the peer of the proudest, but on a steamboat or [rail]car I am not equal to the most degraded. Is not this most anomalous and ridiculous?"

In his riveting speech Rapier showed his colleagues their shared country through his eyes. Only with an open mind could his colleagues fully appreciate how "anomalous and ridiculous" America's racial system is. Rapier described his travels in Europe as the United States commissioner for the Paris World's Fair and the State of Alabama's official representative to the Vienna Exposition, during which he experienced no discrimination whatsoever. "I left home last year and traveled six months in foreign lands," Rapier recounted, "and the moment I put my foot upon the deck of a ship that unfurled a foreign flag from its mast-head, distinctions on account of my color ceased." In the cruel American paradox of race, African-Americans are treated as outsiders in their homeland while "it was in other countries than my own that I was not a stranger, that I could approach a hotel without the fear that the door would be slammed in my face." Rapier gave voice to the open secret of American racism—that the races were already mixed in individuals like himself and that the mixing continued in every generation, yet it did nothing to temper the racist hypocrisy. African-American women in the capital, he noted, were routinely giving birth to the children of white fathers but "I venture to say that if they [the fathers] were members of this body [they] would vote against the civil rights bill." In America, the same white man who would "throw up [his] hands in holy horror" if a black man shows up in his restaurant will later "leave and go to the arms of his colored mistress and there pour out his soul's complaint, tell her of the impudence of the 'damned nigger' in coming to a table where a white man was sitting."

Alonzo Ransier, the author of South Carolina's state civil rights law, had also been elected to congress in 1872. He was the third Brown Charlestonian in the House, though all represented different districts. Like Rapier of Alabama, Ransier of South Carolina drove home the point that America's hard-and-fast color line was anything but: "These negro-haters would not open school-houses, hotels, places of amusement, common conveyances, or the witness or the jury box to the colored people upon equal terms with themselves, because this contact of the races would, forsooth, 'result injuriously to both.' Yet they have found agreeable associations with them under other circumstances which at once suggest themselves to us." No American adult could gaze on Congressman Ransier, with his crown of tight curls and his flowing Gallic beard, and not understand the "agreeable associations" to which he was referring. If America wanted to be a society with distinct races, it was about two hundred years too late for that. His South Carolina colleague, Joseph Hayne Rainey, had made a similar point on the floor of the House in the previous session, noting archly that keeping blacks and whites apart had not become a priority until emancipation. "Why this fear of the negro since he has been a freedman," Rainey wondered aloud, "when in the past he was almost a household god, gamboling and playing with the children of his old master? And occasionally it was plain to be seen that there was a strong family resemblance between them." Like the civil rights test-case plaintiffs, the congressmen of color were interrogating the American idea of race itself.

It was the Rev. Congressman Cain, with his Afro-Cherokee background and rhetorical training in the church, who transmuted this critique into a soaring vision. To the preacher from "Mother Emanuel," it was the nation's very mission—our New World destiny—to harmoniously blend all the peoples of the earth. As he told his House colleagues, "I believe God designed us to live here together on this continent, and in no other place, to develop this great idea that all men are the children of one Father. We are here to work out the grand experiment of the homogeneity of nations, the grand outburst of the greatness of humanity, by the development in us of the rights that belong to us, and the performance of the duties that we owe each other." In this work, Senator Sumner's equal rights bill was crucial. "Let the civil-rights bill be passed this day," Cain urged, and "put the cap-stone on the mighty structure of government."

Even with its church and cemeteries clause removed, the

integrated-schools plank that Cain so zealously defended against Congressman Vance remained a stumbling block. Shortly after Cain offered his House floor defense of the integrated University of South Carolina, Senator Sumner suffered a debilitating heart attack. His supporters insisted that the head wounds he had endured in 1856 from Preston Brooks's cane had contributed to his declining health. Languishing on his deathbed in March 1874, Sumner voiced a final wish: "If my Works were completed and my Civil Rights bill passed, no visitor could enter that door that would be more welcome than death."

Sumner's last words before he gave out rekindled a sense of idealism in many citizens that had been lost as the economy faltered and the war receded from view. Congressmen who had been silent on civil rights began publicly backing the late senator's bill. At the University of South Carolina, special exercises were held in Sumner's memory, attended by Governor Moses and leading state officials. The program featured an oration by Thomas McCants Stewart, the Charleston-born future valedictorian, poignantly delivered from a stage that had once hosted Preston Brooks. Professor Richard T. Greener, in a eulogy composed on behalf of his fellow "educators . . . executors and promoters of that policy of Equality in Matters of Education to whose successful vindication [Sumner] devoted his . . . talent," noted the "reasons peculiar to our University" that necessitated the ceremony. The late senator died, Greener intoned, "wait[ing] only for Civil Rights, and the coming of the day . . . when the races of our varied nationality should dwell together in mutual harmony." But even with the outpouring of posthumous support, the groundswell was inadequate to overcome opposition to the bill's controversial schools plank in the House of Representatives.

As Northern public opinion wavered on civil rights, particularly over school desegregation, revanchist white Southerners grew more bold. Violent threats and assassinations had long been regular occurrences in the rural South but now white supremacists broadened their sights. In the spring of 1874, a new white supremacist group calling itself the White Leagues sprang up in Louisiana's backwoods parishes. Though sharing the same goals as terrorist organizations like the Ku Klux Klan, the White Leagues made no effort to disguise their members' identities. Composed of white Confederate veterans organized into units under the command of retired Confederate officers, the White Leagues drilled in the open and rode unmasked through the countryside with hangman's noose in hand.

Initially a rural phenomenon, on July 1, 1874, a Crescent City White League formed in New Orleans. Ostensibly, the New Orleans group assembled in response to a rumor that on the coming Fourth of July holiday, the city's African-Americans would, in the words of the New Orleans *Daily Picayune*, mount "a grand *coup* on the white people to enforce their 'civil rights,' if need be, at the point of the bayonet; certainly, in so far as drinking-saloons, soda-water and refreshment stands are concerned" that would culminate in "every white man [being] killed and every negro hav[ing] a white wife." The rhetoric elevated the utterly anodyne reality of desegregated lunch counters into a slippery slope to race war and mass miscegenation.

The White League's platform made clear it opposed not only the ever-controversial "social equality" but the supposedly settled matter of political equality as well. Among the long series of grievances its platform ticked off was universal male suffrage. "The right of suffrage was, as we believed, and as we still believe, accorded too hastily to a race in the infancy of freedom," the platform read in its signature style of primly edited racism. On the stump, White Leaguers were less circumspect, foaming at the mouth over, as one speaker railed, "the crime against nature itself which subjected

the high and ancient civilization of free-born Anglo-Saxon com-
monwealths to the rule of debased and ignorant Africans."

Considering this narrow rhetoric of "Anglo-Saxons," it is remarkable how widely the group recruited in New Orleans. Though
mostly composed of Uptown Anglos—the *Américains*, as the
French-speakers called them—the corps made inroads among the
international immigrants and Mediterranean-Americans who had
previously shown sympathy for equal rights. The White League's
platform embraced a more broadly defined whiteness, stating
that since "our hereditary civilization and Christianity [are now]
menaced by a stupid Africanization, we appeal to the men of our
race, of whatever language or nationality, to unite with us against
that supreme danger." As a public organization, the Crescent City
White League, unlike the Ku Klux Klan or the Mistick Krewe of
Comus, published its membership rolls and, while dominated by
Anglo-Saxon last names (Richards, Smith, White), the rolls show
a significant representation of French family names (Bouligny,
Berault) and even a smattering of German (Blankensteiner), His-
panic (Garcia), and Jewish (Hyman) surnames. The Crescent City
White League was clearly more multicultural than the Klan. In
fact, the group was so diverse that a Creole of color had no trouble
passing undercover as a spy at one of the group's meetings, his
complexion well within the White League's spectrum of "whiteness." The man was expelled only when, unable to bite his tongue
any longer, he outed himself and began heckling the speakers.

The French Creole newspaper *Le Carillon*, which had only
recently embraced the *Américains*' racial notion that "one must
be either WHITE OR BLACK," endorsed the White League and
justified the group's big-tent approach to whiteness through a circuitous logic. The paper offered a new set of racial boundaries that
crossed lines of nationality, language, religion, and skin tone. In a
pseudoscientific disquisition on race, *Le Carillon* pleaded no con-

test to the idea that Spaniards had mixed with Arabs during the centuries-long Moorish occupation of the Iberian Peninsula but, regardless, the paper insisted, Spaniards remained white. "Our fellow Spanish citizens . . . are descended to a large extent from Arabs [but] Arabs are white," the newspaper informed its readers, "just tanned by exposure to light and to the sun, as are all whites who live out in the open in hot countries . . . like the Jews." Those still beyond the widening boundaries of whiteness found themselves pushed towards the growing category of blackness, which was expanded to encompass Creoles of color and anyone else known to have a drop of African blood regardless of complexion or status before the Civil War.

It was this multiethnic congealing into categories of "white" and "black" that doomed New Orleans's Unification Movement's rainbow coalition for equal rights. After its grand platform-unveiling ceremony in the summer of 1873, it fizzled as non-Anglos who had initially embraced universal human rights as a way to secure their future now embraced white identity as a route to the same goal, disowning their former allies and dooming them to discrimination. The *Américains* had long insinuated that all Creoles had at least "a touch of the tarbrush," but what could be a better defense against the charge of not being white than loudly and publicly supporting white supremacy? Even P. G. T. Beauregard, Unification's most famous endorser, distanced himself from the movement. Some Unification leaders defected outright to the White League. In the words of one of them, "last summer one hundred of us, representing fairly *all* the grades of public and social status, humbled ourselves into the dust in an effort to secure the cooperation of the colored race in a last attempt to secure good government, and failed. . . . To this complexion it has come at last. The niggers shall not rule over us."

The Crescent City White League was, to a striking extent, an armed wing of the local Democratic Party, so the paramilitary group rallied to the cause of seating the Democratic ticket that had lost the last statewide election. The White League's strategy for ousting the integrated Republican government was to mount a coup d'état. A few months after its creation, the drilled and trained White League leapt into action. White Leaguers cut down the city's telegraph lines and erected barricades of debris piled high around streetcars, making Canal Street impassable. This effectively cut the city, long divided socially between the French and English sides, in two. The White League held the Uptown *Américain* districts where New Orleans's stately, columned city hall housed the municipal administration, while the besieged Republicans held the downtown Creole wards and the French Quarter with the makeshift statehouse in the St. Louis Exchange Hotel.

On September 14, the armed White League membership assembled on Canal Street, chanting threats to hang the state's elected governor. White League leader Davidson Penn declared himself "acting governor" and promptly appointed former Confederate major general Frederick N. Ogden provisional commander of his "state militia." The scion of a New Orleans real estate family and a Confederate veteran, Penn was so dark in his features that he was beyond racial suspicion only on account of his vociferous white supremacism. Upon "taking office," Penn issued a carefully worded "proclamation to the colored people" of the state assuring them that "no harm is meant towards you, your property or your rights. . . . The rights of the colored, as well as of the white race, we are determined to uphold and defend." Coming from the leader of a self-described White League, it, of course, had no credibility.

Besieged in the French Quarter, James Longstreet, the Confederate-general-turned-scalawag who now commanded federal forces in the city, plotted with state authorities over how to put down the coup. They decided to have the integrated Metropolitan Police march from the French Quarter to the White League lines on Canal Street and command them to disperse.

When the police arrived, a sniper hidden in a commercial building shot one sergeant dead. Chaos reigned as a street battle between the White League guerrillas and America's leading, albeit badly outnumbered, integrated police force ensued. In the melee, Longstreet was thrown from his horse, reinjuring a right arm that had never fully recovered from a Civil War battle injury. Algernon Badger, the white New England transplant who commanded the Metropolitan Police, sustained four gunshot wounds but survived; his horse succumbed to its injuries. By the end of the skirmish, eleven Metropolitan Police officers lay dead—six white men and five men of color.

Overwhelmed by the White Leaguers, the police retreated to the French Quarter. While the elected Republican governor remained uncaptured, holed up in the federal Custom House, in the early morning hours of September 15 White League forces overran the makeshift state capitol and hastily inaugurated their own "governor," Penn. Following events from Washington via telegraph, President Grant gave the coup plotters an ultimatum: resign peacefully within five days or be forced from office. Facing the threat of overwhelming federal force, the White Leaguers did not even wait that long. The self-styled governor surrendered power after only one full day in office.

The federal authorities prevailed in the military standoff, but the White League won the propaganda war. With America's economy reeling and white Northerners perceiving a new racial threat from their increasingly diverse neighbors, solidarity grew among elite whites nationwide. Even *The Nation*, once a stalwart defender of civil rights, bought the Orwellian line that white mob rule was law and order while interracial democracy was mob rule. During the brief moment of White League power, *The Nation* informed its readers, "The city in the hands of the insurgents seems to have been perfectly quiet and orderly, and numerous despatches testifying to this fact were sent to the North." Spurred by this and similar propaganda, in the November 1874 midterm elections Northern voters handed Congress back to white supremacist Democrats. Since 1867, Congress had been driving Reconstruction policy; now it looked poised to slam it into reverse.

Emboldened by its public relations victory, in December the Crescent City White League launched a wildcat campaign to resegregate the New Orleans public schools. The League called on whites to boycott the district. White students at the Upper Girls High School, who around the time of the attempted coup had attempted to chase out their African-American classmates "armed with broomsticks," vowed to skip their own graduation ceremony unless students of color were barred. District officials were also targeted. Integrationist city schools superintendent Charles Boothby was attacked by a group of armed white youths who forced him to sign a statement disavowing integration; Judge Henry Dibble, whose court order had integrated the school district, was insulted to his face, an incident a local newspaper dubbed the "hooting of Judge Dibble." For several days, vigilante squads of young white men and boys, calling themselves "Regulators," rampaged through the integrated schools, attempting to expel nonwhite students by force. A confrontation with civil rights activists outside one school left a policeman wounded and one African-American boy, Eugene Ducoslange, dead.

An attempt to resegregate the New Orleans schools was no simple task. To do it correctly would require preparing a detailed family tree for each student. As a *Harper's* reporter described for its national readership, given the

mixture of all shades and colors, including Indians and even Chinese . . . nowhere, indeed, would it be so difficult, so invidious, to establish a government founded upon a distinction of color as in New Orleans. Here all shades and tints are blended in harmonious confusion. The dark bronze of the creole inhabitants, the descendants of French and Spanish blood, is sometimes of a deeper shade than the traits of negro descent [and] even the pure Caucasian, white and red from the misty climate of England, grows tawny and atrabilious beneath the sun . . . and there are persons of negro descent apparently so purely white as to surpass in this particular the emigrants from New York and Connecticut.

Even with the White League's broad definition of whiteness, in practice it was difficult to figure out who should be included and who excluded. An elaborate system of identification was implemented at the Upper Girls School, where students who were certified as white were given makeshift badges to wear and escorted to and from school by the mob. In another school the Regulators raided, they expelled "several Jewish maidens, touched with the olive tint of an Orient clime," having mistaken them for Creoles of color. In response, the "parents [of the] Israelite children [made] much noise over the grievance." In another incident, a girl deemed too dark to remain in school outed several students who, passing for white, had been overlooked, and she also fingered one of the boys doing the "regulating" as secretly biracial. In the most embarrassing episode of all, the Regulators attempted to expel the daughter of their own leader, Davidson Penn of the White League. When the girl was asked to leave, she indignantly responded, "Do you know who I am?"

"No," the Regulator in charge responded, "nor do I desire to know you. You are a negro, and must leave this school."

"A negro!" the girl screamed. "I am the daughter of your leader. My name is Miss P[enn]."

In fact, she was both the daughter of Davidson Penn *and* of African descent. Like so many wealthy New Orleans gentlemen before the Civil War, Penn had fathered a child with a biracial lover. Penn's mixed-race daughter, Blanche, had been born to Josephine

Keating, a teenaged quadroon, in January 1859, and had grown up in the downtown Creole wards with her aunt and her grandfather. When the census takers came by her Aunt Olivia's boarding house in 1870, they recorded Blanche's race as white. But, even assuming the dark-skinned Penn's lineage was as purely European as he claimed, Blanche, having seven white great-grandparents and one great-grandparent of African descent, was an octoroon, still outside the boundaries of the White League's standard for whiteness.

Blanche apparently was dark enough to attract the attention of the Regulators yet light enough to rebuff them. After standing up for herself, the young ruffians "made no further attempt to eject her, and retired in confusion." Ultimately, according to *Harper's*, the "young 'regulators' . . . were baffled at every step [and] gave up their [schools] crusade in shame."

Even in failure, the Regulators' days of disruption upended the district. With chaos sweeping the schools, the Orleans Parish School Board saw no solution save to close early for Christmas break. When the schools reopened, they remained integrated, but precariously so. The virulence of the Regulators' racism left the *Harper's* correspondent pondering how distant the Unification Movement of 1873 now felt. It was just a year and a half ago, he lamented, when "General Beauregard . . . leant his aid to the extinction of the race-quarrel, and a wiser spirit seemed about to animate the people." Only the most radical of Republicans kept up a brave face, laughing off the incident as a humiliation to a self-styled White League that couldn't even police the bloodlines of its own membership. But centrist white Republicans began openly calling for activists to give up on school integration. As the white liberal *New Orleans Republican* argued, "If the movement against mixed schools had ceased with the first outburst," much like white opposition to streetcar integration, then the issue might have been "left . . . to its natural and gradual solution." But since it didn't, the newspaper suggested, the local school board should craft "some plan whereby the colored children can be provided with educational advantages equal in all respects to those enjoyed by the whites, without attempting to carry out the obnoxious one of mixed schools."

In mid-December, as the Regulators marauded through the Crescent City's schools, Republicans in Washington surrendered on school desegregation nationally. With the loss of the Congress to the Democrats in the November election, the lame-duck Republicans decided to pass whatever watered-down version of the late Senator Sumner's civil rights bill could get the votes to clear the House. After lengthy negotiations, the Radicals agreed to strike the school integration mandate from the bill. A proposed compromise read, "If any State or its authorities having control of common schools or other public institutions of learning shall establish and maintain separate schools or institutions, giving equal educational facilities in all respects to all classes entitled thereto, such schools shall be in compliance" with federal law. Rather than have the federal government go on record affirming the legality of segregated schools, Congressman Butler removed all mentions of schools from the bill. The final text prohibited discrimination in "inns, public conveyances on land or water, theatres, and other places of public amusement," but was mute on the question of schools as well as churches and cemeteries. It passed the House without a single Democratic vote. After two days of sparse debate, the lame-duck Senate passed the House version and sent it to the White House. On March 1, President Grant signed the Civil Rights Act of 1875. It would be the last federal civil rights law passed until 1957.

Immediately, African-American activists all over the country began testing their newly guaranteed rights. On the evening of Thursday, March 4, four African-American men in Tennessee purchased dress circle tickets to the New Memphis Theater and were duly seated. But the following night, in Louisville, the manager of the Public Library Hall theater refused to seat an African-

American man in its still-designated whites-only section. The following week, two African-American politicians bought tickets to the formerly whites-only dress circle of the St. Charles Theatre on the uptown Anglo side of New Orleans. Though the pair was seated, the white audience members around them left the section in protest. The two men stayed in the abandoned section for the entire play, but their white neighbors had made their point. Even if the theater abided by the letter of the new federal civil rights act, they could still resist "social equality" by ostracizing fellow citizens on the basis of race.

More worrisome still was the disdain the new law drew from leading organs of the national press. The *New York Times* counted itself lucky to be based in a city with a relatively small African-American population that, in its editorial opinion, knew its place: "The negroes in this part of the country . . . have no desire to intrude where they are not welcome." The problem arose "in the South" with its myriad civil rights activists or, as the *Times* called them, "colored men and women who delight in 'scenes' and cheap notoriety." The newspaper dismissed the activists, despite so much evidence to the contrary, as riff-raff in league with rabble-rousing politicians rather than the prosperous, educated women and men that they overwhelmingly were:

> The large class of educated colored people who have their homes in Savannah, Charleston, New-Orleans, and other Southern cities . . . will never take advantage of the provisions of the new law. The very fact that they are educated and refined will deter them from forcing their presence upon their white neighbors. They have a certain aristocracy, a *caste* of their own; many of them are even proud of their blood; in New-Orleans they are among the richest property-owners and heaviest tax-payers. They do not desire, nor will they seek, admission to places frequented by white people.

> The negro politicians, however, the ignorant field hand, who, by his very brutality has forced his way into, and disgraces, public positions of honor and trust—men of this stamp, who have no feeling and sensibility, will, under the protection of the Civil Rights bill, take every opportunity of inflicting petty annoyances upon their former masters.

Most troubling were the publications that had once supported Sumner's civil rights bill that now, with its passage, railed against it. In 1872, *The Nation* had argued, "It is preposterous to allow a steamboat captain, navigating American waters, under the American flag, or a railroad company owing its very existence to the law, or an innkeeper carrying on his business with peculiar privileges, to degrade and harass a people because their complexion raises disagreeable associations in other people's minds." But the week the civil rights bill became law, *The Nation* sneered that "The negroes of the South, being mainly occupied in tilling the soil, or in labor of some kind, are not as a rule in the habit of travelling much . . . and when they do go from time to time . . . they are apt to move in crowds on foot, or in wagons not subject to the jurisdiction of Congress. [Moreover,] they do not frequent hotels much." Similarly, "the number of theatres and opera-houses in the South is not so great" apparently rendering that provision, in *The Nation*'s Manhattanite opinion, moot.

At the University of South Carolina, Richard T. Greener took up his pen to respond to *The Nation*'s new conservatism. "The New York *Nation* [has] intimated that the colored people are not interested in the assertion of their civil rights," he wrote. "I know of no question in which we colored people are more interested, or one on which our opinion, as a class, has been more emphatically expressed. . . . Decent, human treatment in schools, in traveling and in public are decidedly essential to the happy enjoyment of . . . life." The mixed-race professor attacked not only the notion of race-based rights but of race itself—a supposedly biological fact that, rather suspiciously, could never quite be pinned down. "[Segregation's] proscriptions are ostensibly based on race," Greener wrote, "but its judgments are visited universally upon those who, either by reason of hair, complexion or feature, are supposed to be allied to that race." Enforcement of such unjust rules couldn't help but be capricious. Greener noted an incident in which a federal tax collector was welcomed into a hotel at check-in only to be "dragg[ed] out of his bed [later] because *he did not tell them he was a colored man*" and of "women, so fair as to be mistaken for white, [forced] into a filthy [second-class] car filled with drunken negroes and poor whites" when her ancestry was discovered. "What reasonable, fair-minded or honorable American ought to object to a specific law which shall prevent the possibility of such outrages?" Greener concluded. With universal equality enshrined in law, there would be no need to adjudicate Americans' racial backgrounds on sight. But his argument was falling on deaf ears.

Sensing the turn in the public mood, the president of Louisiana State University, David Boyd, gladly buried his draft proposal to desegregate the college. Even activists began to lose hope. In Atlanta, an African-American barber who had celebrated the passage of the Civil Rights Act with a bar crawl through formerly whites-only taverns found his white customers now boycotting his business as retaliation. Reeling from the financial hit and devastated by the disdain of his once-loyal customers, he shot himself through the heart with a pistol.

9.

THE GREAT BETRAYAL

Randall Lee Gibson, the "Redeemer" congressman from New Orleans.

(Brady-Handy Photograph Collection, Library of Congress,

Prints & Photographs Division [LC-DIG-cwpbh-04008])

In 1876, with Klansmen and White Leaguers marauding through the South, America geared up for a presidential election. Up North, liberals—even *Nation* editors and suffragettes—had turned against civil rights. The shift in opinion leached into Washington and onto the Supreme Court itself.

Over his two terms, Ulysses S. Grant had been given four opportunities to make appointments to the high court, and each time he had chosen a Northern white Republican like himself. While the South Carolina state supreme court and the halls of Congress had been integrated during his time in office, Grant never challenged the nation's troubling tradition of a United States Supreme Court composed exclusively of white men. Ultimately, those white men in black robes on the Supreme Court would do more to turn back civil rights than the white men in white robes of the Ku Klux Klan.

Just a month after President Grant signed the late Charles Sumner's Civil Rights Act of 1875 into law, the Supreme Court heard arguments in a civil rights case out of backwoods Louisiana. In the spring of 1873, in the tiny hamlet of Colfax, three hundred and fifty miles inland from New Orleans, rival claimants to various parish political offices sparred. A multiracial group of Republicans had successfully ousted a white Democratic sheriff and judge who had won their offices through voter intimidation; the Republicans then called in a local African-American militia to patrol the parish courthouse. In response, the Democrats spread a dastardly rumor that the armed defenders of the courthouse were hell-bent on "go[ing] into the country and kill[ing white males] from the cradle up to old age," and then "seduc[ing]" the women to create a "new race." A request to the Metropolitan Police in New Orleans for backup went out but was met too late.

Spurred by the fictional menace of a massacre at the hands of the black militia and the racial amalgamation of their supposedly purebred community, the white townspeople of Colfax launched a massacre of their own. On Easter Sunday, around 150 armed white men besieged the courthouse and set it alight. As fire and smoke spread through the building, those trapped inside raised a white flag of surrender. They were shot on exit nevertheless. After the fight, even those African-American militiamen who had been captured alive were summarily executed.

In the months after the massacre, three white vigilantes were successfully indicted and convicted in federal court for conspiring to deprive the victims of their constitutional rights to assemble, to bear arms, and to be safe from punishment without trial. The convicts took their case to the Supreme Court, arguing that the Fourteenth Amendment only prohibited *states* not *individuals,* from depriving fellow citizens of their rights. For the crimes alleged in this case, their legal team, led by Crescent City White Leaguer R. H. Marr, argued that the three individuals could only be tried in state courts. The defendants knew full well that in many parts of the South white supremacists ran the local criminal justice systems and would never convict white men for killing African-Americans, especially as a means of political retribution and voter suppression. In a five-to-four decision issued on March 27, 1876, the Supreme Court backed the white terrorists. While the Fourteenth Amendment had been broadly understood to confer citizenship on African-Americans, the high court narrowly read its clause, "No State shall make or enforce any law which shall abridge the privileges or immunities of the citizens of the United States; nor shall any State deprive any person of life, liberty, or property, without due process or law," as having no relevance to the vigilante massacre in Colfax. The justices left it to the local state prosecutors to charge the perpetrators with murder, arson, or nothing at all.

The same day that this Fourteenth Amendment decision in *United States v. Cruikshank* came down, the Supreme Court issued a similarly crippling decision on the Fifteenth Amendment. When it was passed, that amendment—"The right of citizens of the United States to vote shall not be denied or abridged by the United States or by any State on account of race, color, or previous condition of servitude"—was universally understood to confer the right to vote upon African-American men. But now, in a case coming out of Kentucky, *United States v. Reese*, the Supreme Court ruled that the amendment meant only that African-Americans could not be deprived of the right to vote *because* they were African-American; they could still be disenfranchised for other, ostensibly race-neutral, reasons. To the plain intent of the amendment, Chief Justice Morrison Remick Waite, a Grant appointee from Ohio, retorted, "The Fifteenth Amendment to the Constitution does not confer the right of suffrage upon anyone." Instead, he wrote, it simply prohibits the "wrongful refusal to receive the vote of a qualified elector . . . because of his race, color, or previous condition of servitude." Eight of the nine white men on the Supreme Court agreed, essentially daring states to come up with ways to disenfranchise their black populations through supposedly race-neutral policies, like literacy tests. In practice, determining who was literate would be left to prejudiced, capricious, unaccountable registrars who were free to hold white and black citizens to different standards of "literacy."

With federal civil rights enforcement hamstrung by the high court and the turn in Northern public opinion, even the outgoing commander in chief was wary of using his full powers. "The whole public are tired out with these annual autumnal outbreaks [at election time] in the South," President Grant lamented in a

September 1875 telegram to his attorney general, "and the great majority are ready now to condemn any interference on the part of the government [in Washington]."

As the public appetite for federal intervention waned, white reactionaries in Mississippi, the most vulnerable of the three black-majority states, got to work. In 1875, James Z. George, a Confederate general, and Ethelbert Barksdale, a newspaper editor, hatched a plan to ensure a Democratic electoral victory in a Republican-majority state in the upcoming statewide election. Armed white men began intimidating Republican Party rallies, often wearing red shirts as an unofficial uniform. In tandem, wealthy whites organized what amounted to a statewide protection racket. African-American tenants and employees who signed "certificates of loyalty" vowing to vote the Democratic ticket would be protected from firing, eviction, and assault; those who refused faced consequences, up to and including being lynched. Abandoning hope, the white Republican governor of Mississippi resigned his post and fled the state rather than stand for reelection.

The Mississippi Plan, as it came to be known, inspired white supremacists in the other black-majority states to imitate it. The fawning coverage in the upstate South Carolina *Spartanburg Herald*'s article, "What Was Done in Mississippi," served as a how-to guide for voter suppression. That summer, an election "expert" from Mississippi was brought to South Carolina to offer detailed tutorials on how to steal an election. A thirty-three-point plan drawn up by a former Confederate general turned South Carolina Democratic Party operative endorsed the electoral equivalent of man-to-man defense: "Every Democrat must feel honor bound to control the vote of at least one negro, by intimidation, purchase, keeping him away or as each individual may determine, how he may best accomplish it." Another plank called for flat-out political assassination: "Never threaten a man individually if he deserves to be threatened, the necessities of the times require that he should die. A dead Radical is very harmless—a threatened Radical or one driven off by threats from the scene of his operations is often very troublesome, sometimes dangerous, always vindictive." While "fusionists" in Charleston held fast to a platform of interracial governance, "straight-outs" in the rest of the state backed unabashed white rule.

On the Fourth of July, 1876, a replay of Louisiana's 1873 Colfax massacre occurred in South Carolina—only this time without the federal courts willing to determine whether anyone's civil rights had been violated. In upstate Hamburg, across the Savannah River from the larger city of Augusta, Georgia, the South Carolina State Militia (resented as "the black militia" by local whites) paraded in honor of the nation's hundredth birthday. The anniversary of the nation's founding declaration that "all men are created equal" was heartily commemorated by African-Americans in the years following emancipation with marches, barbecues, and public readings of Thomas Jefferson's century-old words. Unrepentant white Southerners often interpreted these celebrations as gloating over the United States victory in what they called the "War Between the States." When the son and son-in-law of a local white farmer rode up in a carriage and demanded that the parading militia step aside for them, tempers flared. To defuse the situation, the African-American Civil War veteran in command, Dock Adams, who had moved to South Carolina from Georgia after that state's white supremacist "redemption," ordered his men to clear a path for the buggy.

With the matter seemingly settled, Adams was surprised to learn later that the two men had subsequently gone to state authorities and gotten him charged with obstructing a public roadway. On July 8, Adams arrived in the courtroom of Judge Prince Rivers, an African-American born in slavery, now elevated to magistrate by Reconstruction. Tensions ran high. Adams's militia turned out at the courthouse to support him, while a group of Red

Shirts, under former Confederate general Matthew Butler, arrived to intimidate them. Butler was particularly resentful of the new order in South Carolina, since he had lost his bid for Congress to African-American civil rights leader Alonzo Ransier.

Hoping to avoid trouble, the state militia repaired to a local armory. But the Red Shirts followed, joined by white vigilantes from neighboring Georgia who had poured over the border eager for a fight. When shots rang out, leaving one white Georgian dead, the enraged Red Shirts overran the armory. Militiamen fled in disarray into the countryside and the Red Shirts followed. Those captured were subjected to hastily arranged show trials and executions. The white mob then rampaged through the African-American section of Hamburg, burning it to the ground. They looted Judge Rivers's home and bludgeoned the town's African-American police chief to death. Days later, in Washington, South Carolina congressman Joseph Hayne Rainey begged a skeptical administration to send a post-massacre show of force, to little avail.

Reeling from news of the rural outrage, Charleston civil rights activists led by congressman-cum-reverend Richard Cain called for a mass protest. On the night of July 17, a unified assembly of one thousand African-Americans and five hundred whites turned out at the city's Market Hall. As the speeches rolled, the overflow crowd stretched into the middle of the street, overrunning the streetcar tracks. When a trolley attempted to pass, it was blocked by the crowd, which refused to move for it. In this metaphorical replay of the Fourth of July incident at Hamburg, this time the assembled citizens refused to make way. "This is no Hamburg!" the crowd began to chant. Eventually the city's integrated police force had to step in to clear the street and arrest one particularly recalcitrant protester. The streetcar passed, but the point had been made. Charleston was no Hamburg; its residents would not be intimidated.

Once the mass meeting settled down, it culminated with the issuing of a public statement, reprinted by newspapers far beyond

Charleston. "Although many miles from the scene of action, we do unite in mass-meeting to express our just indignation," the activists began. They demanded that Matthew Butler, the leader of "the Regulators [and] a private citizen, having no authority whatever," be subjected to the same "swift . . . arrest, trial, conviction, and punishment . . . as are always visited on colored criminals." And they vowed—pointedly ignoring the Supreme Court's *Cruikshank* decision—that "in case this one legal demand be not granted, and the protection of our lives, liberty, and property be not to our satisfaction guaranteed and secured in the future, by the State Government, then [we will] petition the National Government through legal channels 'for redress of grievances.'"

The protesters were correct that Charleston was no Hamburg— but, unfortunately, more and more of South Carolina was. The Democrats' gubernatorial nominee, the grandly mustachioed former Confederate cavalry officer Wade Hampton III, kicked off his campaign on August 16 in the center of the state with a mounted torchlight parade of night riders toting "Carolina, Home of the White Man" signs. Hampton's campaign beat a dramatic path through the black-majority state, beginning in the reactionary hinterlands before marching on cosmopolitan Charleston.

Meanwhile, Republican rallies were plagued by Red Shirt violence. At an August campaign event in Edgefield, twenty-five miles north of Hamburg, Robert Smalls, the African-American Civil War hero, now a congressman, was harassed with racial slurs, forced from the stage, and run out of town by armed men on horseback. Professor Richard T. Greener, often the lone African-American speaker at Republican events, was repeatedly heckled with vile language and threatened by gun-toting white supremacists.

Only Charleston, with its African-American majority, organized activist community, and prosperous Brown middle class, remained safe. There was no parallel in the city to the overwhelming economic leverage for intimidation white landowners held in the countryside. In the city, the Charleston *News and Courier* still urged its conservative white readership to stop shopping at black-owned businesses—"Withdraw [y]our patronage . . . from those who make war upon us"—and a Democratic Party leader exhorted "white men [to] walk rather than use a 'hack' drawn by a Republican [and to] go unshaven rather than patronize a Republican barber," but the effects were limited. Sure, some white customers grew out their sideburns in protest, but others did not; regardless, it didn't pack the same economic knock-out punch as a rural landlord's threat to evict a tenant farmer.

Charleston's civil rights activists simply were not intimidated. And when there were racial altercations in or near Charleston, African-American Republicans typically came out on top. On the night of September 6, an armed group of white Democrats ran into trouble escorting several black Democrats through the city after they had spoken out for the Democratic ticket. While rural African-Americans typically only backed the Democrats when threatened with violence, a subset of well-to-do African-Americans in Charleston supported the Democrats out of sincere fiscal conservatism, and others did so to prevent white customers from boycotting their businesses. Among the Democrats' small cadre of African-American supporters was Sydney Eckhard, one of the activists whose civil disobedience had launched the Charleston streetcar integration campaign in 1867. In exchange for their support, black Democrats had been assured by Wade Hampton himself that he would safeguard their rights. As Hampton wrote in a campaign pamphlet, "I pledge my faith that if we are elected . . . we will observe, protect, and defend the rights of the colored man as quickly as [we would] any man in South Carolina." Behind the scenes, Hampton quietly backed a strategy of "bloodless coercion"— using open-carry parades rather than outright murder—to cow black citizens into not voting.

As the African-American speakers from the Democratic Party

rally walked up King Street to Citadel Square, the Republican ward meetings were letting out. Soon a crowd of black Republicans began stalking the outnumbered Democrats. Panicking, their white guards fired into the air. The Republicans returned fire first with stones, then bullets. The speakers were spirited out under police escort, but the rioting continued through the night as African-American Republicans looted white-owned businesses and beat two reporters from the conservative Charleston *News and Courier.* By the time order was restored two men, one African-American and one white, lay dead.

A month later, an interparty debate twelve miles upriver from Charleston, in Cainhoy, South Carolina, similarly devolved into violence. The audience had come well armed but, in a time and place where pistols were considered men's fashion accessories, no one thought much of it. All seemed calm as Republican William McKinlay took the stage. The wealthy biracial real estate baron, who had been born free and was an active member of the Brown Fellowship Society, was now Charleston's recorder of deeds. As he began his speech, a shot rang out, and a melee ensued. Democrats and Republicans exchanged fire. The outnumbered Democrats soon found themselves outgunned and they fled down the road from Cainhoy as Republicans fired after them. In the end, six men were dead, all but one of them white. Of the three African-Americans who sustained injuries that day, all were Democrats. But increasingly, Charleston was a tiny Republican-dominated island in a vast sea of Democratic voter intimidation.

By the time candidate Wade Hampton concluded his campaign with a parade through Charleston, his party was already celebrating statewide victory. After attending a formal dinner in Hampton's honor, James Conner, a Charleston aristocrat and Confederate veteran, who was running down-ticket for attorney general, gloated to his wife that the campaign had "scare[d] the darkies and astonish[ed] the Governor," referring to African-

Americans with a slur and to Hampton with the title that was not
yet his. Republican officials put on a brave face but their faith was
giving out. As one Republican poll manager wrote on the eve of
the election, despite Democratic "deception[,] force [and] fraud . . .
I shall do my part without fears of intimidation. I shall die [at]
the polls—in the defense of the Republican Party—[for] once we
allow the Democrats in the State to get in power, then we will see
a Second Georgia. What right has a colored man in Georgia today?
None whatever [save to be] treated like a dog." On election day,
even Charleston was plagued by violence. When a brawl broke out
between white Democrats and black Republicans, the Republican
mayor had to call in federal troops to restore order.

The fall campaign in Louisiana went similarly. The Democratic candidate for governor, Francis T. Nicholls, was, like Wade
Hampton, a Confederate veteran with flamboyant facial hair who
insisted publicly that he would safeguard civil rights but was privately hostile. In New Orleans, African-Americans were unafraid
to openly campaign and vote, but in rural areas fear was palpable.
As a member of a congressional fact-finding committee later sum-
marized, "Organized clubs of masked, armed men, formed as rec-
ommended by the central Democratic committee, rode through the
country at night, marking their course by the whipping, shooting,
wounding, maiming, mutilation, and murder of women, children,
and defenseless men, whose houses were forcibly entered while
they slept, and, as their inmates fled, the pistol, the rifle, the knife
and the rope were employed to do their horrid work. Crimes like
these, testified to by scores of witnesses, were the means employed
in [the] Louisiana [election]."

Under these conditions of violent voter intimidation, even after
the votes had been counted in November 1876, no one could agree
on who had won. Both the Republicans and Democrats claimed
the governorships of South Carolina and Louisiana and both went
about inaugurating rival governors and sending rival slates of rep-

resentatives to the state capitals and to Washington. On South Carolina's capitol building grounds in Columbia, state militiamen stared down vigilante Red Shirts in a tense standoff, each hoping to seat their preferred ticket.

At the national level, neither the Democratic presidential candidate, Samuel J. Tilden, nor the Republican, Rutherford B. Hayes, could claim the presidency. The electoral votes from South Carolina, Louisiana, and Florida were all in dispute over allegations of ballot fraud and voter suppression. Facing this chaos, outgoing President Grant and the lame-duck Congress appointed a bipartisan committee of five House members, five senators, and five Supreme Court justices—all white men—to resolve the dispute. Privately, Grant now told his cabinet that passing the Fifteenth Amendment had been a grave mistake. "It ha[s] done the Negro no good," he concluded. Instead, "[it has] been a hindrance to the South, and by no means a political advantage to the North."

The impaneled committee met and, by a vote of eight to seven, awarded the disputed electors to the Republican Hayes. But with Democrats threatening to block the official tallying of the electoral college in the House of Representatives, four Southern Democrats and five Northern Republicans met on February 26, 1877, at Washington's Wormley Hotel to resolve the matter in secret. That the establishment was owned by James Wormley, the wealthiest African-American in the city, was painfully ironic, considering that the deal the nine white men cut there to cede the South to white supremacists would scuttle civil rights for nearly a century.

According to the terms of the backroom deal, in exchange for not blocking the Republican nominee, Hayes, from the White House, the new administration would accept Democratic governors Hampton and Nicholls in South Carolina and Louisiana. Hampton personally assured Hayes that if given the governorship he would protect African-American civil rights; Nicholls made similar vows. In Washington, incoming president Hayes personally met with South Carolina's top African-American Republicans, including Congressmen Joseph Hayne Rainey, Richard Cain, and Robert Smalls and State Treasurer Francis Lewis Cardozo, but what he told them was chilling. "The use of the military forces in civil affairs," Hayes said, "is repugnant to the genius of American institutions, and should be [dispensed] with if possible." A secret protocol of the deal that made him president included a promise to end federal military protection of civil rights in the South. Soon after his swearing in, the new president ordered the federal troops stationed in southern cities back to their barracks.

Most of white America congratulated itself on what it called the Great Compromise that finally laid to rest the fractious era of disunion. But others slammed it as the Corrupt Bargain, even the Great Betrayal. How could Hayes "go back on us," one black South Carolinian muttered, "when we had to wade through blood to help place him where he is now." Though the compromise gave lip service to protecting equal rights, enforcement of civil rights laws would be left to Southern state governments now solidly in the hands of white Democrats.

Hampton and Nicholls had both made vague campaign promises to protect African-American rights, but civil rights activists, reeling from the Great Betrayal, braced for a backlash. While Hampton would appoint nearly a hundred men of color to office during his term and publicly dine with African-Americans—taboo among those who feared "social equality"—his attitude was paternalism, not egalitarianism. The most glaring success of the civil rights era—the desegregated state university—was firmly in his cross hairs.

On the afternoon of June 25, 1877, annual commencement exercises were held in the library on The Horseshoe. With ceremonial grandeur, both white and African-American graduates were duly presented with their diplomas, all hand-signed by Governor Hampton, the chairman *ex officio* of the university board. A faculty member noted pointedly that the students of color "had done as well as any of the great men of the old South Carolina College" but all present knew that it would not be enough to stave off resegregation. The nation's increasingly intolerant intellectual climate of pseudoscientific racism was already seeping into the curriculum. On a history exam that spring, students had been asked to "name the Caucasian races; also, trace the supposed origin of the Hamites, Semites, and especially the Aryans and their migrations."

In his capacity as outgoing president of the student literary and debating club, the Clariosophic Society, one of the African-American graduates of 1877, Cornelius Chapman Scott of Charleston, duly turned over its records to the incoming board. The new, all-white panel was headed by Perry Butler, a nephew of Matthew Butler, the butcher of Hamburg. Record book now in hand, the new board got to work defacing it. Every page of the ledger filled out during integration was written over in dark ink with a tombstone pictograph blotting out the meeting minutes and budgetary figures. "Negro Regime" and "Not Clariosophics" was scrawled on every page.

A week after commencement, the final integrated faculty meeting was held in Richard T. Greener's university library with Governor Hampton present. The negotiations, such as they were, echoed the Corrupt Bargain struck that winter in Washington. In exchange for accepting the faculty members' resignations, a trumped-up charge that it had been current students, not the departing racists, who had vandalized the university library years ago, would be dropped. Shortly after the meeting with Governor Hampton, the highest-profile African-American at the school, Professor Greener, left South Carolina for Washington, D.C. African-American students who were midway through their course of studies would be permitted to complete their degrees on condition they transfer to Claflin University, an all-black institution.

While Hampton preferred to operate behind closed doors, other white supremacists were more openly confrontational. Over

Hampton's public objections, the newly seated legislature withheld the salaries it owed to the outgoing faculty members. A rural
newspaper cheered on the legislators, backing their move against
the university's "dirty and infamous . . . so-called professors" and
exulting that "our beloved and honored university is freed forever
from the Radical and the negro!"

Democrats went on settling scores with their integrationist enemies statewide. Republicans who remained in office after the federal
troops stood down were forced out. Alleging voter fraud, the new state
legislature dismissed seventeen Republican representatives from
Charleston and made them rerun for their seats in a special election
that was swept, under suspicious circumstances, by the Democrats.
In the state senate, so many besieged Republicans resigned that it
flipped the majority to the Democrats without an election.

The now-Democratic legislature set its sights on purging the
state supreme court of the man who had desegregated it: Justice Jonathan Jasper Wright. The judge whose complaints over
segregated seating at a public lecture had sparked the desegregation of the state university was impeached for alleged drunkenness. The legislators' investigation was based entirely on secret
testimony, and even Governor Wade Hampton suggested its conclusions were unproven. But seeing no hope of beating the charges,
Wright resigned rather endure a show trial.

The new legislature also impaneled a Commission on Public Frauds to investigate corruption and issued a highly parti-
san report that fingered only Republicans. No doubt there was
plenty of graft—the so-called Gilded Age after the Civil War was
an unparalleled era of greased palms—but the corruption was
national and bipartisan. The real sin the Republicans were being
called to account for was their racial egalitarianism. Tellingly, for
all the dozens of Republican politicians implicated in the report,
fewer than twenty were ever indicted, and only three were ever
tried in court. The Commission on Public Frauds's report was a

forum for slander; public trials, on the other hand, with their rules of evidence, the right of the accused to confront his accusers, and the burden of proof beyond a reasonable doubt, would only undermine the allegations, so few were held.

The pair who pushed the hardest to integrate the University of South Carolina, former governor Franklin Moses Jr. and his secretary of state, Francis Lewis Cardozo, were both arrested. Moses, who had almost certainly committed financial improprieties, was publicly disgraced but never charged with any crimes. Cardozo, who was almost certainly clean, was among the handful of politicians put on trial. In a private letter, the state attorney general who charged Cardozo called his trial an attempt "to politically guillotine" the state's Republican Party.

Cardozo had been reelected as state treasurer in the 1876 election until the backroom deal at the Wormley Hotel had allowed South Carolina Democrats to remove him. Soon after relinquishing his office, Cardozo was arrested for embezzlement of public money and other crimes. He quickly posted bond and moved his family to Washington, D.C., but returned to South Carolina in the fall of 1877 to stand trial before a racially mixed jury.

Weaving an implicitly anti-Semitic conspiracy theory, the prosecution alleged that Cardozo and Moses—both practicing Christians of partial Jewish descent—had filched taxpayer funds in league with Hardy Solomon, a South Carolina banker. The judge, in a biased charge to the jury, all but convicted Cardozo himself and, after twelve hours of deliberation, the jury did as it had been instructed. At the reading of the verdict, one newspaper reported, Cardozo's "eyes became dilated and his whole visage denoted his grief. He was a picture of despair." The civil rights champion was sentenced to two years in prison but, less than six months into his sentence, Governor Hampton pardoned him in what was almost certainly a quid pro quo political deal. Soon after his release Cardozo wrote to President Hayes to request that he pardon three

South Carolina Klansmen who had been convicted on federal charges. To put it mildly, clemency for the Klan had never before been a pet cause of Cardozo's.

The quashing of the public school desegregation experiment in New Orleans was hard fought. In the 1876 election, Democrats had run the rabidly racist Robert Mills Lusher against Louisiana's African-American state superintendent of education, William G. Brown. With the results in dispute, Lusher waited through the winter, quietly laying plans for reconquest. He even worked a half day on Mardi Gras before going out to enjoy what he termed the "organized frivolity" of the parades. The Mistick Krewe of Comus's theme that year—"The Aryan Race"—was particularly inspiring to him. A "gorgeous display," Lusher gushed in his diary of the torchlight parade.

Lusher's integrationist rival, William G. Brown, had predicted that he would need "five or six more years" of mixed schools before the state would produce a new generation, free of prejudice, that could lead it into the future. He would not get them. The deal at the Wormley Hotel seated Louisiana's entire Democratic slate, including Lusher. Taking office, Lusher ordered armed guards posted at the doors of city hall "so as to prevent the Radical Board of Directors"— which insisted, with justification, that it had won the election—"from meeting." He tapped his old henchman, William O. Rogers, who had scrupulously fought integration in the uncertain days after the Civil War, to serve as local superintendent. With Lusher back in charge at the state level and Rogers in the city, the pair began resegregating the schools. Rogers handled the bureaucratic wranglings locally, while Lusher agitated to amend the state constitution to remove the integration plank he dubbed an "unwise and unnecessary . . . obstacle of an embarrassing character [not] to be found in the constitution of any other American State."

The city's African-American leaders feared Lusher, and they didn't trust the new governor, Francis T. Nicholls. On the eve of taking office, Nicholls professed his intentions to preserve civil rights: "I have earnestly sought to obliterate the color line in politics and consolidate the people on the basis of equal rights." But he also specifically endorsed "a system of public education, to be supported by equal and uniform taxation upon property, so that all without regard to race or color may secure equal advantages thereunder." This position shrewdly opened the door to separate albeit ostensibly equal public schools for white and nonwhite children.

In June, the Orleans Parish School Board met to formally vote on school resegregation. Rogers and his allies put out a statement that "personal observation and universal testimony concur . . . that public education has greatly deteriorated [by] the ill-advised action of our predecessors in forcing the children of both races into the same schools." Rather than discipline the vigilante Regulators who had tried to reestablish segregation by force in 1874, the board used their violence as an excuse to meet their demands. "The turbulent spirit of the white boys . . . exhibited in quarrels, bickerings [and] ostracism—attended with humiliation—which one race inflicts upon the other, and which cannot be remedied by the best of teachers, convince [the] committee that the education of both races would be greatly promoted by conducting it in separate schools," the board members wrote. Whether this strife was the result of "a prejudice [or] an instinct," was irrelevant, they concluded, since it was interfering with the mission of the school district regardless. To justify their reactionary proposal, Rogers's allies cynically asserted that "giv[ing] the best education possible . . . to the whole population, without regard to race, color or previous condition . . . can be best attained by educating the different races in separate schools." They predicted that "nine-tenths of both races [would] warmly approve it."

When the floor was finally opened for debate, one biracial board member, Louis A. Martinet, rose to object. Martinet was a living, breathing testament to the transformative power of education. To his white supremacist colleagues, he was precisely what they feared could result from educating nonwhite children. The son of a French Creole father and an enslaved African-American mother, Martinet had been born into slavery and educated in schools for freedmen after the war. He had gone on to study law and had served in the Louisiana House of Representatives from 1872 to 1875. The impassioned board member pleaded with his colleagues to leave the district's racial policy alone, noting that it was a modest school-choice program that didn't force integration but simply allowed it. If the change went through, he vowed, he would resign his school board post in protest and upend the board's plans for a public consensus on resegregation. Faced with Martinet's appeal, the board agreed to a short delay, postponing the vote until their meeting the following week.

Knowing he would be outvoted when the school board reconvened, Martinet scrambled to block the plan by going over his colleagues' heads. Days after the school board met, Martinet and thirty other prominent African-American men, calling themselves the Colored Committee on Mixed Schools, arrived at the governor's office. Being some of the wealthiest men in the state—their combined net worth in real estate and taxable property was, according to (likely inflated) news reports, $20 million—they could not be easily ignored. The Colored Committee was led by Unification Movement veteran Aristide Mary, the biracial real estate heir and philanthropist who was likely the wealthiest person of color in the city. Famed for his posh style, never seen on the city streets without gloves, silk hat, and cane, Mary cut a striking figure. Governor Nicholls, who had lost an arm and a leg in the Civil War, was less imposing. He hobbled over to meet the Colored Committee and directed them to the lieutenant governor's office, where the unwieldy group squeezed in around a conference table.

Mary opened the meeting, pointedly reminding Nicholls of his pledge to uphold civil rights. "We have come to you, sir, to right our wrongs," Mary began. "The late report of the School Board, which has resolved to have separate schools for white and colored children is, I consider, a violation of . . . your own pledge [that our] rights, liberties and lives should be protected [and] that those rights given to us by the constitution shall not be violated. We thought it best to call upon your Excellency, and lay before you this indignity offered to the colored race, and we look to you to enforce the rights of the colored race."

"I have not before given the subject much thought," Nicholls dissembled. He was merely the *ex officio* president of the state board of education, he offered, "and your grievances (if there be any) belongs exclusively to the [Orleans] parish [school] board." Sensing that this did not satisfy the group, but still trying to end the meeting quickly, he goaded the men to bring a case in the state courts that he knew they would lose. "If you believe that there has been a violation of the constitution, the courts are open, and there lies your redress [but] I believe the [segregated] mode adopted by our board exists all over the United States." School desegregation in New Orleans had been pioneered by civil rights activists as an experiment which, if successful, could be replicated in locales all over America. Now its experimental nature was being used to destroy it.

"I believe the constitution says that 'all public schools shall be open to all children,'" Mary countered. Indeed, that was a direct quote from the state's 1868 constitution, still the governing document of the state.

Nicholls snapped back that he wouldn't comply without a court order. "I disagree with you," he told Mary. "But if you believe that your legal rights are infringed upon make application for one of your children to the public schools, and if rejected, then the courts are open to you."

Frustrated that his gentlemanly approach was failing, Mary stepped aside. Taking a tougher line, Louis Charles Roudanez, the Paris-educated physician and newspaper publisher, rose to confront Nicholls. "Governor," he began sternly, "that the rights, the liberties, the lives of the colored children should be protected, was your pledge when you took your office. . . . Do you mean to say you have not the moral influence to enforce our rights? If not . . . it is a gross injustice [and] we shall sound the tocsin of alarm throughout the country."

Nicholls tried to steer the conversation back into legalistic minutiae but George T. Ruby, decades younger than Mary or Roudanez, rose in a rage. The Manhattan-born son of a white clergyman and a free woman of color, Ruby had spent most of Reconstruction in Texas before moving to New Orleans to work as a journalist and customs official. Now he played the ultimate race card on the governor. The Creole of color community, he told Nicholls, knew which families were passing for white in New Orleans society, even if their white lies had gone on for generations. If the governor insisted on segregating the schools, the Colored Committee would start outing prominent white families as the one-drop-rule people of color they were. If the activists' own children were forced into segregated schools, he warned, they would drag out scores of ostensibly "white" students with them. "I believe it dangerous in a community like this—of doubtful ancestry—to push this matter further," Ruby told the governor in a thinly veiled threat. "For we have those facts in our possession which it would be unpleasant to some in high circles were we to use them, which we must do in the event of separate schools." Ruby and his committeemen were not the only Americans of mixed background—mixing was rampant and had gone on for centuries—they were just the rare Americans who never tried to cover it up.

Racial passing went to the very highest levels of Louisiana

society. Even Randall Lee Gibson, the white supremacist Democrat who, with the coming of "redemption," now represented New
Orleans in the United States Congress, was secretly descended
from a free man of color. Gibson family lore long attributed the
family's off-white complexion to their descent from "an English
lord" who had fallen for "a Gypsy maid." Later generations speculated that their family was variously part Portuguese, Native
American, Sephardic Jewish, Moroccan, or Turkish—anything
but the sub-Saharan truth.

With the specter of a mass racial outing raised, the meeting
with the governor threatened to overheat. Dr. Roudanez, trying to
lower the temperature, appealed to Nicholls's humanity. "Governor," he beseeched him, "put your prejudices aside. Place yourself
in my humble position and when you leave your Executive office
and go to your home converse with your conscience and let your
moral integrity conquer all, if any, prejudices that may exist."

As tempers cooled, the governor ended the meeting. "If a point
of violation of your legal rights is established by law, I shall
bring everything to bear that is in my power to see that you are
righted . . . but believing as I do that your complaint is based
solely upon a feeling among you, and no violation of your rights,
I am powerless to act." With that, committee members shook the
governor's sole hand and departed.

Convinced that Nicholls was an enemy of the Colored Committee, Dr. Roudanez delivered on his threat to "sound the tocsin of
alarm throughout the country." The following day, the *New York
Times* published an uncharacteristically sympathetic article on
the meeting, clearly sourced from committee members. "The colored committee," the paper informed its readers back in New York,
a city with its own segregated school system,

> stated its intention to oppose this flagrant violation of dis-
> tinctive pledges and constitutional obligations, and left the

Governor's presence determined to defeat and overcome the proposed violation of their common rights. When it is remembered that the public schools of New-Orleans have been common for the past 10 years, and that even before the war classes of colored citizens had access for their children to the schools, the outrage of the proposed act is the more glaring. Indignation is a mild term for the feelings of this class of citizens whose rights are thus threatened.

The following week, the school board reconvened to vote on its plan to resegregate the schools. Again, Louis Martinet rose to register his opposition, reminding his colleagues that the Fourteenth Amendment to the United States Constitution mandated equal citizenship regardless of color and that the Louisiana state constitution explicitly prohibited school segregation. In their own oaths of office, mandated by the state constitution, he noted, each board member had sworn "that I accept the civil and political equality of all men, and agree not to attempt to deprive any person or persons, on account of race, color or previous condition of any political or civil right." Now his colleagues were openly violating their oaths. Facing this betrayal, Martinet swore, "our duty, both as your fellow citizens and constituents, and of the class against whom you have been at pains to express this wrongful intent is, firmly and respectfully, in the full dignity of Americans citizens, to protest."

Martinet's righteous eloquence won over only two of his colleagues. The resegregation plank was passed by a vote of fifteen to three. Later that month, the city's African-American community honored Martinet's call for protest, rallying in a mass meeting against the board's decision and adopting a resolution that "no distinction shall exist among citizens of Louisiana in any of our public schools or state institutions of education." In reality, this was less true by the day.

With Nicholls's tacit support, Rogers and Lusher moved to

resegregate the schools with as little friction as possible. Reviving an old canard that racial equality was a Creole of color obsession with little support among rank-and-file freedmen, the segregationist duo attempted to buy off their well-to-do mixed-race critics by giving them their own school. Four elite "academic schools" were set up in New Orleans—one for white boys, two for white girls, and, crucially, a fourth "for advanced colored students." Located in the French Quarter in a rented building on the corner of Royal Street and Hospital Street (later renamed for Governor Nicholls), the school was explicitly set up for Creoles of color; "advanced colored students" was a blatant euphemism for the children of mixed-race New Orleanians who had been free before the Civil War. As Superintendent Lusher would explain in his 1877 report to the state legislature,

It has long been apparent, in the city of New Orleans, that nine-tenths of our colored fellow citizens prefer separate schools for the education of their children, and that the desire to enter white schools, in contravention of the natural law, is peculiar to the children of mixed white and colored blood, whose parents have always been free. These children undoubtedly merit special consideration; and, as they have a strong aversion to association in the schools with children of darker hue, it would seem wise to establish a separate, intermediate class of schools for their instruction. This the City Board of School Directors have already done by opening an "Academy No. 4."

The Creole of color community, however, did not take the bait. When the schools reopened that fall with tripartite segregation—schools for whites-only, blacks-only, and biracial-students-only—one member on the Colored Committee took Governor Nicholls up on the dare to see him in court. Paul Trévigne, the biracial editor of

the *L'Union* and *New Orleans Tribune* newspapers and a veteran of
the integrationist school board that Lusher had physically barred
from office, brought a lawsuit in Louisiana state court against
Superintendent Rogers and his new school board. The Fourteenth
Amendment coupled with the integrationist planks of the Louisiana state constitution prohibited school segregation, Trévigne
argued, and he sought an injunction to block the board's resegregation policy. In court he was represented by Simeon Belden,
a scalawag who had served as Louisiana's attorney general and
speaker of the state House of Representatives before "redemption."
Expecting a long legal battle, Trévigne's community supporters
created a fund to support his lawsuit.

At the initial hearing, Judge Nicholas H. Rightor granted a preliminary injunction barring the school board from implementing
its resegregation plan. But a week later, at the next court hearing,
the board's attorneys moved to dismiss the case. Their argument
was simple: Paul Trévigne did not have standing to sue. Trévigne had based his suit on the facts that he was "a citizen of the
United States and of Louisiana, resident in this city, of which he
is a native, [and] avers that he is a colored man of African descent
and origin; that he is a married man, has a minor now under his
tutelage of schoolable age; that he is the owner of real and personal property in the city, upon which he pays taxes." But to have
standing to sue, the Board's attorney argued, Trévigne would have
to attempt to enroll his son in an all-white school and get turned
away. Since the schools had not yet been segregated—on account
of the very injunction Trévigne had won—he had not yet been able
to be discriminated against.

Remarkably, Judge Rightor agreed with this preposterous argument and dissolved the injunction he had issued. And his written
opinion went further, launching a legal theory that would make
it all but impossible to challenge the new segregation policy even
after it was implemented. Since students are required to enroll in

their neighborhood schools, Judge Rightor ruled, Trévigne's hypothetical subsequent case—to be filed after his son was discriminated against—would only affect his particular neighborhood school. Trévigne, the judge wrote "cannot assume either the tasks or the prerogatives of a public functionary nor constitute himself the champion of any rights but his own." With this flourish, Judge Rightor was attempting to invalidate all potential civil rights test cases through which one aggrieved plaintiff files suit on behalf on an entire class of similarly injured people. It was a bizarre move that, if followed to its logical conclusion, would revoke the courts' coveted power to judge the constitutionality of a law based on an individual case.

Trévigne appealed to the state supreme court. Against Rightor's claim that his case involved one child and one parent, Trévigne argued, "This case is one of great magnitude, involving as it does a question of civil liberty and constitutional right, with all the sacred guarantees of citizenship, and is really a test, judicially, of the status of that class termed 'colored,' whose rights to citizenship ought to be protected." The state's high court waited over a year to consider the matter before dismissing Trévigne's appeal with an opinion it never even deigned to publish.

Meanwhile, with Judge Rightor's preliminary injunction dissolved, the school board began implementing its separate schools policy. As children were forced into segregated schools, civil rights activists regrouped and plotted two new test cases, one to be filed in state court and one at the federal level.

The new state court case was brought by Ursin Dellande three weeks after Rightor's decision against Trévigne. A real estate owner and broker, Dellande was a pillar of the community and a fitting test-case plaintiff. On October 30, 1877, he had attempted to enroll his sons, Arnold, fourteen, and Clement, eleven, in the Marigny district's long-integrated Fillmore Boys School. It was located only 150 feet down St. Claude Avenue from the Dellande home, while the nearest school for children of color was six blocks away. When the Dellandes arrived, Principal George H. Gordon, who, the day before, had finished transferring all of his students of color to their new, segregated schools, refused to enroll the brothers, citing the school board's new policy.

In court, Dellande, like Trévigne, was represented by Simeon Belden and his case was similarly routed to Judge Rightor. On February 18, 1878, Ursin Dellande took the stand. When the school board's attorney asked him "Your children are colored?" Dellande responded with a simple "Yes, sir." But on redirect, Belden dove deeper into the vexing question of race.

"Can it be ascertained that your children are colored by their appearance, without being told?" Belden asked Dellande.

"No. The children are as white in color as anybody," he responded.

As with earlier civil rights plaintiffs, Ursin Dellande hoped to use his case to question and undermine the pseudoscientific concept of distinct races. But now the stakes were much higher. During Reconstruction, when the position of the state had been that people of different races must be treated equally, the question of race's reality was largely academic. Now that the position of the government was shifting towards treating members of different races differently, whether race was a reality or a fiction became crucial.

It was not until the spring, after nearly an entire school year had passed under the new segregated conditions, that Judge Rightor finally issued his decision. In it, Rightor accepted the fluidity of New Orleans's racial system only to use it against the civil rights plaintiffs. Rightor admitted that Dellande and his children were of mixed descent but concluded that because they do "not belong exclusively to any separate race," they had no grounds to object to being assigned to any school the board saw fit to make them attend. Then, seeking to blot out the New Orleanian racial system Rightor had just used to vindicate segregation, he adopted the

Anglo-American one-drop rule. Since "by American traditions and the language of common parlance . . . the relator may be classed as a negro," the judge wrote, his children should rightly attend the schools for colored children. For decades, by the common parlance of Louisiana, Dellande was a multiracial "Creole of color." Now, by the judge's vaunted "American traditions," the plaintiff was, even in Louisiana state court, "classed as a negro," even though physically, his children were "white in color as anybody."

The activists' parallel federal challenge faced similar odds despite its compelling test-case plaintiff, Arnold Bertonneau. The wine merchant who had lobbied President Lincoln for African-American voting rights in 1864 had, over the past decade, become a relatively private man. Shortly after representing New Orleans at the state constitutional convention of 1868, Bertonneau married a mixed-race woman, Eulalie Marie Adelaide Monfort. Now they were raising three sons—a nine-year-old, a seven-year-old, and a newborn. On November 19, a few weeks after Ursin Dellande's ill-fated integration attempt, Bertonneau had taken his two school-age children, Arnold John and François Henry, to enroll at Fillmore Boys School. As he had done with Dellande's sons, Principal Gordon barred them from enrolling.

To dodge Judge Rightor and the rest of the "redeemed" Louisiana bench, the week after the incident Bertonneau filed suit in federal court. He demanded cash damages of a thousand dollars and the vindication of the right of his children "to be educated [in any public school] just as the children of white parents are." Like Trévigne and Dellande, Bertonneau argued that the new policy violated both the state and federal constitutions and, like them, Bertonneau, though fair-skinned, swore in his court filings that he was "of African descent." Again, this self-outing raised pointed questions about the nature of race, a supposedly biological fact for which there can be no observable evidence.

In February 1879, the federal judge, William B. Woods, decided

Bertonneau's case. It was the first federal decision on school seg-regation in American history and it was devastating. "Both races are treated precisely alike" in segregated schools, Judge Woods wrote, openly accepting the principle of separate-but-equal. "White children and colored children are compelled to attend different schools. That is all." As for Bertonneau's claim that the state con-stitution of Louisiana prohibited school segregation, Woods replied that it was a matter to be raised in the state courts of Louisiana. Of course, Woods knew full well that Trévigne and Dellande had already done that and had lost their state court cases. The federal courts were retreating as fast as the federal military from defend-ing Reconstruction.

10.

FADE TO BLACK AND WHITE

THE SCREENS THAT DIVIDE THE RACES.

Lithograph of a resegregated New Orleans streetcar
published in the *Daily Picayune*, 1902.

(Louisiana Division/City Archives & Special Collections, New Orleans

Public Library, Photograph by Cameron Wood)

Graduating from the University of South Carolina in 1877, with a degree signed by Governor Wade Hampton, Cornelius Chapman Scott tried to make a decent life for himself under difficult circumstances. Scott worked in upstate South Carolina as a public school teacher and Methodist preacher, striving to help the most vulnerable members of the state's African-American community cope with the new realities. But in the spring of 1880, the well-educated, well-to-do, mixed-race Charlestonian caught a glimpse of the apocalypse.

A local theater was presenting the biblical Book of Revelation through a panorama—a high-tech, immersive, virtual reality conjured by a moving set with simultaneous narration. Hearing good reviews, Scott was eager to watch the four horsemen rampage across the palm-bedecked, subtropical landscape.

On a springtime Thursday night, Scott arrived at the Greenville Opera House box office and paid his fifty cents for a ticket. Seating at the theater had long ago been desegregated, so Scott was taken aback to receive a "half-ticket" entitling him to a balcony seat and twenty-five cents in change. He insisted he wanted a "full ticket" and, after pushing his half ticket and twenty-five cents back to the clerk, he was given one. But, when Scott took his assigned seat, a white man approached, pointed to the balcony, and instructed, "The gallery is for colored people." Scott stayed put. As the music began and the panorama commenced, Scott again thought the matter resolved. But midway through the show, a policeman arrived—"a contemptible 'poor white trash' who look[ed] more like a colored than a white man," as Scott later recalled—and tried to remove him by force. Scott refused to move, telling the officer that he could arrest him, but he would not comply voluntarily nor would he physically resist. Only when the policeman grabbed Scott by the shoulders did he budge. As Scott was escorted through the theater lobby, the management attempted to refund his money but, to show he was leaving against his will, Scott refused. "I was now sick of the thing," Scott recounted soon after in a letter to his father. "I was boiling with indignation, but kept perfectly cool."

No matter how bad things were in South Carolina, Scott knew he could bring a case under the federal Civil Rights Act of 1875. Scott had done everything a civil rights plaintiff should do to win a case—not leave voluntarily, not resist the police, and not accept a refund—but when he approached an attorney, the lawyer was dubious. Trying to recover money from the policeman would be hopeless as he was almost certainly had no savings, but suing the Greenville Opera House raised other problems. One of its owners was a county official. And justice was anything but blind in the now "redeemed" State of South Carolina, especially upstate. "I shall not undertake to bring an action against them," Scott concluded, "unless I could have the case take place in Charleston."

But even a victory in a federal courtroom in Charleston would face hostility at every step of appeal. Despite all the civil rights laws on the books, an ominous warning shot had come down from Washington, D.C., in 1878. In a unanimous decision, the Supreme Court invalidated a landmark transportation discrimination case: Josephine DeCuir's $1,000 recovery from the Louisiana riverboat that had barred her from the "ladies' cabin."

The high court's reasoning was bizarre. The decision, authored by Chief Justice Morrison Remick Waite, argued that because the vessel's full route crossed state lines, journeying upriver to a final destination of Vicksburg, Mississippi, it should be considered interstate commerce even though DeCuir had bought an in-state

ticket from New Orleans to Hermitage, Louisiana. Being interstate commerce, only Congress, not a state legislature, could regulate it; thus Louisiana's civil rights statute had no bearing on
DeCuir's journey. "If the public good requires such legislation," the
elderly Northerner wrote for the unanimous court, "it must come
from Congress and not from the states." But in the time between
the 1872 incident and the 1878 Supreme Court decision, Congress
had taken this very action. In 1875, it had passed Charles Sumner's Civil Rights Act, which stipulated clearly that "all persons
within the jurisdiction of the United States shall be entitled to
the full and equal enjoyment of . . . public conveyances on land or
water . . . applicable alike to citizens of every race and color." The
decision read as if Sumner's law had not passed, never suggesting that plaintiffs in similar situations could now sue in federal
court under the 1875 civil rights law. With the unanimous decision
in *DeCuir,* an earlier Supreme Court decision from 1875, upholding New Orleans sheriff Charles St. Albin Sauvinet's award from
The Bank coffeehouse which had refused to serve him on racial
grounds, began to seem like a fluke.

Given carte blanche from the high court in Washington, white
supremacists throughout the newly Solid South moved to elimi-
nate all vestiges of multiracial democracy. In 1879, Louisiana
called a new constitutional convention. With African-Americans
too terrified to vote in much of the state, only thirteen of the 133
delegates were men of color. The new constitution went back on
the promises of the 1868 document, eliminating the guarantees
of integrated schools and public accommodations. Taking its lead
from the Supreme Court's *U.S. v. Reese* decision, the new constitution guaranteed "no qualification of any kind for suffrage or
office . . . on account of race, color or previous condition" but instituted a poll tax to dissuade the state's poor, disproportionately
African-Americans, from exercising their right to vote. While well-
to-do Creoles of color would have no trouble coming up with the

annual poll tax, the Republican base of freedmen was effectively disenfranchised.

The 1879 constitution also moved the state capital upriver from New Orleans to Baton Rouge. A seemingly trivial change, it was quite telling. At the time, New Orleans was one of the ten largest cities in America while Baton Rouge was a town less than a tenth New Orleans's size. And the Crescent City's cosmopolitan mix of immigrants, Northern transplants, and mixed-race freeborn people of color was unknown in Baton Rouge. Moving the capital was an attempted political exorcism by white supremacists who hoped to fade an unwieldy, threatening technicolor society into a controllable black and white.

South Carolina's white supremacists mounted a similar attempt to lock in their counterrevolution. Upon taking power, the general assembly gerrymandered electoral districts to dilute African-American voting strength and closed many rural voting precincts. On election days poor, disproportionately African-American voters would have to walk up to twenty miles to cast ballots and contend with ferry boats that went mysteriously out of service. Rural landowning whites, by contrast, got to the polls on private boats and horses. An insidious measure enacted in 1882 made it quite literally harder to vote. Called the Eight Box Law, the legislation required that the ballot for each political office be deposited in a separate, specifically labeled ballot box. Votes cast into the wrong box would not count. The legislators knew that freedmen, subjected in childhood to legally enforced illiteracy, would be less able to comply with the law, and that even though assistance was officially prohibited white poll workers were likely to help illiterate whites get their ballots into the right box. While well-educated Browns in Charleston had little trouble complying with the new law, their political base of freedmen was swept out from under them. Such bald-faced efforts to undermine the Fifteenth Amendment's guarantee of universal male suffrage were

cunningly crafted to comply with the *Reese* decision's legalization
of racially targeted disenfranchisement for officially race-neutral
reasons like illiteracy or poverty.

As the states retracted their civil rights guarantees, in 1883
the Supreme Court fully revoked federal support. In a consolida-
tion of five lawsuits that became known as the Civil Rights Cases,
the Supreme Court struck down the Civil Rights Act of 1875 as
unconstitutional. In all five cases, African-Americans refused
the use of public accommodations guaranteed to them by Senator Sumner's law had pressed federal charges against the proprietors. Notably, only one of the cases originated in the South—that
of a Tennessee railroad conductor who had attempted to physically
push an African-American woman out of a whites-only railcar. He
only backed down when the fair-skinned, blue-eyed man who had
boarded with the woman outed himself as her nephew and firmly
requested that the conductor cease manhandling his aunt. The
Midwest cases concerned a Kansas restaurateur and a Missouri
innkeeper who refused to serve black patrons. The most famous
of the cases came out of San Francisco and Manhattan, where
recalcitrant theater owners had refused to seat black ticket holders despite the federal law. In the San Francisco case, a black man
was refused a seat at a minstrel show at Maguire's New Theater
on Bush Street in 1876. In the New York case, a South Carolina
transplant was denied a seat at the Grand Opera House in 1879 at
a tragedy starring Edwin Booth, the brother of the man who had
shot President Lincoln.

As the cases headed towards the Supreme Court, public support
for civil rights continued to erode. In an 1879 editorial, the *New
York Times* sneered that

> to invoke the Civil Rights laws is becoming very fashionable.
> Within a few days a holder of a ticket to an up-town theater
> was refused his seat on account of color, and he threatens a

civil rights action. Not many weeks ago a colored clergyman called for refreshments at an ice-cream saloon in Jersey City; the proprietor refused to serve him, and at last reports he was consulting a lawyer about suing under the Civil Rights laws. At the South, two or three married couples have lately been prosecuted because, contrary to the law of the State, the husband was black and the wife white, and their lawyers have argued that such law amounted to nothing, because [it is] contrary to the Civil Rights laws. At the North, when the Jews are excluded from Saratoga or Coney Island hotels, they are counseled that by virtue of the Civil Rights laws they can insist on being received. . . . What are these 'Civil Rights laws'? . . . If a [businessman] does not wish to employ negroes, or . . . sell to negroes, there [ought be] no compulsion.

It was in this hostile climate that the Supreme Court heard the cases and issued its eight-to-one decision striking down the Civil Rights Act of 1875. Writing for the majority, New York native Justice Joseph Bradley explained that the federal government lacked the authority to prevent "every act of discrimination which a person may see fit to make as to the guests he will entertain, or as to the people he will take into his coach or cab or car, or admit to his concert or theater, or deal with in other matters of intercourse or business." In the high court's view, the federal requirement that a theater owner must seat African-American ticket holders was tantamount to forcing him to host black guests at his house for dinner. But in the decision's most stunning section, Bradley condescendingly told African-Americans to quit whining. "When a man has emerged from slavery," he scolded, "there must be some stage in the progress of his elevation when he takes the rank of a mere citizen and ceases to be the special favorite of the laws." Bradley's opinion conflated all African-Americans with freedmen regardless of whether they had ever been enslaved and insisted that, despite this, the state owed them nothing—not even equal rights.

Only a single justice, John Marshall Harlan, dissented. Born to a slaveholding family in Kentucky, Harlan seemed an unlikely defender of civil rights. But, like many Southerners of his class, Harlan was part of a multiracial family—he had a mixed-race half sibling—and, unlike many Southerners of his class, Harlan's half sibling was acknowledged by his family. Young John's blue-eyed, straight-haired, enslaved half brother Robert, born to one of the family's mixed-race slave women, was sent to the same whites-only elementary school as the rest of the children until he was outed by a janitor as a child of color and expelled. Reaching adulthood, Robert's father-owner had him live independently and encouraged him to open a barbershop and grocery store in Lexington. In 1848, Robert, though still legally his father's property, moved west to California, where he made a fortune. Returning home wealthier than his father, Robert bought his freedom from him for five hundred dollars and settled in Cincinnati, where he opened several businesses and married a white woman. Perhaps because Justice Harlan was loath to sentence his half brother to a lifetime of discrimination, he cast the only vote on the Supreme Court to uphold the Civil Rights Act of 1875.

In his dissent, Harlan did not mention his multiracial family, but he did call out his colleagues for using word games to subvert the will of Congress. "I cannot resist the conclusion that the substance and spirit of the recent amendments of the Constitution have been sacrificed by a subtle and ingenious verbal criticism," Harlan wrote. "The court has departed from the familiar rule requiring, in the interpretation of constitutional provisions, that full effect be given to the intent with which they were adopted." Whatever Justice Bradley had written, equal rights were not special rights:

My brethren say that, when a man has emerged from slavery . . . there must be some stage in the progress of his elevation when he takes the rank of a mere citizen, and ceases to
be the special favorite of the laws. . . . It is, I submit, scarcely
just to say that the colored race has been the special favorite
of the laws. The statute of 1875, now adjudged to be unconstitutional, is for the benefit of citizens of every race and color.
What the nation, through Congress, has sought to accomplish
in reference to that race is what had already been done in
every State of the Union for the white race—to secure and
protect rights belonging to them as freemen and citizens,
nothing more.

Harlan directed his dissent to his metaphorical "brethren" on
the Supreme Court in Washington but, as he was making this
argument, how could he not have been thinking also of his biological half brother John in Cincinnati?

White supremacists nationwide hailed the Supreme Court's
nearly unanimous decision. At the Atlanta Opera House, the management interrupted a minstrel show to announce the news from
Washington. For the theater managers, the decision was no academic matter; a case against the venue, challenging its segregated
seating policy, was working its way through the courts. Now the
highest court in the land had, essentially, invalidated the suit. The
civil rights–weary *New York Times* reported on the "wild scene in
the [Atlanta] opera-house last night when the announcement of
the civil rights decision was made. . . . While [white] men stood on
their feet and cheered and ladies gave approving smiles, the qui-
etude of the colored gallery was noticeable. Not a note of applause
came from those solemn rows of benches; their occupants were
dum-founded." The *Atlanta Constitution* crowed the news from
Washington with alliterative abandon: "A Radical Relic Rubbed
Out." It was left to an African-American paper in Harlan's home

state, the *Louisville Bulletin*, to assail the Supreme Court's logic, editorializing bluntly: "Our government is a farce."

With even liberal outlets like *The Nation* firmly behind the ruling, it fell to Richard T. Greener to tilt at windmills in the New York *Evening Post*. Greener had organized a petition drive urging the passage of Sumner's civil rights bill when it was first introduced, called out progressives for getting cold feet as the bill languished in committee, and celebrated its passage after Sumner's death. Now, with what Greener slammed as "the most startling decision of the Supreme Court, so far as the colored people are concerned, since the infamous [*Dred Scott*]," the high court had buried it. In response, Greener hoped to muster a coalition of the misfits, like the one he had been part of in South Carolina, to continue the fight for civil rights. If "a pious and venerable negro bishop [can] be thrust from a railway car in Georgia although he had paid his fare," he said, what protects New York "Archbishop McCloskey [from being] thrust from a car in some Roman Catholic hating community. It may deny Mr. Adler or Mr. Weiss, distinguished Hebrews, the comforts of some third-rate hotel by some anti-Semitic community." But few answered the call. The McCloskeys and Adlers of America were increasingly finding themselves sheltered beneath the big tent of whiteness, despite their Celtic or Semitic ethnicities.

In the wake of the fall of Reconstruction, the expanded boundaries of blackness were ossifying. Greener himself felt it in his quotidian existence. For him, the everyday dignity of the tabooed "social equality" was, if anything, more important than political equality. "I myself would rather be deprived of my political rights than my social ones," Greener wrote. "I can live without suffrage; I can exist without [holding public] office; but I want to have the privilege of travelling from New York to California without fear of being put off a car or denied food and shelter solely because I have a trace of negro blood in my veins."

Greener was referencing the so-called one-drop rule. Though only formulated on the eve of the Civil War, it was being viewed ever more widely as sound science. The theory was the brain-child of an editor in Charlottesville, Virginia, down the road from Thomas Jefferson's sotto voce experiment in race mixing, who had formulated it to challenge the State of Virginia's antebellum racial definitions. According to the widely accepted definition of his day, when a European-American and an African-American had a child together, the child was "mulatto." If the progeny then had a child with a white person, the offspring would be a "quadroon," the next generation following the same pattern would yield an "octoroon," and the next what was known as a "mustee." But if the pattern continued one more generation and the "mustee" had a child with a white person, the child, according to Virginia law and scien-tific consensus, would be a white person. The idea that someone with one great-great-great-grandparent of African descent and thirty-one great-great-great-grandparents of European descent was white greatly perturbed the editor. How, he wondered, could a white man be "manufactured" from a "negro"? Surely such a thing was impossible. Africanness would be evident in anyone with an African ancestor no matter how remote, he insisted, in the form of "black and curly hair, nails dark and ill-shaped, feet badly formed, and much of the negroes propensities."

Needless to say, this one-drop concept was deeply threatening to the South's white elite. Many supposedly lily-white family trees harbored hidden African-American forebears. Louisiana remained completely mute on racial definitions. Even Virginia refused to implement the theory hatched on its soil. With the collapse of Reconstruction, the Old Dominion State defined a person of color as someone with one or more grandparents of African descent; even "octoroons" were legally white in Redemption-era Virginia. When South Carolina adopted its first post-Reconstruction racial definitions, in 1879, it opted for the relatively lax standard that anyone with one or more African-American grandparents was a person of color. That same year it banned interracial marriage— something that had been legal throughout the entire history of the state save for three brief years between the end of the Civil War and the dawn of Radical Reconstruction. In Charleston, where integrated streetcars continued to ply the streets, the social space for mixed-race people was shrinking; America's black/white binary system of race was closing in.

Of most immediate concern to many leading white families was hacking off the African-American branches of their family trees, the result of mixed-race relationships over the centuries ranging from rape to concubinage to committed love. When Reconstruction collapsed, fervent denial of interracial realities became the norm— even in Charleston, where it had always been tacitly understood that the elite whites were kin to the elite Browns.

In 1876, the leading church of the Charleston Browns, St. Mark's, had attempted to join the Protestant Episcopal Diocese of South Carolina, but the white leadership of the state's wealthy, mainline churches resisted. At the diocese's statewide convention, a representative of St. Mark's made the thinly veiled argument that his congregation was being ostracized not in spite of its congregants' blood relationships to leading whites but because of them. "I attribute a great deal of our present depression," the representative explained, "to the fact that we have been so closely allied with wealth in times past, and with the social position which usually accompanies wealth, especially it if be ancient wealth." Even with this careful circumlocution, all understood what he meant when he spoke of the congregation members' close alliance with ancient wealth. The church's application was rejected; the diocese would be for white churches only.

In practice if not law, the one-drop rule began to impose itself on South Carolina. As Professor Greener testified to Congress when asked by a senator why, given his complexion, he was even considered black: "They call everybody a negro that is as black as the ace of spades or as white as snow [in South Carolina], if they . . . know that he has negro blood in his veins." In time, even the mixed-race community itself began to surrender to the black/white binary. The Brown Fellowship Society, on the hundredth anniversary of its founding, in 1890, rechristened itself the Century Fellowship Society, burying its neither-white-nor-black identity as a relic of times past.

A similar imposition of the color line struck the mixed-race Creoles of New Orleans. Even in a city where *plaçage* relationships between white men and their mixed-race concubines were recorded in the church archives, a new racial amnesia was imposed. Creoles of ostensibly pure French and Spanish descent worked to prove their European ancestry by disowning mixed-race family members. Mixed-race relationships, once celebrated in sumptuous quadroon balls, became guarded secrets, though the Louisiana legislature balked until 1894 before outlawing interracial marriage.

As part of the cover-up, the city's French and Spanish community increasingly insisted that the term *creole* referred only to people of pure European descent. In an 1885 lecture at Tulane University, historian Charles Gayarré grumbled that it was "impossible to comprehend how so many intelligent people should have so completely reversed the meaning of the word *creole*, when any one of the numerous dictionaries within their easy reach could have given them correct information of the subject." The term, he insisted, denoted a New World "native of European extraction, whose origin was known and whose superior Caucasian blood was never to be assimilated to the baser liquid that ran in the veins of the Indian and African native." Gayarré proclaimed, "It [is] high time to demonstrate that the Creoles of Louisiana . . . have not, because of the name they bear, a particle of African blood in their veins."

The following year, the city's leading French and Spanish

families formed the Creole Association of Louisiana so that the "descendants of the original Creoles of Louisiana" could "disseminate knowledge concerning the true origin and real character . . . of the CREOLE RACE of Louisiana." The organization barred mixed-race Creoles of color from joining while opening its membership to "all white male persons of age and of good standing" even if they had no French or Spanish ancestry at all, so long as they were "desirous to co-operate in disseminating knowledge of the true character and origin and in furthering the advancement of the Creole race." To join the Creole Association of Louisiana, one need not actually be Creole, one need simply be white.

Faced with the rapidly bifurcating racial system, many Creoles of color opted to pass for white, often leaving Louisiana to do so. Historians estimate that in the last quarter of the nineteenth century hundreds of mixed-race Louisianans became "white" every year. But others chose to resist.

As disenfranchisement and segregation metastasized through the "redeemed" South, New Orleans's Creoles of color came to constitute a lost battalion, fighting on as if they had never gotten the telegram that their side had already conceded defeat. Despite failing to halt the resegregation of the New Orleans public schools, Louis Martinet continued to lead the activist circle in New Orleans as editor of the *Crusader*, launched in 1889 as the successor to the Reconstruction-era *Tribune*. A rare Creole of color who had been born into slavery, Martinet could bridge the freemen/freedmen fault lines in the city's African-American community like few others. Even as America's racial system congealed, Martinet's colleague on the newspaper, Rodolphe Desdunes, a mixed-race man with Caribbean roots, relentlessly pointed out how ill-fitting it was for New Orleans. Desdunes noted that the *Crusader*'s "proprietors are men of as pure Caucasian blood as any, and perhaps purer than some on the [white supremacist] T-D [*Times-Democrat*] staff." As for Martinet himself, Desdunes noted, though born a slave he's "as white as the editor of the *Times-Democrat*, as any who will see both together can judge." With their enduring confidence in the power of reason to expose the patent absurdity of the new racial system, the activist cadre around the *Crusader* would soon mount the most significant civil rights test case America had ever seen.

In 1890, Louisiana state representative Joseph St. Amant, a white Democrat representing a rural district fifty miles from New Orleans, introduced a bill to segregate the state's railcars. St. Amant's proposal, the Separate Car Act, would "promote the comfort of passengers in railway trains" by mandating "equal but separate accommodations for the white and colored races."

A multiracial coalition of activists organized as the American Citizens' Equal Rights Association (ACERA) came out against the bill. Too intimidated to organize in rural parishes—early on the group conceded that "in communities where lawlessness exists [the only option is to] abstain from any participation in politics"—activity was largely limited to New Orleans. At the statehouse in Baton Rouge, ACERA's official letter of protest condemning St. Amant's bill as "unconstitutional, un-American [and] unjust" was read into the record. "Will it be seriously contended that such a problematical proposition as the ethnical origin of color is a sufficient cause for a deliberate interference with settled rights?" the letter asked rhetorically, raising New Orleans's vast ethnic diversity and rampant intermixing to challenge the concept of distinct races.

> We do not think that citizens of a darker hue should be treated by law on different lines than those of a lighter complexion. Citizenship is national and has no color. We hold that any attempt to abridge it on account of color is simply a surrender of wisdom to the appeals of passion. It strikes us that the immediate effects of such legislation would be a free license to the evilly-disposed [*sic*] that they might with impunity insult,

humiliate, and otherwise maltreat inoffensive persons, and especially women and children who should happen to have a dark skin.

Refusing to give credence to binary racial categories of "Negro" and "Caucasian," the petitioners hoped to win allies across Louisiana's broad color spectrum. But with white supremacy hardening under big-tent whiteness, the activists had few allies with any authority left in the state. The 1879 constitution's poll tax had long since disenfranchised most freedmen. Despite Louisiana's non-white majority, only sixteen of the ninety-seven statehouse representatives were now men of color.

One of the sixteen, J. J. Williams, an African-American blacksmith representing Baton Rouge, rose to savage St. Amant's bill as the result of "the prejudices of . . . intellectual dwarfs [and] pigmies [who have] learned nothing during our century of progress." C. F. Brown, another of the sixteen, took a gentler approach, trying to coax his colleagues into understanding that it was the civil rights activists who were colorblind and their opponents who were creating color-coded disharmony. "If a number of colored men meet to discuss any question betwixt the races, they are charged with drawing the color line," he explained, "but here we find the Democratic party drawing the color line [in] laws such as will be a disgrace to any State in the Union." In a plea to his fellow representatives, Brown offered, "the color of our skin is no fault of ours. . . . If you should harbor any prejudices in your hearts on this subject, I would ask you . . . to forget them. Your oath binds you to be fair and impartial to all men, and to see that the Constitution and laws of our land are just and impartial." He concluded, "Considering this bill unconstitutional I vote no."

For some of the bill's supporters, the question was not whether to draw the color line, only where. Georgia-born planter W. C. Harris found its presumed boundaries of whiteness too permissive. He complained that under the bill, Asian-Americans and Italian-Americans could be classified as white while, in his opinion, "Chinamen and Dagoes [are] not as desirable citizens as the colored people."

Echoing Harris, a member of the state senate railed against the bill's potential inclusion of Asian-Americans under the big tent of whiteness. The Chinese were, in his opinion, "more obnoxious than most colored persons." He also sniffed that the bill ought to permit class-based discrimination—"[The bill] fails to exclude low white people of the worst possible stamp"—in case the ticket prices in the first-class cars weren't enough.

Shocked at his colleagues' prejudice but knowing he would be outvoted, one African-American senator warned, "When this bill shall have passed it is the last indignity left for you to heap . . . upon us. . . . But the time will and must come . . . when we will rise and strike, for our liberties, let the chips fall where they may or consequences be what they will."

The bill passed both houses and was sent to Governor Francis T. Nicholls. Louis Martinet feverishly telegrammed the governor to lobby him for a veto. "Governor," he wrote in the pay-by-the-word brevity the form inspired, "thousands good and true men petition you to veto separate car bill." Nicholls, who had famously pledged to protect civil rights when he took office back in 1877, ignored the plea. On July 10, 1890, he signed the bill into law.

Just nine days after the signing, Martinet published an editorial in the *Crusader* vowing "We'll make a case, a test case, and bring it before the Federal Courts on the ground of the invasion of the right [of] a person to travel through the States unmolested." Led by Martinet, Creole of color activists formed the Citizens' Committee to Test the Constitutionality of the Separate Car Law. Better known by its abbreviated French name, the Comité des Citoyens, the group was backed by philanthropist Aristide Mary. To the New Orleans activists, equality was an all-or-nothing proposition. If Americans of color had fewer rights than white Americans in any respect, their rights could be stripped in every respect. The routine humiliation of being asked to move to a Jim Crow railcar could lead, the group argued, to "every manner of outrage, up to murder without redress." The Comité vowed to mount "legal resistance" to the new law.

Beyond the confident Creole elite of New Orleans, African-American leaders looked with skepticism on the endeavor. Many Southern blacks saw their best hope in insisting that separate institutions be truly equal—a position that would be codified in Booker T. Washington's Atlanta Compromise speech of 1895 that explicitly eschewed "seat[s] in Congress or [the] opera-house." Even for those who still backed full civil rights, why give the most powerful all-white jury in the land—the United States Supreme Court—the opportunity to sanctify "separate but equal" public accommodations? When the Comité reached out to Frederick Douglass to get his backing for their proposed suit, he refused, warning that the case was more likely to end with the Supreme Court establishing a precedent for segregation than against it.

Yet the Comité pressed ahead, hatching a methodical plan for a test case. In their careful setup, a racially ambiguous passenger would buy a train ticket and board the first-class car where a private detective, a plant in the Comité's pay, would already be seated. When the conductor arrived, the passenger would out him- or herself as a person of color, refuse to move to the Jim Crow car, and get arrested by the detective. Then he or she would take the case all the way to the United States Supreme Court on the grounds that Louisiana's Separate Car Act was unconstitutional, setting a national precedent against segregation. After a successful fund-raising campaign, in October 1891 the well-heeled group hired a leading civil rights attorney, Albion Winegar Tourgée.

An idealistic white Ohio native of French descent, Tourgée was nationally known as one of the last unrepentant Radical Republicans. Thrice-wounded as a Union soldier in the Civil War, Tourgée was blind in one eye and walked with a limp. During Reconstruction, he had lived in North Carolina and worked as an attorney, judge, journalist, and founder of a college for freedmen. When Klan threats against his wife and daughter became too much, he fled North and settled in upstate New York.

As the country turned its back on civil rights, Tourgée stuck to his increasingly unpopular beliefs. From his idyllic country house, he dedicated himself to the vindication of his lost cause, writing political tracts like his Klan exposé, *Invisible Empire*, and taking on public-interest legal work. Seen as a late-Sixties relic adrift in the modern world, Tourgée was tolerated as a charming if ridiculous figure with his bushy walrus mustache and realistic-looking glass eye. Even as he comforted himself that in the land of the blind, the one-eyed man is king, he had enough self-knowledge to entitle his 1879 roman-à-clef on Reconstruction *A Fool's Errand, By One of the Fools*. The book sold well enough that Tourgée refused payment from the New Orleans activists and took their case pro bono.

In written correspondence between Louisiana and New York, Martinet and Tourgée brainstormed over their ideal test-case client. Tourgée suggested that a fair-skinned, mixed-race woman might be best. She would have no trouble buying a ticket to a whites-only car and she would sidestep the white South's psychopathic fear of black men and white women rubbing up against each other on crowded trains. At the same time, her racially indeterminate appearance would expose the absurdity of categorizing Americans as "white" or "colored" after centuries of overt and covert race mixing.

Martinet disagreed and he vetoed the idea of enlisting a female. Precisely because a mixed-race woman, no matter how she was racially perceived, wouldn't arouse Dixieland's psychosexual obsessions, she might not get asked to switch cars. At the other extreme, once the train left the city limits there was the danger that vigilantes might physically eject the passenger from the train—a risk to which they could not, in good conscience, subject a lady. At the height of Radical Reconstruction, "respectable" mixed-race women were the go-to test-case clients, but the times had grown too dangerous for that.

Though they disagreed on gender, Martinet seconded Tourgée's idea of using a racially ambiguous client. A racially unplaceable rider would challenge the entire pretense that Americans were racially pure and could be racially sorted. Finding such an individual would be easy. "There are the strangest white people you ever saw here," Martinet wrote Tourgée. "Walking up & down our principal thoroughfare—Canal Street—you would [be] surprised to have persons pointed out to you, some as white & others as colored, and if you were not informed you would be sure to pick out the white for colored & the colored for white. . . . In this respect New Orleans differs greatly from the interior towns."

Agreeing to recruit a biracial man, the Comité sprang into action. Martinet tapped Daniel Desdunes, the son of his *Crusader* colleague Rodolphe Desdunes, and hired a private detective to witness his lawbreaking and make the arrest. Then he went searching for a railroad company willing to cooperate. Contacting the business community, Martinet learned that the railroad companies, like the streetcar companies before them, supported their effort to overturn the law if only out of economic interest. Running extra, often half-empty, cars for different races threatened their profit margins. In fact, the first railroad company Martinet approached for cooperation told him it couldn't participate since it didn't even enforce the costly law on its trains. Instead, it put up a sign designating a Jim Crow car, as required, but never monitored who sat in it nor made anyone move to it. A second railroad company agreed to help. It would have its employees ensure an orderly arrest for the test case but, fearing a white customer backlash, it would not publicly support the lawsuit.

With all the proper arrangements in place, on February 24,

1892, Daniel Desdunes boarded the first-class compartment of a Louisiana and Nashville Railroad train bound for Mobile, Alabama. Just as planned, Desdunes outed himself, was asked to move, refused, and got arrested by a private detective hired by the Comité.

In June, Desdunes was brought before Judge John Howard Ferguson. It seemed a lucky break for the activists. Ferguson had been born on the island of Martha's Vineyard, Massachusetts, and had married the daughter of Thomas J. Earhart, a rare white New Orleans abolitionist before the Civil War. But the Northern-born judge was, if anything, too sympathetic. He threw the case out entirely, citing a recent Louisiana Supreme Court decision on behalf of the Pullman Company, which similarly opposed the new segregation law because it was expensive and had successfully argued that only the federal government could regulate interstate travel. Pared back by the state supreme court decision, the Separate Car Act now applied only to in-state travel. Even as Martinet's *Crusader* crowed after Ferguson's decision, "the Jim Crow car is ditched and will remain in the ditch. Reactionists may foam at the mouth . . . but Jim Crow is dead as a door nail," it was a pyrrhic victory. Though the activists had ostensibly won—Desdunes's charges were dismissed—they had no case to send to the Supreme Court in Washington.

Regrouping, the Comité plotted a new test case, this time on an in-state train. It recruited Homer Adolph Plessy, a twenty-nine-year-old cobbler. Though an octoroon, having a single nonwhite great-grandparent, Plessy had grown up in New Orleans's Creole of color community and lived in the downtown wards that had been its heart for over a century. Born free in 1863, he had come of age during the heyday of racial equality and had first become involved in civil rights activism as a teenager during protests against the resegregation of the public schools.

Just two weeks after Daniel Desdunes's case was dismissed,

Homer Plessy took up the cause. The Comité timed Plessy's civil disobedience for June 7, 1892, to coincide with the first day of the Republican National Convention kicking off in Minneapolis. The activists hoped the publicity might tweak the conscience of the Party of Lincoln and move civil rights back onto its agenda.

That afternoon, Homer Plessy bought a first-class ticket from New Orleans to Covington, a small town just across Lake Ponchartrain from the city. After waiting in the yet-to-be-segregated station hall, he took his assigned seat on the train. At 4:15 p.m., with a great puff of smoke the locomotive pulled out of the Marigny neighborhood station.

Within minutes, the conductor, J. J. Dowling, came by punching tickets. Encountering Plessy, the ticket taker's routine walk down the aisle came to a halt. Dowling asked Plessy if he was a person of color.

It was an odd question to ask Homer Plessy, who looked, in the words of the *Crusader*, "as white as the average white Southerner." But Plessy gave his assent that, indeed, he was a person of color. As Plessy surely knew, Louisiana had no fixed racial definitions; racial status in Louisiana could only be legally determined on a case-by-case basis in court. But by identifying himself as a person of color, Plessy was essentially goading Dowling into evicting him, which he did. As per the Separate Car Act of 1890, the conductor explained, Plessy must leave the cushions of the whites-only first-class compartment for the wooden slats of the Jim Crow car at the front of the train, just behind the smoke-belching locomotive. Plessy, of course, refused to move and moments later, Chris Cain, a private detective, materialized and arrested the recalcitrant passenger.

In short order, the train was halted and Cain marched Plessy to the nearby Fifth Police Precinct. As the cobbler waited among that day's haul of streetwalkers and petty thieves, a retinue of the city's most prominent Creoles of color, including Louis Martinet, arrived. Cash in hand, the group paid enough temporary bail to spare Homer Plessy a night in jail. The next morning, these friends from the Comité produced a remarkable sum—five hundred dollars bond—to keep the cobbler free until trial.

On October 13, 1892, Homer Plessy arrived in court and stood before the same judge who had thrown out the charges against Daniel Desdunes. Plessy's local attorney, James Walker, presented Judge Ferguson with an erudite brief, largely prepared by Tourgée. It cited the postwar amendments to the Constitution that prohibited discrimination on the basis of race or color and urged the judge to dismiss the case on the grounds that the Separate Car Act was unconstitutional. By this point, however, the reactionary series of Supreme Court decisions, most crucially the devastating 1883 decision in the Civil Rights Cases, had largely neutered those amendments. The following month, when the court reconvened, Ferguson issued his decision. Though the judge noted that the legal filings showed "great research, learning, and ability," he had no choice but to find for the prosecution on account of the Supreme Court's new precedents.

Plessy's attorneys immediately appealed Ferguson's decision to the Louisiana state supreme court in a subcase called *Plessy v. Ferguson*. They had no illusions—or even intentions—of winning the case there. The sitting chief justice was Francis T. Nicholls, the now-former governor who had signed the Separate Rail Car Act in the first place.

As expected, Plessy lost his case badly at the state supreme court. The December 1892 decision went out of its way to declare that the Fourteenth Amendment "created no new rights." For the activists, of course, the loss at the Louisiana Supreme Court was what they had wanted. Now they had a test case to take to the United States Supreme Court.

Bringing the case before the all-white tribunal might have seemed, in Tourgée's phrase, a fool's errand. But there were a few potential paths to victory. One was a change in the makeup of the court over the years it would take to be heard. With a few deaths or retirements among the justices and a few lucky appointments, the panel could tilt towards Plessy. Those hopes suffered a setback on Election Day in 1892, when the incumbent president, Republican Benjamin Harrison, was ousted by Grover Cleveland, a Democrat whose base came from the nascent Solid South, where African-Americans had been overwhelmingly disenfranchised.

A few weeks after Cleveland's 1893 inauguration, the leading backer of Plessy's legal fund, Aristide Mary, gave up. In his luxurious French Quarter mansion, the prosperous civil rights leader turned his Smith and Wesson .38 on himself, pumping three rounds into his abdomen. He died bleeding out, slumped in an armchair. In its Aristide Mary obituary, the *New York Times* noted with apparent befuddlement the "singular coincidence that many of the very wealthy colored men of this city have taken their own lives." Surely many were in despair from watching their rights get revoked one by one.

When the backlogged Supreme Court finally heard oral arguments in *Plessy v. Ferguson*, on April 13, 1896, the makeup of the court was ominous and the public had moved beyond hostility into indifference. Unlike the Civil Rights Cases, which spurred dueling editorials and wire-service reactions from all over America, *Plessy* garnered little media attention. The courtroom press gallery was nearly empty the day the case was heard.

Representing Plessy in Washington, Albion Tourgée was joined by Samuel F. Phillips, a veteran North Carolina scalawag and an experienced Supreme Court advocate. Phillips had served as solicitor general under Republican president Chester A. Arthur and had represented the administration before the Supreme Court on the losing side of the Civil Rights Cases.

In their twin briefs, Phillips played the realist, hoping to win over a difficult audience with moderation, while Tourgée wrote for the history books. Phillips's brief asked for a limited ruling in favor of Plessy, taking pains to assure the justices that even if they were to outlaw railcar segregation, such a ruling need not invalidate segregated schools or antimiscegenation laws. "*Separate cars*, and *separate schools* . . . come under different orders of consideration," Phillips wrote. "A conclusion as to one of these does not control determinations as to the other [or to] *intermarriage*."

Tourgée, by contrast, openly mocked the faux egalitarianism of the law's separate accommodations. "The claim that this act is for the common advantage of both races," he wrote, "is simply farcical." To Tourgée, the Louisiana law violated not only the Fourteenth Amendment's guarantee of equal citizenship but even the Thirteenth Amendment's abolition of slavery. The Thirteenth Amendment, in his broad reading, was meant to free the slaves but was also "meant to undo all that slavery had done in establishing race discrimination." Thus, "the establishment of a statutory difference between the white and colored races in the enjoyment of chartered privileges" by the Louisiana railcar law constituted "a badge of servitude which is prohibited by that amendment." That this "badge of servitude" was being affixed to his client, Homer Plessy, who, though born in slavery times, had never been enslaved, only made it more absurd.

Audaciously, Tourgée brought the Creole of color community's long tradition of courtroom challenges to the reality of race to the highest court in the land. "Is not the question of race, scientifically considered, very often impossible of determination?" Tourgée asked. And yet, the Louisiana law leaves this oft-impossible task of racial categorization to the "casual scrutiny of a busy conductor" deputizing a marginally educated ticket taker as "the autocrat of Caste, armed with the power of the State conferred by this statute." The only way to accurately enforce the law, Tourgée chided, would be to have every Louisianan "carry a certified copy of his pedigree" every time he or she boarded a train. Short of that, conductors would be required to walk the aisles making spot judgments about the ethnicities of each passenger's various great-grandparents. This bizarre nightmare of racial autocracy, Tourgée warned, would be the endpoint of any Supreme Court decision upholding the law. The only solution was a determination that the postwar amended constitution was colorblind. "Justice is pictured blind and her daughter, the Law, ought to be color-blind," the one-eyed attorney declared.

It took the justices a month to issue their near-unanimous decision. Justice Henry Billings Brown, a Massachusetts-born Republican, wrote for the majority. A proud member of the American Association for the Advancement of Science, Brown fancied himself a renaissance man and he kept up with all the latest developments in the science of race. In his autobiography, the justice bragged of his own inbreeding, crediting it for making him so healthy and wise. "I was born of a New England Puritan family in which there has been no admixture of alien blood for two hundred and fifty years," Brown wrote in his book's very first sentence. Perhaps realizing that some might find this touting of his racial purity potentially racist, his second sentence noted, "my ancestors were neither bigoted nor intolerant."

Having inherited his broad-mindedness from generations of inbred Anglo-Saxon forebears, Brown based his decision not on benighted backwoods bigotry but on a hardheaded realism built upon the scientific facts he had imbibed as a student at Harvard and Yale. Racial animosity, the justice wrote, is "in the nature of things." It was government's role to deal with this fact of human nature rather than engage in a quixotic crusade to stamp it out. To this end, racial segregation on a separate but equal basis seemed, to him, eminently reasonable. If African-Americans felt targeted by legislation that barred blacks from white cars with the same force that it barred whites from black cars, well, that was the result of their own self-loathing. "We consider the underlying fal-

lacy of the plaintiff's argument to consist in the assumption that
the enforced separation of the two races stamps the colored race
with a badge of inferiority," Brown wrote. "If this be so, it is not by
reason of anything found in the act, but solely because the colored
race chooses to put that construction upon it." As for Tourgée's
attack on the reality of distinct races or the racially unplaceable
Homer Plessy's physical, phenotypic questioning of the whole
concept, Brown demurred: each state could define race however
it saw fit. The justice freely admitted that he personally couldn't
say whether Plessy was white or colored and that different states
would no doubt categorize him differently. Still, Brown insisted,
each state was free to make whatever determination it saw fit.

As in the Civil Rights Cases, there was a lone dissenter: John
Marshall Harlan of Kentucky. Despite two decades of deliberate
misinterpretation by the high court, Harlan wrote, the postbellum
amendments "if enforced according to their true intent and meaning, will protect all the civil rights that pertain to freedom and
citizenship."

Harlan's argument echoed Tourgée's brief. And it was no less
stirring for its self-conscious hopelessness. "There is no caste
here," Harlan wrote. "Our Constitution is color-blind, and neither knows nor tolerates classes among citizens. In respect of civil
rights, all citizens are equal before the law. The humblest is the
peer of the most powerful. The law regards man as man, and takes
no account of . . . his color when his civil rights . . . are involved."
But for all his soaring rhetoric, Harlan was outvoted. There would
be caste here.

Stung by defeat at the high court, the Comité issued a statement defending their rights even as those rights were trampled by
the justices. "Notwithstanding this decision, which was rendered
contrary to our expectations, we, as freemen, still believe that we
were right, and our cause is sacred . . . [W]e are encouraged by the
indomitable will and noble defense of Hon. Albion W. Tourgee, and

supported by the courageous dissenting opinion of Justice John Harlan in behalf of justice and equal rights. In defending the cause of liberty, we met with defeat, but not with ignominy." The cause might be lost but that didn't make it any less worth fighting for.

In his dissent, Justice Harlan prophesied that "the judgment this day rendered will, in time, prove to be . . . pernicious [and will keep] alive a conflict of races." Indeed, in the wake of the decision state after state passed railcar segregation laws. By the turn of the century, Southern states were outdoing each other in identifying new areas of life to segregate. But the *Plessy* decision also contributed to racial division because segregation made it necessary to firmly define who was white and who was not. In antebellum times, the slave/free distinction was central and that line was crystal clear. The child of an enslaved mother was a slave no matter how light the child's coloring and no matter the color or status of the father (in many cases, the mother's owner). By the same iron law, the child of a free mother was free no matter who the father was, how dark the child's complexion was, or how many African forebears the baby may have had. Under the laws of Reconstruction, racial definitions were unnecessary since all were equal citizens regardless of race, color, or previous condition. Now, with "redemption," a new, ostensibly biological distinction of "race" would determine every American's rights. Each state created its own definitions. That they never matched or that states changed their definitions over time somehow did little to undermine their scientific authority in the popular mind.

As Jim Crow laws became more common, pressure grew to police bloodlines more punctiliously. At South Carolina's 1895 state constitutional convention, convened to replace the egalitarian constitution of 1868, delegates considered stricter racial definitions. African-American disenfranchisement was now so widespread that only six of the delegates at the convention were not white. But even the overwhelming white majority found little consensus

on defining race. Those backing the one-drop rule were silenced
when one member took to the podium to declare that "there [i]s
not a full-blooded Caucasian on the floor of this Convention." Panicked by the potential outing of the state's entire ruling class—
Charleston's leading newspaper, the *News and Courier*, slapped
its reprint of the speech with the salacious headline "ALL NIG-
GERS, MORE OR LESS!"—the convention delegates scaled back.
They agreed to define a person of color as anyone with at least one
African-American great-grandparent, tightening the state's standard by moving it back one generation.

In Louisiana, the notion of defining race was so threatening to
the supposedly pure white supremacists that even as the legislature passed ever-greater restrictions on people of color, it never
explicitly defined who such people were. The state's 1898 constitution, which included a poll tax to purge freedmen from the voter
rolls, offered no definition of race whatsoever. When questions
arose about an individual's status—increasingly common as Jim
Crow laws proliferated—they were still settled in the courts on a
case-by-case basis. As had been the situation for centuries, Louisiana courts continued to give deference to higher status, lighter-
skinned biracial people. As a 1910 Louisiana state supreme court
ruling put it, "We think . . . that any candid mind must admit that
the word 'Negro' of itself, unqualified, does not necessarily include
within its meaning persons possessed of only an admixture of
Negro blood; notably those whose admixture is so slight that in
their case even an expert cannot be positive." The occasion for the
decision was a claim by a white man and his octoroon concubine
that they were not violating the state's 1908 interracial cohabitation ban since it only applied to "a person of the negro or black
race." That bill had initially defined a "negro" as anyone who had
one or more great-great-great-grandparents of African descent,
but the provision was struck during debate and, tellingly, replaced
with nothing at all.

As usual, the rest of America was blazing a trail towards a black/white binary far ahead of South Carolina and Louisiana. Most states hewed ever closer to the one-drop rule in their racial definitions. The federal government changed with the times as well. The 1890 census asked in detail if a person was "white, black, mulatto, quadroon [or] octoroon." A decade later, it required a singular "color or race."

As rights became ever more race-based, police departments were turned back into all-white forces. By the 1890s, most places that had desegregated their forces during Reconstruction had resegregated them, sometimes with violence. In Texas, the Klan bragged that it hunted down and killed every African-American member of the Reconstruction-era state police.

In Charleston, resegregation moved slowly but inexorably. A new police chief, hired in 1896, fired Lieutenant James Fordham, an antebellum free man of color who was then the highest-ranking African-American policeman in America. The other officers of color were purged through attrition. By the early twentieth century, the number of African-American policemen in Charleston could be counted on one hand and when they retired, they were replaced by whites. When resegregation was finally complete, most living Charlestonians had never known an all-white force. At the height of Reconstruction, about half the city force was African-American, and even after the reestablishment of white supremacist rule in the state, in 1878, the Charleston police had remained one-third men of color.

In New Orleans, the corps was resegregated in a similar fashion. The department simply stopped hiring new African-American officers, pressured others to resign, and waited for the final veterans of the Reconstruction era to age out. While nearly two hundred African-Americans were serving as New Orleans police officers during the height of Reconstruction, by 1880 there were sixty; in 1890, twenty-five; and in 1900, five. In 1909, the last two

African-American officers died in their boots. The 1910 federal census showed not a single African-American police officer in the entire Deep South.

In the face of voter suppression and poll taxes, African-American members of Congress dwindled; the last African-American representative gave up his seat in 1901, resurrecting the color line in the Capitol Building. Even in the rare cities where well-to-do African-Americans remained on the rolls, their ballots were routinely discarded. As one Louisiana Republican bitterly quipped after "redemption": "Colored . . . republicans may here be allowed to vote, but after the polls are closed the election really begins." When the Scottish author Thomas Archer traveled to Charleston in the early twentieth century, he interviewed a clique of men from the biracial elite brought low by Jim Crow. Of the group, he recounted, "Only one member (a doctor) was dark-brown in complexion; two were very light-brown; while two others . . . were indistinguishable from white men. . . . Meeting him in England, you would have said he was a trifle sunburnt." From his discussions with the gentlemen, he relayed to his British readers that "when a negro happens to be a man of such property, education, and position that it is absolutely impossible to reject his vote, there is always the last resource of omitting to count it. One of the Charleston group spoke of a particular election in which he himself, and others of his people to his certain knowledge, cast Republican ballots; but the result, as announced, showed not a single Republican vote."

With African-Americans stripped of political power, public officials could safely ignore the legal requirement that separate facilities be equal. In 1880, South Carolina's segregated public schools were funded at plausibly comparable levels: $2.75 per white pupil, $2.51 per African-American. By 1885, they were savagely unequal. White funding had risen to $3.11 per student, while African-American funding had dropped to $1.05. New Orleans founded its public library system in 1897, but it would not open its first branch for readers of color until 1915.

The final rollback of integration took place where it had all begun: on the streetcars. In 1900, Harry Wilson, a representative of Tangipahoa Parish, across Lake Ponchartrain from New Orleans, introduced a bill in the statehouse requiring streetcar segregation in all cities with more than fifty thousand people—a category that included only New Orleans. Unlike his colleagues who had passed the separate-but-equal railcar law a decade before, Wilson did not hide the purpose of his bill. He baldly stated that the legislation's main aim was to "demonstrat[e] the superiority of the white man over the negro."

Though reeling from the *Plessy* defeat at the Supreme Court and the rash of suicides that had culled their leadership ranks, New Orleans's civil rights activists vowed to boycott the system if the bill passed. Those with capital sought to leverage it. As the *Southwestern Christian Advocate*, an African-American newspaper, noted, "There are colored persons of wealth in the city [of New Orleans who] own stock in the street railroads. . . . Where is the conductor who would attempt to debar them from riding in the white car?" But having been overwhelmingly purged from the voting rolls, African-American citizens were easy to ignore at the statehouse in Baton Rouge. Voters of color had made up nearly a quarter of New Orleans registrants as late as 1896; by 1900, they constituted just over 3 percent. The main obstacle to the bill's passage was no longer activist opposition but the streetcar company executives who saw segregation in New Orleans as an expensive—and ultimately impossible—task. Their powerful corporate bosses lobbied hard against Wilson's bill and got it bottled up in a committee.

Frustrated by the gridlock in Baton Rouge, a white member of the New Orleans city council introduced his own segregation ordinance, requiring streetcar companies to run separate cars for

African-American passengers or "divid[e] their cars by a wooden partition." Fearing the cost, the presidents of all four of the city's streetcar lines came to council to testify against the bill. One after another, an array of the most successful and respected business-men in the city—a hodge-podge of *Américains*, French Creoles, and Jews—explained their opposition.

R. M. Walmsley of the New Orleans and City Railroad Company led off. "I regard the proposed separate car ordinance as a very unwise measure," he began.

> The authorities might as well designate a certain portion of the city sidewalks to be traversed upon by white people and colored people separately. Street car travel is a necessity to all alike, the rich, the poor, the black, the white [and besides] it would be impossible for the conductors to discriminate. Among many of the Latin races it is impossible to distinguish them from those of African races. Wherever the races mingle freely it is difficult to tell which are not Caucasian. All of our conductors are men of intelligence, but the greatest ethnolo-gist the world ever saw would be at a loss to classify street car passengers in this city. Many bright mulattoes are apparently whiter than a great number of the Spaniards, Italians, etc., their features are regular, and there is nothing to indicate that they are negroes.

Following Walmsley, J. K. Newman, who ran the New Orleans and Carrollton Railroad Company, desegregated in 1867 under P. G. T. Beauregard, argued from a purely economic per-spective. The streetcar system was working fine, so why "tamper with existing conditions?" Newman asked. "A 'Star Car' ordinance would require the setting aside of a large percentage of cars for a small percentage of the riding public, while the great majority of patrons would have to be contented with a proportionally smaller percentage of cars."

Emilien Perrin of the Orleans Street Railroad Company continued this line of argument. "Under the ordinance," President Perrin explained, "it would be impossible to maintain the present schedule [since] it would require double the number of cars." African-Americans, he estimated, made up only 5 percent of his line's passengers, so why should his company so expensively accommodate this tiny subset of customers? Why should "the same privileges . . . be given to 5 per cent of the public as to 95 per cent?"

Finally, Albert G. Phelps of the St. Charles Street Railroad Company rose to inveigh against "this absurd proposition." After venting for a bit—"there is no call on earth for this measure, and there never was any"—he gave up the floor with the words, "You must excuse me further. I have not the patience to discuss it more than to hope and trust that our good Council will not give Northern cities a chance to laugh at us."

It was left to the *Southwestern Christian Advocate* to raise the specter that the law could out prominent whites as people of color. Adjudicating race, the paper noted, would be "a dangerous game to play [considering] the reports as to how things are mixed. . . . [Thus,] it would seem that our city should be extremely liberal on the color question." Besides, no conductor could possibly get it right: "The man who is given the task, by law or otherwise, of deciding this question for the citizens of New Orleans will find that he has undertaken more than he can possibly do."

Swayed by these arguments, the week after the streetcar company presidents testified, the city council voted down the proposal overwhelmingly, by a vote of twelve to four. But the integrationists' victory was short-lived. In 1902, Representative Wilson reintroduced his streetcar bill in the statehouse. New Orleans's African-American press again resorted to mockery. "The measure is brought forward now as two years ago by a member from one of the country parishes. He seems extremely solicitous that the races should be separated on the street cars of this city [though he represents] a parish . . . that hasn't a street-car in it," the *Southwestern Christian Advocate* noted. This time, however, Wilson hoped to placate his streetcar company opponents by mandating a cheaper solution: a movable mesh screen that could be adjusted by the conductor based on the number of passengers of each race in his car.

To plan their opposition, roughly two hundred representatives from sixty African-American organizations met in a New Orleans Masonic hall "for the purpose of determining upon some concerted course of action which will in some way free us from being separated from other civilized races in street cars by means of wire screens." In the new political climate, many just wanted to ensure that separate-but-equal accommodations would truly be equal. Reverend E. A. Higgins proposed at the meeting, "If they want to keep us from riding with white people, why don't they give us separate cars, with negro conductors and motormen. . . . Before I would ride in a screened 'Jim Crow' car I would walk my feet off."

Wilson's revised bill passed easily. In a spotty boycott, African-American ridership dropped by half, leaving the seats behind the screens largely empty while whites were crammed into the front of the cars. Even the conservative *Daily Picayune* conceded that "almost everyone said it looked ridiculous for people to stand up when there were vacant seats." As many had warned, adjudicating race on sight proved difficult. In one car, a fair-skinned man took an empty seat in the colored section. When the conductor told him to move up, he told him he was African-American. As the *Times-Democrat* reported it, "[hearing his response,] the conductor's face wore a look of disbelief, but the case was closed so far as he was concerned." The newspaper headlined its coverage of the incident, "The Law A Farce."

Among the first arrested under Representative Wilson's law

were the president and officers of the newly consolidated New Orleans Railway Company for not installing screens in every car. The group sought out arrest intentionally in the hope of overturning the law with a test case in the courts. But in March 1903, the Louisiana state supreme court ruled against the company. Movable screens were installed systemwide. They would divide New Orleans streetcars for more than half a century.

In Charleston, too, segregation came slowly but steadily. The Charleston Academy of Music, integrated to great fanfare during Reconstruction, was resegregated around the turn of the twentieth century. Unleashed by the United States Supreme Court's *Plessy* decision, the South Carolina legislature in Columbia went to work segregating ever more areas of life, including railroad cars (1898), steamboats and ferries (1904), and train station dining facilities (1906). Charleston's consolidated streetcar company began insisting that African-Americans and white passengers not share a given bench even though the benches remained colorized on a first-come, first-served basis. It was not until 1912 that a state legislator introduced a bill requiring cities of thirty-thousand inhabitants or more—a category that included only Charleston— to segregate passengers in separate cars. A less expensive segregation bill was introduced that year in the Charleston city council, to require separate white and colored sections within the same streetcar. In the summer, a group of eight African-American community leaders met with Charleston mayor John Grace to lobby him against it—a course of action that had worked on an earlier, similar bill. Two days later, a group of segregationists met with the mayor to lobby him to pass the new bill. The mayor remained publicly silent on the issue.

At the city council hearing on the legislation, the hall was packed with African-Americans, including the eight men who had lobbied the mayor. The president of the city's consolidated streetcar lines took the floor. He accepted segregation, he explained, but he urged the council to adopt a more "flexible" plan in which whites would be seated from the front and African-Americans from the rear with no fixed section sizes. The African-American speakers, now seeing some form of segregation as unavoidable, pushed for the least bad option. They urged the council to vote down the bill and preserve the existing bench-by-bench system.

Two weeks after the hearing, Mayor Grace publicly came out in support of the streetcar company president's "flexible" plan on the risible grounds that it "was not likely to cause any race feeling [because] it would give the negroes a fair amount of seating room." The measure was amended in accordance with the mayor's request, passed, and signed.

As in New Orleans, adjudicating race on the fly in Charleston proved difficult. That Charleston's Brown community had ceased to self-identify as "Browns" didn't make their skin tones any less ambiguous. In local parlance, Charlestonians began speaking of "black Negroes" and "white Negroes." As the memoir of one African-American Charlestonian recalled, "At one time, mulattos who looked like white[s] used to do what they wanted to do in Charleston. But after the Jim Crow laws made everything strict . . . we got to the place where they had to identify themselves as a race."

Even after formal protests fizzled from a combination of intimidation and hopelessness, mixed-race people still relished the chance to highlight the system's absurdity. As the memoirist recounts,

> We used to get together in pairs of black and white Negro young women [and board a street] car . . . keep laughing and talking, put in your money and walk right past the conductor, nonchalant, don't know what he is looking at, don't even notice that he is looking. We would go exactly halfway down the streetcar, where nobody else was sitting, and take seats. Now the conductor would start to fidget [and] the white pas-

sengers . . . looked   at . . . the   conductor. . . . The   looking
would start to bear down on the conductor, because it was
his streetcar: on *his* streetcar he was supposed to uphold Jim
Crow on behalf of all white people. The pressure on him got
worse as each new white man, woman, or child got on and
looked—until he couldn't take it: "You don't belong back there
with the colored." The first time a conductor said anything,
we pretended not to know who "you" was. However, when he
finally did say something, the game was almost over. . . . [A]t
last he would stop the car and tell us, "You girls sit the way
you are supposed to!" Then we would both get up together and
walk to the very last seat in the back that was empty. How the
white stripe would blush at that moment. The blacks stripe
in the back chuckled. But there was nothing much anybody
could do about it. We never said anything disrespectful, and
we obeyed the law, to the letter.

The law was a farce but that didn't make it any less binding;
race was a myth yet it became the most important factor in every
American's life. As W. E. B. Du Bois—himself of French, English,
Dutch, and African descent—would write in 1923, "There are no
races [since] we are all so [thoroughly] mixed. [And yet] the black
man is a person who must ride 'Jim Crow' in Georgia." His bitter
joke was that there was no scientific reality of race outside the
painful social reality of racism. With race-based rights now the
law of the land, racism was real even if race was not.

CONCLUSION

LIVING THE LIE

The CRISIS

Vol. 13—No. 4   FEBRUARY, 1917   Whole No. 76

Richard Theodore Greener in the Jim Crow era.

(NAACP)

In the fall of 1907 Richard T. Greener returned to his old haunts on the University of South Carolina's Horseshoe campus for the first time in three decades. After "redemption," Greener had moved to Washington, D.C., and become dean of the Howard University law school. During Republican presidential administrations, Greener, like many loyal veterans of Reconstruction's noble lost cause, had been given patronage jobs to support himself. As a member of the foreign service, he had served as U.S. consul in Bombay, India, and Vladivostok, Russia, both cosmopolitan Asian port cities where Greener's national identity took precedence over his racial identity.

Jim Crow–era South Carolina operated differently. When Greener gave a lecture in Charleston recounting his international travels, a local newspaper marveled at the Philadelphia-born Harvard alum's "fine command of English." At The Horseshoe, Greener found the remaining African-Americans on campus all relegated to servile roles. One alumnus, a graduate of the Reconstruction-era "Radical University," worked in the school's executive offices as a janitor. Demoted to manual labor, William "Willis" Mitchell was patronized on campus as an ostensibly beloved figure akin to a university mascot. As a Columbia newspaper, *The Record*, oozed in its obituary twenty years later, "Willis" was entrusted with "keys to all of the [executive offices as well as] important messages and [i]s faithful and dependable at all times."

Given this campus racial climate, Greener approached the university with caution. Always racially ambiguous, the self-described "smoked Yankee" passed for white more readily in old age, once his jet-black hair had gone gray. Entering the library incognito, Greener spotted the very same African-American library assistant who had helped him organize and modernize the collection in the 1870s. The man hurried down a bookshelf ladder and rushed over to shake his old colleague's hand. Thinking fast, Greener whispered, "No names!" The reigning white librarian could tell the two men knew each other but when he inquired, Greener told him obliquely, "I had met him when I visited the library years ago."

The mixed-race generation coming of age in this new, segregated, one-drop-rule America faced a stark choice. While Richard T. Greener lived his life on the knife's edge, passing for white one day and embracing blackness the next, his daughter fully crossed over. She continued the family tradition of library building but hid the family truth of African descent. Cutting herself off from her family and her community, she moved to New York City and reinvented herself as Belle da Costa Greene, a Latina librarian supposedly of Portuguese background. In 1905, she began working for tycoon J. P. Morgan to amass the peerless collection for his eponymous Manhattan library.

Other mixed-race veterans of Reconstruction crossed the color line. Arnold Bertonneau, the New Orleans wine merchant who had lobbied President Lincoln for voting rights and filed the first federal case against school segregation on behalf of his sons, François Henry and Arnold John, moved to California and passed for white. His son Arnold John went even further. The child civil rights plaintiff from New Orleans grew up to become a pillar of Pasadena's white business establishment, a partner in West Coast hotels, banks, and grocery stores. Perhaps still smarting over bitter memories of exclusion from the all-white Mardi Gras parades of his Crescent City youth, Bertonneau gravitated towards the Tournament of Roses parade thrown annually by the whites-only Pasadena Valley Hunt Club. In 1913, Arnold John Bertonneau was given the honor of running the parade that coming New Year's Day. In the parade that winter, among the marching bands and children dressed as Mother Goose characters, was a motorized Ku Klux Klan float, its terrifying insignia made of flowers. By 1920, even the most famous civil rights test-case plaintiff of them all, Homer Plessy, was officially "white" on the United States Census.

Those too dark or simply unwilling to pass bore unfathomable humiliations. The fall of "Willis" Mitchell, the university graduate turned university janitor, was minor compared to the fate of Alonzo Ransier. The mixed-race Charlestonian, who had written and enforced South Carolina's public accommodations law and served in the United States Congress from 1873 to 1875, spent the last years of his life in abject poverty. Ransier lived in a boarding house and worked as a day laborer, a night-shift Custom House security guard, and a street sweeper for the City of Charleston. According to an apocryphal story, on one of his street-sweeping shifts, the former congressman came upon an old newspaper clipping in the gutter with an article about him from his days as a statesman.

Across the South, the white branches of mixed-race families, like Charleston's Cardozos, disowned their biracial relatives, leaving them to fend for themselves in the harsh new world of Jim Crow. After his conviction and pardon in South Carolina, Francis Lewis Cardozo moved to Washington, where he worked for the Treasury department for six years before returning to his vocation as an educator. In the segregated schools of the capital, Cardozo served as principal of the leading all-black public high school. He died in 1903, mercifully two years before novelist Thomas Dixon Jr. published his reactionary roman à clef, *The Clansman: An Historical Romance of the Ku Klux Klan*, which cast Cardozo as its cartoonish mixed-race villain, Silas Lynch. Dixon painted Lynch as "a mulatto, who had evidently inherited the full physical characteristics of the Aryan race, while his dark yellowish eyes beneath his heavy brows glowed with the brightness of the African jungle." A preacher like Cardozo, the literary alter ego Lynch mobilizes black voters by plastering South Carolina towns with "placard[s of] the Civil Rights Bill," and gets himself elected to statewide office. Lynch then schemes to publicly humiliate former slaveholders and seduce white women until the local Klan intimidates him into fleeing. In 1915, *The Clansman* was turned into the Hollywood blockbuster movie, *The Birth of a Nation*, the first film to be screened in the White House.

Cardozo's descendants, living in Washington at the time, surely felt the sting of this slanderous portrayal of the family patriarch. In a pattern repeated again and again, the openly mixed side of the Cardozo family saw their opportunities evaporate under Jim Crow while the other side climbed ever higher. By the 1930s, Francis Lewis Cardozo's biracial granddaughters were running a blacks-only hair salon near Howard University called Cardozo Sisters while the scion of the other side of their family, Benjamin Nathan Cardozo, was serving as a justice on the still-all-white United States Supreme Court. A Latino Jew, Benjamin Nathan Cardozo found shelter beneath the big tent of whiteness while his cousins across town, though descended from a South Carolina state treasurer and secretary of state, were limited to less exalted fields by their one-drop-rule blackness.

Many Reconstruction leaders of all colors fled the South but kept the faith, continuing the fight against segregation in the North and West. Henry Dibble, the Indiana-born attorney and judge who had fought for streetcar integration in New Orleans and ordered the desegregation of the city's public schools, moved to San Francisco and ran for office. In 1888, his urban district sent him to Sacramento, where he championed an array of progressive causes including women's suffrage, campaign finance reform, and, his lifelong passion, civil rights. In 1897, Dibble introduced "An Act to Protect All Citizens in Their Civil and Legal Rights," a pub-

lic accommodations bill meant to reinstitute for Californians the
rights the Supreme Court had stripped in its Civil Rights Cases
decision. The bill, which included both civil and criminal penalties, barred racial discrimination in "inns, restaurants, hotels,
eating houses, barber shops, bath houses, theaters, skating rinks,
and all other places of public accommodation or amusement." Initially judged too radical to pass, after a compromise was reached
eliminating the criminal penalties, the bill became law. It was the
first civil rights statute ever passed in the state of California.

Back east, Thomas McCants Stewart, the first African-
American graduate of the University of South Carolina, was notch-
ing similar victories. After "redemption," the freeborn mixed-race
Charlestonian moved to the still-independent City of Brooklyn,
where he worked as a minister and civil rights activist. Brooklyn
had been known for its surprising Confederate sympathies during
the secession crisis and, even after taking in an influx of African-
American refugees from the devastating 1863 Manhattan draft
riots, it remained unfriendly ground. Brooklyn's public schools had
been founded on a segregated basis in 1817, the same year New
York State began its gradual abolition of slavery, and even these
schools did not escape racists' wrath. White Brooklynites fought
to keep blacks-only schools out of their neighborhoods, claiming
that they would lower their property values. It was not until 1883
that an African-American was finally appointed to the local school
board and a resolution was passed mandating that "all principals
be directed to receive all colored children on the same terms as
white children." Foot-dragging in the courts continued until Stewart himself got on the school board in the 1890s and finally pushed
integration through.

By fighting on at the local level, these activists helped ensure
that one day a nationwide civil rights movement could rise again.
In the mid-twentieth century, the movement was reborn. Again,
activists took up the toolbox forged in Reconstruction—marches,

sit-ins, legislation, and test cases. Yet something had gone missing that had been central to the earlier struggle of Charleston Browns and New Orleans Creoles: the critique of race itself.

In 1954, in *Brown v. Board of Education of Topeka*, the Supreme Court ruled segregation unconstitutional, overturning its 1896 precedent from *Plessy v. Ferguson*. But the *Brown* decision was not a complete posthumous victory for Homer Plessy. The Kansas plaintiffs in *Brown* argued that Americans had different races but should all be treated equally nonetheless. Homer Plessy of New Orleans had argued a far more radical point—that Americans didn't have distinct races. We had all been mixing for centuries, whether we acknowledged it openly or not.

After Homer Plessy's loss, the racial binary had become the law of the land. Complex identities were jammed into the straitjackets of "white" and "colored." Some suffered far more than others, but liberation came for no one. Every ten years, even Homer Plessy himself duly checked a unitary racial box. Whatever he chose, it was a lie and an insult to the full richness of his heritage.

After losing *Plessy v. Ferguson* at the Supreme Court, the Comité des Citoyens had issued the statement, "Notwithstanding this decision . . . we . . . still believe that we were right." What they believed they were right about was not merely that separate could never be equal but that, in America, separate was not even possible. As New World people, we were too mixed up to sort back out. Say what we may, Americans would never be black or white. We are *mestizos*, Creoles, misfits all.

BIBLIOGRAPHIC NOTE

New battles.—After Buddha was dead, they still showed his
shadow in a cave for centuries—a tremendous, gruesome
shadow. God is dead; but given the way people are, there may
still for millennia be caves in which they show his shadow—
And we—we must still defeat his shadow as well!
—*Friedrich Nietzsche*

It's up to you. As long as you think you're white, there is no
hope for you. As long as you think you're white, I'm going to
be forced to think I'm black.
—*James Baldwin*

The Accident of Color is intended for a general readership, so
citations have been provided only for direct quotes and statis-
tics. Nonetheless this book is greatly indebted to works from the
academy. For anyone writing about Reconstruction, the twin 700-
page monuments of W. E. B. Du Bois's *Black Reconstruction in
America* (1935) and Eric Foner's *Reconstruction: America's Unfinished Revolution* (1988) constitute the Old and New Testaments
of the Bible. Ira Berlin's *Slaves Without Masters* (1974) remains
an invaluable overview on antebellum free people of color and

C. Vann Woodward's *The Strange Career of Jim Crow* (1955) a pioneering touchstone on the postbellum era. I have also benefited from the painstaking work by authors of various monographs on urban communities of color, including but not limited to Bernard Edward Powers's *Black Charlestonians* (1994) and John Wesley Blassingame's *Black New Orleans* (1973).

Undergirding this book are several brave new works that powerfully, if belatedly, subject race in America to the genealogical method pioneered by Friedrich Nietzsche and Michel Foucault. By exposing the social construction of race, their authors have begun the crucial task of expunging Jim Crow's tremendous, gruesome shadow from the wall of our American cave. Among them are *Racecraft: The Soul of Inequality in American Life* (2012) by Karen E. Fields and Barbara J. Fields, *A History of White People* (2010) by Nell Irvin Painter, and *Brown: The Last Discovery of America* (2002) by Richard Rodriguez. Daniel Sharfstein's *The Invisible Line: Three American Families and the Secret Journey from Black to White* (2011) showed how this theoretical work can be applied to the narrative of American history, providing an inspiring if intimidating template for *The Accident of Color.*

ACKNOWLEDGMENTS

This work would never have taken the shape it did without the friendship of expatriated Englishman Nicholas Jackson. Watching his flailing efforts to comprehend America's anomalous racial system allowed me to see my native land with fresh eyes.

This book would not exist at all without the support of my agent, Larry Weissman, who was enthusiastic from the start, and my editor, Brendan Curry, who was eager to take the requisite leap of faith. As usual, I am indebted to Brendan for savvy edits and for the book's title. His assistants, Sophie and Nat, like the entire staff at Norton, are consummate professionals. Production manager Beth Steidle deserves tremendous credit for turning my disordered, obsessive design demands into this elegant volume.

A Monroe Fellowship from the New Orleans Center for the Gulf South at Tulane University aided with the research at a crucial phase. The support of the Center's leadership and staff, in particular, Joel Dinerstein, Rebecca Snedeker, and Denise Frazier, is greatly appreciated. A reading list, kindly drawn up for me by eminent Reconstruction historian Greg Downs of UC Davis, was helpful in getting my research underway.

This project benefited from the research facilities of many institutions and the assistance of their librarians and archivists. In Charleston: the College of Charleston's Avery Research Center and its Addlestone Library as well as the Charleston County Public Library; in Columbia: the South Caroliniana Library at the University of South Carolina and the South Carolina Department of Archives and History; in New Orleans: the University of New Orleans's Earl K. Long Library, the Tulane University library system and, particularly, its Amistad Research Center and its Louisiana Research Collection, the New Orleans Public Library and, particularly, its Louisiana Division/City Archives and Special Collections; in Baton Rouge: Louisiana State University's Louisiana and Lower Mississippi Valley Collections; in New York City: the New York Public Library Main Branch and the Brooklyn Historical Society; and in Washington, D.C.: the National Archives and the Moorland-Spingarn Research Center at Howard University.

Portions of this book were written during a six-month sojourn in San Francisco that would not have been viable without the San Francisco Public Library. Fact checking would have been difficult without our national treasure, the Library of Congress. I am grateful that the Kluge Center there continues to be my research home away from home. For this, its generous staff, especially Mary Lou Reker, deserves thanks.

The bulk of the book was written, researched, and edited at the Williams Research Center of The Historic New Orleans Collection in New Orleans's French Quarter. I spent so much time in its hushed, grand reading room that it feels wrong to thank the staff formally using their full names, so thank you Bobby, Jennifer, Becky, Mary Lou, Eric, Matt, both Heathers, as well as Albert and Frances, Dorothy and Daniel.

Two deep Deep Southerners offered words of wisdom that I would have been better off heeding immediately. Nicholas Lemann warned me about the pitfalls of Reconstruction-era primary sources. Astra Taylor exhorted: "Keep Daniel Weird."

Three writers offered sage advice at various stages of the drafting process. Journalist and author extraordinaire Brendan I. Koerner passed along writerly tips. University of Michigan history professor Matthew Spooner kindly read the manuscript and gave feedback informed by his academic expertise. Gifted novelist Simeon Marsalis pushed me to think about the material in new ways. All of their comments improved the manuscript. The shortcomings still evident are entirely my own.

My parents have offered unceasing love and support throughout my unconventional career. My father, in particular, born to immigrant parents in Birmingham, Alabama in 1941, kindled my interest in history and civil rights. My dear friend Zachary Lazar kept on me to keep chewing once I'd realized just how much I had bitten off. My partner, Rachel—the best reader I know—helped me check myself before I wrecked myself; her forbearance when faced with the all-consuming nature of this project made its completion possible. The warm furry encouragement of our beloved Elijah Chipster Brozman and Princess Smokey Bear helped, too.

NOTES

PREFACE: DOWN THE MEMORY HOLE

xv **"A study of the civil rights":** Williston H. Lofton, "Civil Rights of the Negro in the United States, 1865–1883" (unpublished master's thesis, Howard University, 1930), Moorland Spingarn Research Center, Howard University, Washington, DC.

xvi **"the material today":** W. E. B. Du Bois, *Black Reconstruction in America* (New York: Harcourt, Brace, 1935), 383.

INTRODUCTION: *LES AMBASSADEURS*

xxi **"Citizens of the United States":** Jean Baptiste Roudanez and E. Arnold Bertonneau, Voting Rights Petition, January 4, 1864 (Select Committee on the Rebellious States; Petitions and Memorials Referred to Committees [HR38A-G25.6]; 38th Congress; Records of the U.S. House of Representatives, Record Group 233; National Archives, Washington, DC).

xxi **"no rights which the white man":** *Dred Scott v. Sandford*, 60 U.S. 393 (1857).

xxiii **"I regret, gentlemen":** Colonel John W. Forney, quoted in Benjamin Quarles, *Lincoln and the Negro* (Oxford: Oxford University Press, 1962), 227.

xxiii **"some of the colored people":** Abraham Lincoln, quoted in Joseph Logsdon and Caryn Cossé Bell, "The Americanization of Black New Orleans," in Arnold R. Hirsch and Joseph Logsdon, eds., *Creole New*

Orleans: Race and Americanization (Baton Rouge: Louisiana State University Press, 1992), 226.

xxiii **"conferred on the very intelligent":** Abraham Lincoln, quoted in Terry Alford, *Fortune's Fool: The Life of John Wilkes Booth* (Oxford: Oxford University Press, 2015), 257.

xxiii **"That means nigger citizenship":** John Wilkes Booth, quoted in ibid.

1. MISFIT METROPOLISES

3 **six of the governors:** Joel Williamson, *New People: Miscegenation and Mulattoes in the United States* (New York: Free Press, 1980), 16.

4 **"Certain [white] young Men":** Peter H. Wood, *Black Majority: Negroes in Colonial South Carolina* (New York: Knopf, 1975), 235, 236.

5 **"free white people":** Nell Irvin Painter, *A History of White People* (New York: W. W. Norton, 2010) 104–5.

6 **"We, free brown men":** *Rules and Regulations of the Brown Fellowship Society* (Charleston, SC: J. B. Nixon, 1844), Avery Research Center, Charleston.

9 **constituted more than a third:** Ira Berlin, *Slaves Without Masters: The Free Negro in the Antebellum South* (New York: Pantheon, 1974), 112.

9 **"all the rights":** Ibid., 118.

11 **"We have already a much greater proportion":** Shirley Thompson, *Exiles at Home: The Struggle to Become American in Creole New Orleans* (Cambridge, MA: Harvard University Press, 2009), 5.

11 **"many worthless free people of color":** Berlin, *Slaves Without Masters*, 115.

11 **"men with their hands still reddened":** Ibid.

11 **"The circumstances which occasion'd":** Bernard E. Powers, *Black Charlestonians: A Social History, 1822–1885* (Fayetteville: University of Arkansas Press, 1999), 28.

12 **"the French negroes":** Berlin, *Slaves Without Masters*, 36.

12 **population had more than tripled:** Joseph Logsdon and Caryn Cossé Bell, "The Americanization of Black New Orleans." in Arnold R. Hirsch and Joseph Logsdon, eds., *Creole New Orleans* (Baton Rouge: Louisiana State University Press, 1992), 206.

14 **most Jewish city in early America:** Henry L. Feingold, ed., *The Jewish People in America*, vol. 1, Eli Faber, *A Time for Planting: The First Migration, 1654–1820* (Baltimore: Johns Hopkins University Press, 1992) 111.

14 **Charleston became majority white:** Wilbert L. Jenkins, *Seizing the*

New Day: African Americans in Post–Civil War Charleston (Bloomington: Indiana University Press, 1998), 3.

14 **"sleek, dandified negroes":** Powers, *Black Charlestonians*, 24

14 **"walk[ing] through the streets":** Edward Laurens, quoted in Powers, *Black Charlestonians*, 45.

14 **free people of color constituted 8 percent:** Jenkins, *Seizing the New Day*, xiii.

14 **Three-quarters of Charleston's millwrights:** Berlin, *Slaves Without Masters*, 221.

14 **half of its butchers and tailors:** Powers, *Black Charlestonians*, 45.

15 **only fifteen streets:** Jenkins, *Seizing the New Day*, 5.

15 **seventy-five whites who were renting:** Berlin, *Slaves Without Masters*, 254–56, 344.

15 **over a hundred slave owners of color:** Larry Koger, *Black Slaveowners: Free Black Slave Masters in South Carolina, 1790–1860* (Columbia: University of South Carolina Press, 1985), 228–29.

15 **"become courteous to the negro":** Powers, *Black Charlestonians*, 24.

15 **"the negroes here":** Ibid., 22.

16 **"systematic common law marriages":** W. E. B. Du Bois, *Black Reconstruction in America* (New York: Harcourt, Brace, 1935), 155.

16 **roughly three-quarters of the lots:** Thompson, *Exiles at Home*, 133.

17 **hundreds of slave owners of color:** Carter G. Woodson, *Free Negro Owners of Slaves in the United States in 1830* (Washington, DC: The Association for the Study of Negro Life and History, 1924).

18 **"distinguished for the equality":** Berlin, *Slaves Without Masters*, 262.

19 **"is not to be determined":** *State of South Carolina v. Cantey*, quoted in Daniel Sharfstein, *The Invisible Line: Three American Families and the Secret Journey from Black to White* (New York: Penguin Press, 2011), 50; Powers, *Black Charlestonians*, 56.

20 **"the evil complained of":** Berlin, *Slaves Without Masters*, 268.

20 **"Like the [biblical] patriarchs":** Mary Boykin Chesnut, *A Diary from Dixie*, ed. Ben Ames Williams (Boston: Houghton Mifflin, 1949), 21–22.

20 **"Free people of color ought never insult":** Logsdon and Bell, "The Americanization of Black New Orleans," 207.

21 **"faces with every shade of colour":** Alexis de Tocqueville, *Journey to America*, trans. George Lawrence, ed. J. P. Mayer (London: Faber and Faber, 1959), 164.

21 **"The first time I attended a theater":** Gustave de Beaumont, quoted in Painter, *A History of White People*, 130.

22 **nearly half of New Orleans's white-classified population:** Eric

Foner, *Reconstruction: America's Unfinished Revolution, 1863–1877* (New York: Harper & Row, 1988), 45.

22 **"not an American scene":** Edward King, *The Great South* (Hartford, CT: American Publishing Company, 1875), 19.

22 **"cosmopolitan":** Ibid., 18.

22 **"lively Gallic versions":** Ibid., 47.

22 **"mulatto fruitseller":** Ibid., 19.

22 **"face in which the struggle":** Ibid., 47.

22 **"mulatto girl hardly less fair":** Ibid., 34–35.

23 **"black urchins [who] grin":** Ibid., 49.

23 **"designated by this single phrase":** Berlin, *Slaves Without Masters*, 123.

23 **"marriages of conscience":** Thompson, *Exiles at Home*, 71.

23 **"illicit connexions":** Ibid., 12.

24 **"dressed or masked balls":** Roger Fischer, *The Segregation Struggle in Louisiana* (Urbana: University of Illinois Press, 1974), 18.

24 **half of each cemetery:** Ibid., 14.

24 **"there is . . . all the difference":** Steve Luxenberg, *Separate: The Story of* Plessy v. Ferguson, *And America's Journey from Slavery to Segregation* (New York: W. W. Norton, 2019), 101.

25 **"white persons and colored persons [to] play cards together":** Fischer, *The Segregation Struggle*, 18.

26 **"our free colored population":** "Hayti and Immigration Thither," *Daily Picayune*, July 16, 1859.

26 **"The union now subsisting":** "Declaration of the Immediate Causes Which Induce and Justify the Secession of South Carolina from the Federal Union; and the Ordinance of Secession" (Charleston: Evans & Cogswell, 1860), 11, http://www.atlantahistorycenter.com/assets/documents/SCarolina-Secession-p1-13.pdf.

26 **"have denounced as sinful the institution of slavery":** Ibid, 9.

27 **"The Little Pale Star from Georgia":** Bruce Catton, *The Coming Fury* (New York: Doubleday, 1961), 46.

27 **"The prevailing ideas entertained by him":** Alexander Hamilton Stevens, "Cornerstone Speech, Savannah, Georgia, March 21, 1861," https://www.battlefields.org/learn/primary-sources/cornerstone-speech.

2. STRANGE CONFEDERATES

32 **standing five feet seven inches:** David Detzer, *Allegiance: Fort Sumter, Charleston, and the Beginning of the Civil War* (New York: Harcourt, 2001), 206.

32 **"unusual coloring for a Creole":** Hamilton Basso, *Beauregard: The Great Creole* (New York: Scribner's, 1933), 29.

34 **"oriental races":** "The Hebrew Race," *Charleston Courier*, April 1, 1867.

34 **"We are by birth":** Wilbert L. Jenkins, *Seizing the New Day: African Americans in Post–Civil War Charleston* (Bloomington: Indiana University Press, 1998), 22–23.

34 **roughly 150 free men of color volunteered:** Bernard E. Powers, *Black Charlestonians: A Social History, 1822–1885* (Fayetteville: University of Arkansas Press, 1999), 66.

35 **donated a sum of $450:** Ibid.

35 **"the free colored population (native) of Louisiana":** "The Free Colored Natives of Louisiana," *Daily Delta* (New Orleans), December 28, 1860.

36 **"We, the undersigned":** "Defenders of the Native Land," *Daily Picayune*, April 21, 1861.

36 **nearly two thousand prosperous free people of color:** Shirley Thompson, *Exiles at Home: The Struggle to Become American in Creole New Orleans* (Cambridge, MA: Harvard University Press, 2009), 210.

36 **loaned the Confederate government thousands:** Loren Schweninger, "Antebellum Free Persons of Color in Postbellum Louisiana," *Louisiana History: The Journal of the Louisiana Historical Association* 30, no. 4 (Autumn 1989): 345–64.

37 **"as cosmopolitan a body of soldiers":** Daniel Sharfstein, *The Invisible Line: Three American Families and the Secret Journey from Black to White* (New York: Penguin Press, 2011), 107.

37 **record-setting 545-day siege:** Joseph Kelly, *America's Longest Siege: Charleston, Slavery, and the Slow March Toward the Civil War* (New York: Overlook, 2013), 16.

37 **three thousand militiamen defended New Orleans:** James M. McPherson, *Battle Cry of Freedom: The Civil War Era* (New York: Oxford University Press, 1988), 418.

39 **"what disposition they [should] make":** Benjamin Butler to Edwin Stanton, May 25, 1862, in *The War of the Rebellion: A Compilation of the Official Records of the Union and Confederate Armies* (Washington, DC: Government Printing Office, 1886), series 1, vol. 15, 442.

40 **"In color, nay, also in conduct":** Ibid.

40 **"I only wish to spend":** James Parton, *General Butler in New Orleans* (New York, Mason Brothers, 1864), 490.

40 **"I am changing my opinions":** Benjamin Butler, quoted in Thompson, *Exiles at Home*, 221.

40 **"Appreciating their motives":** General Orders No. 63, August 22, 1862, in *War of the Rebellion*, 557.

41 ***"progressiste":*** William P. Connor, "Reconstruction Rebels: The *New*

Orleans Tribune in Post-War Louisiana," *Journal of the Louisiana Historical Association* 21, no. 2 (Spring 1980): 161.

41 **"organ of the free colored population":** Thompson, *Exiles at Home*, 216.

43 **"the indefatigable J. R. Terry":** *Minutes of the Loyal National League of Louisiana*, 4.

43 **"the first time on any public occasion":** Ibid., 12.

43 **"Fellow citizens, this is the first time":** Ibid., 13.

43 **"Our country has given us our rights":** Ibid., 14.

43 **"white men and women":** Ibid., 5.

44 **"To His Excellency Abraham Lincoln":** Jean Baptiste Roudanez and E. Arnold Bertonneau, Voting Rights Petition, January 4, 1864 (Select Committee on the Rebellious States; Petitions and Memorials Referred to Committees [HR38A-G25.6]; 38th Congress; Records of the U.S. House of Representatives, Record Group 233; National Archives, Washington, DC).

45 **"We are passing through a revolution":** Peyton McCrary, *Abraham Lincoln and Reconstruction: The Louisiana Experiment* (Princeton, NJ: Princeton University Press, 1978), 229.

45 **"with all their admirable qualities":** William Lloyd Garrison, quoted in Ira Berlin, *Slaves Without Masters: The Free Negro in the Antebellum South* (New York: Pantheon, 1974), 387.

46 **"very intelligent . . . colored people":** Abraham Lincoln, quoted in Joseph Logsdon and Caryn Cossé Bell, "The Americanization of Black New Orleans," in Arnold R. Hirsch and Joseph Logsdon, eds., *Creole New Orleans* (Baton Rouge: Louisiana State University Press, 1992), 226.

46 **"We ask that, in the reconstruction":** E. Arnold Bertonneau, quoted in "Dinner to Citizens of Louisiana," *Liberator*, April 15, 1864.

46 **"United, we stand!":** Paul Trévigne, quoted in Logsdon and Bell, "The Americanization of Black New Orleans," 228.

47 **"nearly white":** W. E. B. Du Bois, *Black Reconstruction in America* (New York: Harcourt, Brace, 1935), 462.

47 **"[Just as] we assert[ed] that the sons":** Editorial, *New Orleans Tribune*, January 17, 1865.

48 **"These two populations":** "National Equal Rights League," *New Orleans Tribune*, December 29, 1864.

49 **a simple banner reading "Liberty":** Jenkins, *Seizing the New Day*, 31.

49 **"We know no masters but ourselves":** Powers, *Black Charlestonians*, 69.

49 **"Equal rights":** Philip Dray, *Capitol Men: The Epic Story of Reconstruction Through the Lives of the First Black Congressmen* (Boston: Houghton Mifflin, 2008), 42.

49 **"We know no caste or color!":** Ibid.

49 **"parvenue free"**: Joel Williamson, *New People: Miscegenation and Mulattoes in the United States* (New York: Free Press, 1980), 91.

49 **"Charleston ha[s] the facilities for a better civilization"**: Gilbert Pillsbury, quoted in Powers, *Black Charlestonians*, 141.

50 **"There is among our people that abiding faith"**: Lewis Hayden, quoted in Dorothy Sterling, *The Trouble They Seen: Black People Tell the Story of Reconstruction* (Garden City, NY: Doubleday, 1976), 47.

50 **"now for the first time"**: Eric Foner, *Reconstruction: America's Unfinished Revolution, 1863–1877* (New York: Harper & Row, 1988), 72.

50 **"nigger citizenship"**: John Wilkes Booth, quoted in Terry Alford, *Fortune's Fool: The Life of John Wilkes Booth* (Oxford: Oxford University Press, 2015), 257.

51 **"many of the 'brown people' here"**: Jane Van Allen, quoted in Powers, *Black Charlestonians*, 185.

51 **Not one of the fifteen richest African-Americans**: Jenkins, *Seizing the New Day*, 37.

51 **"foundation-stone [is] Charity and Benevolence"**: Powers, *Black Charlestonians*, 51.

52 **"It appears that all the jail birds"**: Rev. Richard H. Cain, quoted in Powers, *Black Charlestonians*, 77.

52 **"The old jealousy between blacks and mulattoes"**: Williamson, *New People*, 88.

52 **"These people were not always outcasts"**: Whitelaw Reid, *After the War: A Southern Tour* (Cincinnati: Moore, Wilstach & Baldwin, 1866), 244.

53 **"very frankly said during the evening"**: Ibid.

53 **only one of the twenty African-American delegates was a freedman**: W. E. B. Du Bois, *Black Reconstruction in America*, 462.

54 **fifteen thousand African-Americans running away**: Logsdon and Bell, "The Americanization of Black New Orleans," 232.

54 **returned the city to its traditional black-majority status**: Jenkins, *Seizing the New Day*, xiv, 166.

55 **"aristocracy of color"**: Robert J. Swan, "Thomas McCants Stewart and the Failure of the Mission of the Talented Tenth in Black America, 1880–1923" (unpublished PhD diss., New York University, 1989), 7, Brooklyn Historical Society.

55 **"a prominent Rebel"**: Francis L. Cardozo to George Whipple, January 27, 1866, Amistad Collection, Tulane University, New Orleans.

55 **"It is hard telling who is white here"**: John W. Blassingame, *Black New Orleans, 1860–1880* (Chicago: University of Chicago Press, 1973), 201.

56 **"Are you Beauregard?"**: T. Harry Williams, *P. G. T. Beauregard: Napoleon in Gray* (Baton Rouge: Louisiana State University Press, 1954), 257.

3. LEGALLY BLACK

59 "Insolent [African-Americans] never pretend to give place to you": Bernard E. Powers, *Black Charlestonians: A Social History, 1822–1885* (Fayetteville: University of Arkansas Press, 1999), 79.

59 "jostled by flaunting mulattos": Ibid., 78.

59 "They only required a little encouragement": Ibid., 76.

59 "forming alignments and pelting each other": Ibid.

60 "white man's government": James L. Orr, quoted in Richard Zuczek, *State of Rebellion: Reconstruction in South Carolina* (Columbia: University of South Carolina Press, 1996), 13.

60 "We ask not at this time": Powers, *Black Charlestonians*, 82.

60 "protection and government of the colored population": Ibid., 81.

60 "the general interest of both": Edmund Rhett Jr., quoted in Zuczek, *State of Rebellion*, 15.

61 "stealing a horse": W. E. B. Du Bois, *Black Reconstruction in America* (New York: Harcourt, Brace, 1935), 176.

61 "impersonating [a white woman's] husband": Ibid., 176.

61 "any freedman, free Negro, or mulatto": Ibid., 171.

63 "It is hard to tell where Africa ends": *Proceedings of the Colored People's Convention of the State of South Carolina* (Charleston: South Carolina Leader Office, 1865), 15.

63 "caus[ing] us to make distinctions among ourselves": Ibid., 12.

63 "We simply desire that we shall be recognized": Ibid., 25.

63 "that the phrase 'all men' includes the negro": Ibid., 27, 22, 28, 22, 30.

64 hundreds of South Carolina freedmen had sent a petition: Wilbert L. Jenkins, *Seizing the New Day: African Americans in Post–Civil War Charleston* (Bloomington: Indiana University Press, 1998), 142.

65 "a government of white people": Du Bois, *Black Reconstruction in America*, 454.

65 "It does seem strange that so lovely a climate": William Heyward, quoted in Joel Williamson, *New People: Miscegenation and Mulattoes in the United States* (New York: Free Press, 1980), 92.

66 "If a republican form of government is to be sustained": Du Bois, *Black Reconstruction in America*, 554.

66 "The separation of the races": Abraham Lincoln, quoted in Du Bois, *Black Reconstruction in America*, 146.

67 "a frog pond": Ibid., 434.

68 "Damn the Negroes": Andrew Johnson, quoted in Eric Foner, *Recon-*

struction: America's Unfinished Revolution, 1863–1877 (New York: Harper & Row, 1988), 44.

68 **"The first expression"**: Frederick Douglass, quoted in Du Bois, *Black Reconstruction in America*, 296.

69 **including ten generals**: Foner, *Reconstruction*, 226.

69 **"fed, clothed, educated, and sheltered"**: Andrew Johnson, "Freedmen's Bureau Bill Veto Message, February 19, 1866," http://teaching americanhistory.org/library/document/veto-of-the-freedmens-bureau-bill/, accessed July 13, 2018.

69 **"different punishment[s to people]"**: The Civil Rights Act of 1866, http://teachingamericanhistory.org/library/document/the-civil-rights -act-of-1866/, accessed July 13, 2018.

70 **"no white person shall intermarry"**: Andrew Johnson, "Veto of the Civil Rights Bill, March 27, 1866," http://teachingamericanhistory.org/ library/document/veto-of-the-civil-rights-bill/, accessed July 13, 2018.

70 **"Shall Negroes intermingle"**: "Miscellaneous," *New York Herald*, March 30, 1866.

71 **"Nothing has changed"**: Jean-Charles Houzeau, *My Passage at the New Orleans* Tribune: *A Memoir of the Civil War Era*, ed. David C. Rankin, trans. Gerard F. Denault (Baton Rouge: Louisiana State University, 1984), 45.

71 **"The most odious features of slavery"**: Du Bois, *Black Reconstruction in America*, 178.

72 **at least forty-eight African-American men, women, and children**: Foner, *Reconstruction*, 262.

73 **"niggers and half-niggers"**: Philip Dray, *Capitol Men: The Epic Story of Reconstruction Through the Lives of the First Black Congressmen* (Boston: Houghton Mifflin, 2008), 29.

73 **"all assemblies calculated to disturb the public peace"**: John T. Monroe, quoted in ibid.

73 **"sustain the civil authority"**: Andrew Johnson, quoted in James G. Hollandsworth Jr., *An Absolute Massacre: The New Orleans Race Riot of July 30, 1866* (Baton Rouge: Louisiana State University Press, 2001), 143.

73 **over two-thirds of the all-white corps**: James K. Hogue, *Uncivil War: Five New Orleans Street Battles and the Rise and Fall of Radical Reconstruction* (Baton Rouge: Louisiana State University Press, 2006), 34.

73 **approximately two hundred veterans of color paraded**: Ibid., 41.

74 **white mob of roughly fifteen hundred**: Ibid., 42.

74 **"incised wound of head"**: *Report of the Select Committee on the New Orleans Riots* (Washington, DC: Government Printing Office, 1867), 185.

75 **at least thirty-eight people had been killed:** Du Bois, *Black Recon-struction in America*, 465.

75 **"The more information I obtain":** General Philip Sheridan, quoted in Hogue, *Uncivil War*, 44.

75 **"We have fought for four years":** Dray, *Capitol Men*, 29.

76 **"No meeting whatever, for the purpose":** "The Apology for the Late Massacre," *Harper's Weekly*, August 25, 1866, 531.

76 **"I die for the cause of Liberty":** Elizabeth Hayden Reed, *Life of A. P. Dostie; or The Conflict in New Orleans* (New York: Wm. P. Tomlinson, 1868), 318.

76 **"water[ed] the bricks of the bloody city":** Henry Rey, in Shirley Thompson, *Exiles at Home: The Struggle to Become American in Creole New Orleans* (Cambridge, MA: Harvard University Press, 2009), 251.

76 **"political tricksters":** Dray, *Capitol Men*, 32.

76 **"New Orleans!":** Ibid.

77 **"have full and equal benefit":** Thomas Holt, *Black Over White: Negro Political Leadership in South Carolina during Reconstruction* (Urbana: University of Illinois Press, 1977), 24.

77 **"a revolution in the North":** Houzeau, *My Passage at the New Orleans Tribune*, 46.

77 **"the male citizens of [each] State":** First Reconstruction Act, http://teachingamericanhistory.org/library/document/first-reconstruction-act/.

78 **"The negroes have not asked":** Andrew Johnson, "Veto of the First Reconstruction Act, March 2, 1867," http://www.let.rug.nl/usa/presidents/andrew-johnson/veto-for-the-first-reconstruction-act-march-2-1867.php.

78 **"The old southern leaders":** Andrew Johnson, quoted in Foner, *Recon-struction*, 276.

79 **"Some of the rich old colts":** Ibid., 280.

79 **"For us the war was not ended":** Thomas Pinckney Lowndes, quoted in Zuczek, *State of Rebellion*, 47.

79 **"With regard to the suffrage":** "Letter from General Beauregard [to] Wm. H. C. King, Editor of the New Orleans Times," *Charleston Daily News*, April 2, 1867.

4. FREEDOM RIDERS

83 **Twelve of the thirteen were men of color:** Bernard E. Powers, *Black Charlestonians: A Social History, 1822–1885* (Fayetteville: University of Arkansas Press, 1999), 86–87.

83 **"*Whereas*, the founders of this Republic":** "Public Meeting," *Charleston Daily Courier*, March 22, 1867.

83 **roughly two thousand African-Americans :** "Meeting of the Freed-
    men on Citadel Green," *Charleston Mercury*, March 27, 1867.

84 **"impartial laws, impartial justice":** "Mass Meeting of Freedmen,"
    Charleston Daily Courier, March 27, 1867.

84 **"proper arrangements will, in due time, be made":** "The New City
    Street-Railway," *Charleston Daily Courier*, October 15, 1866.

85 **"seemingly well-organized effort":** "Attack on the Street-cars,"
    Charleston Daily Courier, March 27, 1867.

86 **Eckhard appears in the last antebellum census's list:** United States
    Census, 1860. In the Census records he is listed as "Sydney Eccard."

86 **"The news of the occurrence":** "Attack on the Street Cars," *Charleston
    Daily News*, April 2, 1867.

88 **"no right to a seat":** Judge Albert A. Thompson, quoted in Kyle Volk,
    Moral Minorities and the Making of American Democracy (New York:
    Oxford University Press, 2014), 161.

88 **"hundreds of idle negroes":** Douglas Egerton, *Wars of Reconstruction:
    The Brief, Violent History of America's Most Progressive Era* (New York:
    Bloomsbury Press, 2014), 55.

89 **"EJECTED FROM A STREET CAR":** *Congr. Globe, 38th Cong, 2nd
    Sess.* (1865), 915.

90 **"a colored soldier be received":** Roger Fischer, *The Segregation
    Struggle in Louisiana* (Urbana: University of Illinois Press, 1974), 31.

90 **"the attempt to enforce police laws":** Ibid.

90 **"remind[er to] our friends":** "Star Cars," *New Orleans Tribune*, August
    20, 1865.

90 **"Every negro who is able":** "The City Cars Again," *Daily True Delta*
    (New Orleans), October 12, 1865.

91 **"Attention . . . has been called":** "The Street Car Question—Circular
    From General Scott," *Charleston Mercury*, April 6, 1867.

91 **"very unwell and much fatigued":** "The City Car Difficulty," *Charles-
    ton Daily News*, May 6, 1867.

93 **"it will not be safe for ladies":** "Attack on the Street Cars," *Charleston
    Daily News*, April 2, 1867.

93 **"If the negroes here":** "The Disturbances in Charleston," *New York
    Times*, April 5, 1867.

94 **"is worse now than":** Francis Cardozo, quoted in Powers, *Black Charles-
    tonians*, 236.

94 **"public carriers have no right to exclude":** Freedmen's Bureau
    Assistant Commissioner R. K. Scott to Charleston City Railway Com-
    pany President John S. Riggs, April 22, 1867, Charleston City Railway
    Company Records, Addlestone Library, College of Charleston.

95 **"the cars be thrown open"**: Charleston City Railway Company President John S. Riggs to Freedman's Bureau Assistant Commissioner R. K. Scott, May 3, 1867, reprinted in *Charleston Daily News*, May 6, 1867.

95 **"emphatic testimony of the disposition"**: Daniel Sickles to Charleston City Railway Company President John S. Riggs, May 3, 1867, reprinted in *Charleston Daily Courier*, May 4, 1867.

95 **"the whites took it"**: "The Southern States: South Carolina: Senator Wilson in Charleston," *New-York Daily Tribune*, May 5, 1867.

95 **"leg-weary and tired"**: Senator Frederick A. Sawyer, quoted in Eric Foner, *Reconstruction: America's Unfinished Revolution, 1863–1877* (New York: Harper & Row, 1988), 371.

95 **"because of color or caste"**: Willard B. Gatewood, "'The Remarkable Misses Rollin': Black Women in Reconstruction South Carolina," *South Carolina Historical Magazine* 92, no. 3 (July 1991): 172.

96 **eight rolling cars**: "The Car Question," *New Orleans Commercial Bulletin*, May 7, 1867.

96 **boasted 225 cars**: "Street Railways in New Orleans," *Charleston Daily Courier*, April 25, 1867.

96 **"In every civilized country"**: "The Colored People and Their Friends," *New Orleans Tribune*, April 21, 1867.

96 **"More than a year has elapsed"**: "The Star Cars," *New Orleans Republican*, April 28, 1867.

98 **"not so much"**: "Black Against White," *Daily Picayune* (New Orleans), May 5, 1867.

99 **"The victory is not yet won"**: "The Star Cars," *New Orleans Tribune*, May 4, 1867.

99 **"open riot"**: "Coming to a Head," *New Orleans Times*, May 5, 1867; "Riotous Disturbances," *New Orleans Bee*, May 6, 1867.

99 **"I have been informed this morning"**: J. M. Reid to Mayor Heath, May 5, 1867, P. G. T. Beauregard and Family Papers, 1818–1912, Louisiana and Lower Mississippi Valley Collections, Louisiana State University, Baton Rouge.

100 **"On sabbath evening"**: H. C. Knight, quoted in Joshua Jelly-Shapiro, "In Congo Square," *The Nation*, December 29, 2008, 26.

100 **five hundred protesters**: "The Negroes and the City Railroads," *New Orleans Times*, May 7, 1867.

101 **"spill the last drop of blood"**: Ibid.

101 **"appeared to be the result"**: Ibid.

101 **"systematic attempt"**: "The Car Question," *New Orleans Times*, May 7, 1867.

101 **"Erase your stars":** Philip Sheridan, quoted in Jean-Charles Houzeau, *My Passage at the New Orleans* Tribune: *A Memoir of the Civil War Era*, ed. David C. Rankin, trans. Gerard F. Denault (Baton Rouge: Louisiana State University, 1984), 120.

102 **"Have no interference":** Thomas E. Adams, quoted in "The City Car Difficulties," *New Orleans Crescent*, May 7, 1867.

102 **"For the present":** "Star Car Controversy Ended," *New Orleans Bee*, May 8, 1867.

102 **"The bitterness which has existed":** Philip H. Sheridan to U. S. Grant, May 10, 1867, Philip Henry Sheridan Papers, 1853–1896, Manuscript Division, Library of Congress, Washington, DC.

103 **"Travel on the city buses":** Houzeau, *My Passage at the New Orleans Tribune*, 120.

103 **"[White] Southerners recognized [equality] in the horsecars":** George Washington Cable, "My Politics," in Arlin Turner, ed., *The Negro Question* (New York: W. W. Norton, 1968), 8.

103 **"It will settle all the other questions":** "The Car Question," *New Orleans Tribune*, April 30, 1867.

103 **"We recollect the threats made":** "Talking and Acting," *New Orleans Tribune*, October 29, 1867.

5. PROGRESS ON PARCHMENT

107 **"the first official body ever convened":** "Political Bearing," *New Orleans Tribune*, October 25, 1867.

107 **hundreds of citizens, most of them African-Americans:** "The Convention at Mechanics' Institute," *New Orleans Crescent*, November 26, 1867.

107 **Precisely half were white:** W. E. B. Du Bois, *Black Reconstruction in America* (New York: Harcourt, Brace, 1935), 372.

107 **"The white and colored races are about equally divided":** "Louisiana Constitutional Convention," *New Orleans Republican*, November 24, 1867.

108 **"black . . . as the darkest negro":** State Convention," *New Orleans Republican*, November 23, 1867.

108 **"Economic and social differences":** Du Bois, *Black Reconstruction in America*, 470.

108 **"all conveyances by water or land":** *Official Journal of the Proceedings of the Convention for Framing a Constitution for the State of Louisiana* (New Orleans: J. B. Roudanez & Co., 1867–1868), 35.

109 **"All persons shall enjoy equal rights":** Ibid., 125.

109 **by a vote of sixty-six to fifteen:** Donald DeVore and Joseph Logsdon, *Crescent City Schools: Public Education in New Orleans, 1841–1991* (New Orleans: Orleans Parish School Board, 1991), 58.

110 **"The Legislature shall establish free public schools":** *Official Journal of the Proceedings of the Convention for Framing a Constitution for the State of Louisiana,* 17.

110 **"The General Assembly shall establish":** Ibid., 306.

110 **vote of sixty-one to twelve:** Ibid., 201.

111 **"will not elevate the negroes":** Ibid., 290–91.

111 **"mongrel monstrosity":** Roger Fischer, *The Segregation Struggle in Louisiana* (Urbana: University of Illinois Press, 1974), 58.

111 **"My friends here have requested":** Francis L. Cardozo to E. P. Smith, November 4, 1867, Amistad Collection, Tulane University, New Orleans.

112 **worth tens of thousands of dollars:** Thomas Holt. *Black Over White: Negro Political Leadership in South Carolina during Reconstruction* (Urbana: University of Illinois Press, 1977), 46.

112 **"a large portly mulatto":** "Sketches of the Delegates to the Great-Ringed-Streaked-And-Striped Convention. Charleston Delegation," *Charleston Mercury,* February 24, 1868.

113 **"the most incredible":** *New York Herald,* quoted in Howard Fast, *Freedom Road* (New York: Crown, 1969), 76.

114 **Between seventy and seventy-three:** Richard Zuczek, *State of Rebellion: Reconstruction in South Carolina* (Columbia: University of South Carolina Press, 1996), 48; Bernard E. Powers, *Black Charlestonians: A Social History, 1822–1885* (Fayetteville: University of Arkansas Press, 1999), 90.

114 **between fifty-one and fifty-four:** Zuczek, *State of Rebellion,* 48; Powers, *Black Charlestonians,* 90; Holt, *Black Over White,* 35.

114 **"were of various colors and mixtures":** Du Bois, *Black Reconstruction in America,* 404.

114 **"Distinction on account of race":** *Proceedings of the Constitutional Convention of South Carolina* (Charleston: Denny & Perry, 1868), 353.

116 **"be free and open to all":** Ibid., 266.

116 **"Did any South Carolinian vote":** Ibid., 704.

117 **"made New England great":** Ibid., 694.

117 **"splendour of his elocution":** "Sketches of the Delegates to the Great-Ringed-Streaked-and-Striped Convention," *Charleston Mercury,* February 24, 1868.

117 **"I want to divest":** *Proceedings of the Constitutional Convention of South Carolina,* 706.

118 **"All the public schools":** South Carolina Const. of 1868, art. III, § 10.

118 **"To remove these prejudices":** *Proceedings of the Constitutional Convention of South Carolina*, 900–901.

118 **"gauntlet of . . . jeers and threats":** Quoted in Douglas Egerton, *The Wars of Reconstruction: The Brief, Violent History of America's Most Progressive Era* (New York: Bloomsbury Press, 2014), 253.

119 **"the turbulent political arena":** Francis L. Cardozo to E. P Smith, November 4, 1867.

119 **thirteen of the eighteen candidates:** Powers, *Black Charlestonians*, 96.

120 **"murder and intimidation":** Michael Hahn, quoted in Eric Foner, *Reconstruction: America's Unfinished Revolution, 1863–1877* (New York: Harper & Row, 1988), 342.

120 **"incendiary speeches":** Eric Foner, *Freedom's Lawmakers: A Director of Black Officeholders during Reconstruction*, rev. ed. (Baton Rouge: Louisiana State University Press), 176.

120 **"I tremble for this city":** Rev. Richard Cain, quoted in Powers, *Black Charlestonians*, 230.

121 **"We actually have negroes in Council":** Ibid., 229.

121 **"This Is a White Man's Country":** Foner, *Reconstruction*, photo inset, 386–87.

121 **"race, color, or previous condition":** U.S. Const. Amendment XV, § 1, cl. 1.

121 **"In the grand procession":** Philip Dray, *Capitol Men: The Epic Story of Reconstruction Through the Lives of the First Black Congressmen* (Boston: Houghton Mifflin, 2008), 67–68.

6. BROWNS VERSUS BOARD OF EDUCATION

125 **"there shall be no separate schools":** *Official Journal of the Proceedings of the Convention for Framing a Constitution for the State of Louisiana* (New Orleans: J. B. Roudanez, 1867–1868), 306.

125 **"a story, actively circulated":** "City Intelligence—Absurd Report," *Daily Delta* (New Orleans), September 17, 1862.

125 **"whenever the Principal of any schools":** Minutes of the Orleans Parish School Board, September 10, 1862, Louisiana and Special Collections, Earl K. Long Library, University of New Orleans.

126 **"being patronized solely by the French-speaking children":** *The Picayune's Guide to New Orleans*, 6th ed. (New Orleans: The Picayune, 1904), 46.

126 **"rumors . . . spreading about this city":** Minutes of the Orleans Parish School Board, September 18, 1862.

126 **"are very dark":** Minutes of the Orleans Parish School Board, September 29, 1862.

127 **"very insolent language"**: Ibid.

128 **"precious white children"**: Robert Mills Lusher, *Autobiography of Robert Mills Lusher* (unpublished manuscript, 1889), 16, Louisiana and Lower Mississippi Valley Collections, Louisiana State University, Baton Rouge.

128 **"vindicate the *honor and supremacy*"**: *Report of the Superintendent of Public Education, to the General Assembly of the State of Louisiana* (New Orleans: J. O. Nixon, 1867), 18.

128 **"the mental training of an inferior race"**: Ibid., 22.

128 **"We . . . insist on perfect equality"**: Radical Republican Convention, *New Orleans Times*, June 18, 1867.

129 **"[laboring for] the protection of white students"**: Lusher, *Autobiography*, 16.

129 **"wholly apart from the offensive State System"**: Ibid., 17.

129 **"white children . . . would be properly prepared"**: Ibid., 15.

130 **"some 29 pupils"**: Orleans Parish School Board Records, May 27, 1868, Louisiana and Special Collections, Earl K. Long Library, University of New Orleans.

130 **"knowingly admitt[ing] into [her] school"**: Orleans Parish School Board Records, May 21, 1868.

130 **"inform me if there are any children"**: Superintendent Rogers to Principal Bigot, May 7, 1868, Orleans Parish School Board Records.

130 **"such evidence as may be"**: Superintendent Rogers to Mr. Fremaux, May 25, 1868, Orleans Parish School Board Records.

130 **"the purity of their blood"**: "The School Board," *Daily Crescent*, May 28, 1868.

131 **"Complaints have been made"**: Orleans Parish School Board Records, May 23, 1868.

131 **Six of the families ignored**: "The School Board," *Daily Crescent*, May 28, 1868.

132 **"Sir: Certain responsible and well known citizens"**: Orleans Parish School Board Records, June 8, 1868.

133 **"case of grave doubt"**: Orleans Parish School Board Records, May 21, 1868.

134 **"When I joined the United States army"**: Robert Isabelle, quoted in Eric Foner, *Freedom's Lawmakers: A Directory of Black Officeholders During Reconstruction* (New York: Oxford University Press, 1993), 114.

134 **"I want the children of this State"**: *Debates of the House of Representatives of the State of Louisiana, Session of 1870* (New Orleans: Office of the Republican, 1870), 149.

135 **"Now, I want the children of this State"**: "The Public Schools." *Daily Picayune*, February 9, 1870.

136 **"vested with the sole and exclusive control":** Isabelle Case File (Case No. 153, 8th D. Ct., Orleans Parish, 1870), Louisiana Division/City Archives and Special Collections, New Orleans Public Library.

137 **"It [i]s said that such a decision":** "The School Cases," *New Orleans Republican*, November 22, 1870.

137 **"The Ward District Boards will now":** "State Superintendent of Education: Circular," *New Orleans Republican*, November 22, 1870.

138 **"there is not a single white school":** John W. Blassingame, *Black New Orleans, 1860–1880* (Chicago: University of Chicago Press, 1973), 121.

138 **"accomplished facts, which in their very nature":** Ibid., 120.

138 **"no case has come to the [board's] knowledge":** Annual Report of the State Superintendent of Education, 1871 (New Orleans: A. L. Lee, 1871), 360, The Historic New Orleans Collection.

139 **"Radical rascalities":** Lusher, *Autobiography*, 23.

139 **"I am aware that the old leaven":** Annual Report of the Superintendent of Public Education, 1874 (New Orleans: The Republican Office, 1874), 26, The Historic New Orleans Collection.

139 **"[My] officers are not influenced":** Ibid., 11

140 **"Miss Morris . . . the lady graduate":** "The 'Teachers' Institute' Trick," *Daily Picayune*, June 1, 1871.

140 **African-Americans constituted a tenth of the faculty:** Donald DeVore and Joseph Logsdon, *Crescent City Schools: Public Education in New Orleans, 1841–1991* (New Orleans: Orleans Parish School Board, 1991), 73.

140 **"call[ed] together his corps of teachers":** "The 'Teachers' Institute' Trick," *Daily Picayune*, June 1, 1871.

140 **"[I] was the first to notice":** George Washington Cable, "My Politics," in Arlin Turner, ed., *The Negro Question: A Selection of Writings on Civil Rights in the South by George W. Cable* (Garden City, NY: Doubleday Anchor Books, 1958), 8–9.

141 **"I saw, to my great and rapid edification":** Ibid., 9.

141 **"I saw [that] the day must come":** Ibid., 9, 10.

142 **"Men and boys, women and girls":** James Gill, *Lords of Misrule: Mardi Gras and the Politics of Race in New Orleans* (Jackson: University Press of Mississippi, 1997), 36.

143 **"a different Adam":** Ibram X. Kendi, *Stamped from the Beginning; The Definitive History of Racist Ideas in America* (New York: Nation Books, 2016), 51.

143 **"specimen . . . so amazingly like":** "Mystick Krewe," *Daily Picayune*, February 26, 1873.

144 **"it will be impossible for me":** Ulysses S. Grant, quoted in "Carnival Court Journal," *Daily Picayune*, February 15, 1873.

145 **"I was educated at one of the most prominent universities"**: Louis
     Charles Roudanez, quoted in "The Situation," *New Orleans Times*, May
     28, 1873.

146 **"It is my determination to continue to battle"**: Isaac Marks, Letter
     to the Editor, *New Orleans Times*, July 23, 1873.

146 **"as his name indicates"**: Edwin L. Jewell, *Jewell's Crescent City Illus-
     trated* (New Orleans: Edwin L. Jewell, 1874), 116.

147 **"It is manifest that nothing but the forbearance"**: Pierre Gustave
     Toutant Beauregard, "The Unification Question," *New Orleans Times*,
     July 1, 1873.

147 **"Equal Rights, One Flag, One Country, One People"**: "Equal
     Rights," *New Orleans Times*, July 16, 1873.

147 **"all places of licensed public resort"**: "Grand Unification Mass Meet-
     ing," *Daily Picayune*, July 15, 1873.

148 **described the gathering as majority white**: "Unification," *Daily Pic-
     ayune*, July 16, 1873; "Equal Rights," *New Orleans Times*, July 16, 1873.

148 **"We come here to-night"**: Isaac Newton Marks, quoted in T. Harry
     Williams, "The Louisiana Unification Movement of 1873," *Journal of
     Southern History* 11, no. 3 (1945): 365.

148 **"Mr. President, I want to know"**: "Equal Rights," *New Orleans Times*,
     July 16, 1873.

148 **"What is the state of things now"**: Marks, Letter to the Editor, *New
     Orleans Times*, July 23, 1873.

149 **"the encroachments of the combined carpet-bag"**: "Gen. Beaure-
     gard's Unification Scheme," *Columbia Daily Phoenix*, July 13, 1873.

149 **"It is indeed a great pity"**: "Beauregard," *Columbia Daily Union-
     Herald*, July 11, 1873 (reprint from the *Sumter News*).

149 **"It's time to say it plain"**: *"D'un coté ou de l'autre,"* Le Carillon, July 13,
     1873. Translation courtesy of Nathaniel Dennett.

7. RADICAL UNIVERSITY

154 **"All the public schools"**: South Carolina Const. of 1868, art. X, § 10.

154 **"Everybody, white and black"**: "South Carolina," *New York Times*,
     December 25, 1868.

155 **"neither the ... Board of Trustees"**: *The Constitution of South Caro-
     lina, Adopted April 16, 1868, and the Acts and Joint Resolutions of the
     General Assembly Passed at the Special Session of 1868* (Columbia, SC:
     John W. Denny, 1868), 203.

156 **"the hell-born policy"**: *Fairfield Herald,* quoted in W. E. B. Du Bois,
     Black Reconstruction in America (New York: Harcourt, Brace, 1935), 405.

156 **"the most perfect scalawag":** R. H. Woody, "Franklin J. Moses, Jr., Scalawag Governor of South Carolina, 1872–74," *North Carolina Historical Review* 10, no. 2 (April 1933): 111.

157 **"is worthy of the highest":** Jonathan Jasper Wright, "A Card from Judge Wright," *Daily Union-Herald* (Columbia, SC), April 5, 1873.

157 **"I do not ask or contend for social equality":** Ibid.

158 **"pretensive only—the purpose being":** Edwin L. Green, *A History of the University of South Carolina* (Columbia, SC: State Company, 1916), 412–13.

158 **"the axe continues to descend":** Daniel Walker Hollis, *University of South Carolina,* Vol. 2: *College to University* (Columbia: University of South Carolina Press, 1956), 65.

159 **"The venerable University":** Edward King, *The Great South* (Hartford, CT: American Publishing Company, 1875), 459.

160 **"the busts of [John C.] Calhoun":** Ibid., 462.

160 **"the races can no more agree":** "Resignation of the College Librarian," *Columbia Daily Phoenix*, October 16, 1873.

160 **"*rogues & negroes*":** Paul Hamilton Hayne, quoted in Richard Zuczek, *State of Rebellion: Reconstruction in South Carolina* (Columbia: University of South Carolina Press, 1996), 136.

160 **"This Board accepts the resignations":** Hollis, *University of South Carolina,* 67.

161 **"as white as any of his ancestors":** "The 'Color Line' Policy," *New York Times*, January 2, 1877.

162 **"for the first time":** Franklin J. Moses Jr., "Journal of the House of Representatives of the State of South Carolina for the Regular Session of 1873–74 (Columbia, SC: Republican Printing Company, 1874), 91.

162 **"four different races":** Heidi Ardizzone, *An Illuminated Life: Belle da Costa Greene's Journey from Prejudice to Privilege* (New York: W. W. Norton, 2007), 17.

163 **"isolated from the race":** Ibid., 19.

163 **"a smoked Yankee":** Frances R. Marchant, "Richard T. Greener: Portrait of a Busy Man" (unpublished manuscript, 1882), South Caroliniana Library, University of South Carolina.

165 **"I am going home":** Cornelius Chapman Scott to Tobias Scott, August 6, 1872 (Cornelius Chapman Scott Papers, South Caroliniana Library, University of South Carolina, Columbia).

165 **"I began to feel sick":** Cornelius Chapman Scott to Tobias Scott, October 10, 1872, Cornelius Chapman Scott Papers.

165 **"When the University of South Carolina threw open":** Cornelius Chapman Scott, "When Negroes Attended the State University," *The State* (Columbia), May 8, 1911.

166 **"the grand onward movement"**: King, *The Great South*, 462.

166 **All of the African-American students were native Charlestonians:** Scott, "When Negroes Attended the State University,"
The State (Columbia) May 8, 1911.

166 **"Again you are aware":** Francis Lewis Cardozo, quoted in Thomas
Holt, *Black Over White: Negro Political Leadership in South Carolina
during Reconstruction* (Urbana: University of Illinois Press, 1977), 53.

167 **"meet . . . the educational wants":** Michael David Cohen, *Reconstructing the Campus: Higher Education and the American Civil War*
(Charlottesville: University of Virginia, 2012) 120.

167 **"a scheme to buy students":** "Buying Students," *Columbia Daily Phoenix*, December 30, 1873.

168 **fully twenty-five of the thirty-one students:** Cohen, *Reconstructing
the Campus*, 121.

168 **"dismiss[ing] them to the several Counties":** Richard Theodore
Greener, quoted in Michael Robert Mounter, "Richard Theodore Greener:
The Idealist, Statesman, Scholar and South Carolinian" (unpublished
PhD diss., University of South Carolina, 2002), 140, South Caroliniana
Library, University of South Carolina, Columbia.

168 **the tiny senior class hailed from Charleston:** *Catalogue of the Trustees, Faculty, and Students of the University of South Carolina* (Columbia:
University of South Carolina, 1876), 8, South Caroliniana Library, University of South Carolina, Columbia.

168 **"flourishing":** Franklin J. Moses, quoted in Mounter, "Richard Theodore Greener," 116.

169 **"the Freshman Class [was]":** Fisk P. Brewer to Rev. B. B. Babbit, February 20, 1875, South Caroliniana Library, University of South Carolina,
Columbia.

169 **"Some, even [among the University's] graduates":** Fisk P. Brewer,
Report on the University of South Carolina, reprinted in Fisk Parsons
Brewer and William P. Vaughn, "'South Carolina University—1876' of
Fisk Parsons Brewer," *South Carolina Historical Magazine* 76, no. 4
(October 1975): 230.

170 **"it is an insult to both colored and white":** Ibid., 231.

170 **"The University now numbers one hundred and ten students":**
Thomas McCants Stewart, "From South Carolina," *New National Era*,
July 9, 1874; April 16, 1874.

170 **"It was prophesied that the admission":** "The University," Letter
to the editor of the *Daily Union-Herald*, signed "Students," February
10, 1875.

170 **"annihilated":** "South Carolina," *New York Times*, December 25, 1868.

171 **"there was absolutely nothing in the color":** "The 'Color Line' Policy," *New York Times*, January 2, 1877.

171 **"[When] the reconstructed administration of government":** Franklin J. Moses Jr., quoted in Du Bois, *Black Reconstruction in America*, 650–51.

172 **"what you think will be the result":** Hollis, *University of South Carolina*, 78.

8. LAWS AND OUTLAWS

175 **"The right of citizens of the United States":** U.S. Const. Amendment XV, § 1, cl. 1.

176 **"Fifteenth Amendment in flesh and blood":** Wendell Phillips, quoted in Philip Dray, *Capitol Men: The Epic Story of Reconstruction Through the Lives of the First Black Congressmen* (Boston: Houghton Mifflin, 2008), 59.

176 **"as far back as my knowledge extends":** Hiram Rhodes Revels, quoted in Julius E. Thompson, "Hiram Rhodes Revels, 1827–1901: A Reappraisal," *Journal of Negro History* 79, no. 3 (1994): 297.

177 **"What is the evidence of his being a negro?":** *Cong. Globe, 41st Cong., 2nd Sess.* (1870), 1567.

177 **"All men are created equal, says the great Declaration":** Ibid., 1566–67.

177 **"who had been sitting all day":** Dray, *Capitol Men*, 72–73.

178 **"An act to protect citizens":** *Cong. Globe, 41st Cong., 2nd Sess.* (1870), 3434.

179 **"K.K.K. *Beware! Beware! Beware!*":** "Ku-Klux Outrages," *New National Era*, May 25, 1871.

180 **"Let him appoint colored police officers":** "An Erroneous Statement," *New Orleans Tribune*, May 12, 1867.

180 **"everybody knows that one-half at least":** "No Colored Man Appointed," *New Orleans Tribune*, May 10, 1867.

180 **"newly enfranchised":** W. Marvin Dulaney, *Black Police in America* (Bloomington: Indiana University Press, 1996), 11.

180 **Three of the five commissioners appointed:** Dennis C. Rousey, *Policing the Southern City: New Orleans, 1805–1889* (Baton Rouge: Louisiana State University Press, 1996), 135.

181 **two-thirds were native-born Southerners:** Michael A. Ross, *The Great New Orleans Kidnapping Case: Race, Law, and Justice in the Reconstruction Era* (New York: Oxford University Press, 2017), 38–39.

181 **over 40 percent of the Charleston police:** Dennis C. Rousey, "Black

Policemen in New Orleans During Reconstruction," *The Historian*, 429, no. 2 (1987): 232.

181 **"the present police force of the city":** Edward King, *The Great South* (Hartford, CT: American Publishing Company, 1875), 446–48.

181 **there was not a single black officer:** Rousey, "Black Policemen in New Orleans," 232.

182 **"The seats arranged for the colored people":** "Academy of Music," *Charleston Daily Republican*, December 17, 1869.

182 **"black as well as white 'aristocracy'":** "Negroes at the Academy of Music," *Charleston News*, January 10, 1870.

182 **"persons [shall be] admitted":** Bernard E. Powers, *Black Charlestonians: A Social History, 1822–1885* (Fayetteville: University of Arkansas Press, 1999), 239.

183 **"What right have they":** "Louisiana Legislature," *New Orleans Bee*, September 27, 1868.

183 **"business or public resort shall be open":** Roger Fischer, *The Segregation Struggle in Louisiana* (Urbana: University of Illinois Press, 1974), 67.

184 **"I have always drunk in all houses":** Charles St. Albin Sauvinet, quoted in Joseph Nystrom, *New Orleans After the Civil War: Race, Politics, and a New Birth of Freedom* (Baltimore: Johns Hopkins University Press, 2010), 96.

184 **"for the purpose of vindicating his civil rights":** "The 'Bank' Coffeehouse—Suit of Sauvinet—Judgment of Judge Dibble," *New Orleans Republican*, April 28, 1871.

184 **"I am very much astonished":** *Sauvinet v. Walker*, No. 3513, 27 La. Ann. 14 (1871), 61, Earl K. Long Library, University of New Orleans.

184 **"my general reputation in the community":** Ibid., 11, 10.

185 **"Finnegan and Conklin who were with me":** Ibid., 11.

185 **"I did not know that Sauvinet was a colored man":** Ibid., 69.

186 **"Have you not stated":** Ibid., 63.

186 **"the Plaintiff is reputed to be":** Ibid., 14.

186 **"in full consonance . . . with the thirteenth":** "The 'Bank' Coffeehouse—Suit of Sauvinet—Judgment of Judge Dibble," *New Orleans Republican*, April 28, 1871.

186 **"the plaintiff show[ed] an infringement":** "The 'Bank' Coffeehouse—Suit of Sauvinet."

186 **one of over a dozen lawsuits:** John W. Blassingame, *Black New Orleans 1860–1880* (Chicago: University of Chicago Press, 1973), 184.

187 **had been worked by over a hundred slaves:** Eric Foner, *Reconstruc-*

tion: America's Unfinished Revolution, 1863–1877 (New York: Harper & Row, 1988), 47.

187 **"mental pain, shame, and mortification":** *DeCuir v. Benson*, Supreme Court of LA, No. 4829 (1873), 5, Earl K. Long Library, University of New Orleans.

188 **mockingly referred to the ship's colored cabin as the "Freedmen's Bureau":** Ibid., 99.

188 **the color of a "law book":** Ibid., 176.

188 **"the difference between a white man and a colored man":** Ibid., 175.

188 **"if I did [it was only because] I didn't know":** Ibid., 29.

188 **"The plaintiff in this case":** Ibid., 218.

189 **"You come to some landing":** King, *The Great South*, 72.

190 **"here we found a decided change":** Elizabeth Hyde Botume, quoted in Joel Williamson, *After Slavery: The Negro in South Carolina During Reconstruction 1861–1877*, 3rd ed. (New York: W. W. Norton, 1975), 283.

191 **"Africanization":** James Pike, *The Prostrate State: South Carolina Under Negro Government* (New York: D. Appleton, 1874), 4.

191 **"the most ignorant democracy":** Ibid., 12.

191 **"Destruction of the South Carolina University":** Ibid., 79.

191 **"capture by the blacks is a useless humiliation":** Ibid., 81.

191 **"There is really no way of knowing":** Ibid., 32.

192 **"Think of Patrick and Sambo":** Elizabeth Cady Stanton, quoted in Barbara Goldsmith, *Other Powers: The Age of Suffrage, Spiritualism, and the Scandalous Victoria Woodhull* (New York: Alfred A. Knopf, 1998), 181.

193 **"enjoined it upon his children":** *Congressional Record, Proceedings and Debates of the 43rd Congress, Session I* (Washington, DC: Government Printing Office, 1874), 555.

193 **"If the [white] people are let alone":** Ibid.

193 **"[Congressman Vance] cited, on the school question":** Ibid., 565.

194 **"I cannot view [this bill] through the same optics":** Ibid., 343–44.

195 **"[It is] one of the largest and wealthiest districts":** *Congressional Record, Proceedings and Debates of the 43rd Congress, Session II* (Washington, DC: Government Printing Office, 1875), 945.

195 **"Think of it for a moment":** Ibid.

196 **"You may ask why we do not institute civil suits":** Ibid.

196 **"There is not an inn":** *Congressional Record, Proceedings and Debates of the 43rd Congress, Session I*, 4782.

197 **"I left home last year":** Ibid., 4784.

197 **"I venture to say":** Ibid., 4785.

197 **"These negro-haters would not open school-house"**: Ibid., 382.

198 **"Why this fear of the negro"**: *Appendix to the Congressional Globe, Second Session, 42nd Congress, Part VI, Appendix* (Washington, DC: F. & J. Rives & George A. Baily, 1872), 15–16.

198 **"I believe God designed us"**: *Congressional Record, Proceedings and Debates of the 43rd Congress, Session I*, 903.

198 **"Let the civil-rights bill be passed"**: Ibid., 566.

199 **"If my Works were completed"**: Charles Sumner, quoted in Bertram Wyatt-Brown. "The Civil Rights Act of 1875," *Western Political Quarterly* 18, no. 4 (1965): 769–70.

199 **"educators ... executors and promoters"**: Richard T. Greener, "Charles Sumner: The Idealist, Statesman and Scholar: An Address delivered on Public Day, June 29, 1874, at the Request of the Faculty of the University of South Carolina" (Columbia, SC: Republican Printing Company, 1874?), 8–9, 41,

200 **"a grand *coup* on the white people"**: "A Black League," *Daily Picayune*, June 30, 1874.

200 **"The right of suffrage was"**: "The White League," *Daily Picayune*, July 2, 1874.

200 **"the crime against nature itself"**: J. Dickson Burns, *Address to the White League* (New Orleans: A. W. Hyatt, 1875), 6.

201 **"our hereditary civilization and Christianity"**: "The White League," *Daily Picayune*, July 2, 1874.

201 **while dominated by Anglo-Saxon last names**: *Roster of the 1st Crescent City Regiment* (New Orleans: James Buckley, 1877).

201 **"one must be either WHITE OR BLACK"**: *"D'un coté ou de l'autre," Le Carillon*, July 13, 1873. Translation courtesy of Nathaniel Dennett.

202 **"Our fellow Spanish citizens"**: *Le Carillon*, quoted in Virginia R. Domínguez, *White by Definition: Social Classification in Creole Louisiana* (New Brunswick, NJ: Rutgers University Press, 1993), 141, 294.

202 **"a touch of the tarbrush"**: Ibid., 141.

202 **"last summer one hundred of us"**: J. Dickson Burns, quoted in Foner, *Reconstruction*, 551.

203 **"no harm is meant towards you"**: "Proclamation," *Daily Picayune*, September 15, 1874.

204 **eleven Metropolitan Police officers lay dead**: Joe Gray Taylor, *Louisiana Reconstructed, 1863–1877* (Baton Rouge: Louisiana State University Press, 1974), 294.

204 **"The city in the hands of the insurgents"**: "The Week," *The Nation*, September 24, 1874.

205 **"armed with broomsticks"**: Marion Hoey, diary, 1874, Hoey Family Papers, The Historic New Orleans Collection.

205 **"hooting of Judge Dibble"**: "The Boys and the School Imbroglio," *Daily Picayune*, December 19, 1874.

205 **"mixture of all shades and colors"**: Eugene Lawrence, "Color in the New Orleans Schools," *Harper's*, February 13, 1875.

206 **"several Jewish maidens, touched with the olive tint"**: Ibid.

206 **"parents [of the] Israelite children"**: "The Week," *Weekly Louisianan* (New Orleans), December 26, 1874.

206 **"Do you know who I am?"**: Lawrence, "Color in the New Orleans Schools." *Harper's*, February 13, 1875.

207 **"make no further attempt"**: Ibid.

207 **"General Beauregard . . . leant his aid"**: Ibid.

207 **"If the movement against mixed schools"**: "The Schools," *New Orleans Republican*, December 19, 1874.

208 **"If any State or its authorities"**: "A New Civil Rights Bill," *New-York Tribune*, December 17, 1874.

208 **"inns, public conveyances on land or water"**: "The Civil Rights Bill," *New York Times*, March 2, 1875.

209 **"The negroes in this part of the country"**: "Can the Civil Rights Bill Be Enforced?" *New York Times*, March 6, 1875.

210 **"It is preposterous to allow"**: "The Week," *The Nation*, February 1, 1872.

210 **"The negroes of the South, being mainly occupied"**: "The Week," *The Nation*, March 4, 1875.

210 **"The New York *Nation* [has] intimated"**: Richard T. Greener, "Civil Rights Again," *Daily Union-Herald* (Columbia, SC). January 12, 1875.

9. THE GREAT BETRAYAL

215 **"go[ing] into the country"**: Philip Dray, *Capitol Men: The Epic Story of Reconstruction Through the Lives of the First Black Congressmen* (Boston: Houghton Mifflin, 2008), 143.

216 **"No State shall make or enforce"**: U.S. Const. Amendment XIV, § 1, cl. 2.

217 **"The right of citizens of the United States to vote"**: U.S. Const. Amendment XV, § 1, cl. 1.

217 **"The Fifteenth Amendment to the Constitution does not confer"**: Majority opinion, *United States v. Reese*, 92 U.S. 214 (1875), https://supreme.justia.com/cases/federal/us/92/214/case.html.

217 **"The whole public are tired out"**: John Y. Simon, *The Papers of Ulysses S. Grant*, Vol. 26: 1875 (Carbondale: Southern Illinois University Press, 2003), 312.

218 **"What Was Done in Mississippi"**: Nicholas Lemann, *Redemption: The Last Battle of the Civil War* (New York: Farrar, Straus and Giroux, 2006), 172.

218 **"Every Democrat must feel honor bound"**: Dray, *Capitol Men*, 249–50.

220 **one thousand African-Americans and five hundred whites**: "The Negro Spirit." *New York Times*, July 21, 1876.

220 **"This is no Hamburg!"**: "The Meeting Last Night," *News and Courier* (Charleston, SC).

221 **"Although many miles from the scene of action"**: "The Meaning of Hamburg," *New York Times*, July 24, 1876.

221 **"Carolina, Home of the White Man"**: Richard Zuczek, *State of Rebellion: Reconstruction in South Carolina* (Columbia: University of South Carolina Press, 1996), 173.

222 **"Withdraw [y]our patronage"**: Bernard E. Powers, *Black Charlestonians: A Social History, 1822–1885* (Fayetteville: University of Arkansas Press, 1999), 114.

222 **"white men [to] walk"**: Zuczek, *State of Rebellion*, 168.

222 **"I pledge my faith that if we are elected"**: Dray, *Capitol Men*, 254.

222 **"bloodless coercion"**: Zuczek, *State of Rebellion*, 167.

223 **"scare[d] the darkies and astonish[ed] the Governor"**: Ibid., 174

224 **"deception[,] force [and] fraud"**: Ibid., 189–90.

224 **"Organized clubs of masked, armed men"**: W. E. B. DuBois, *Black Reconstruction in America* (New York: Harcourt, Brace, 1935), 483.

225 **"It ha[s] done the Negro no good"**: Ulysses S. Grant, quoted in Eric Foner, *Reconstruction: America's Unfinished Revolution, 1863–1877* (New York: Harper & Row, 1988), 577.

226 **"The use of the military forces in civil affairs"**: Rutherford B. Hayes, quoted in Zuczek, *State of Rebellion*, 199.

226 **"go back on us"**: Foner, *Reconstruction*, 582.

226 **appoint nearly a hundred men of color**: Thomas Holt, *Black Over White: Negro Political Leadership in South Carolina during Reconstruction* (Urbana: University of Illinois Press, 1977), 211.

227 **"had done as well as any of the great men"**: Edwin L. Green, *A History of the University of South Carolina* (Columbia, SC: State Company, 1916), 414.

227 **"name the Caucasian races"**: T. N. Roberts, "History," 1877, South Caroliniana Library, University of South Carolina, Columbia, http://digital.tcl.sc.edu/cdm/singleitem/collection/sse/id/191/rec/37.

227 **"Negro Regime"**: Clariosophic Literary Society Records, 1873–1882, South Caroliniana Library, University of South Carolina.

228 **"dirty and infamous . . . so-called professors"**: "General Legislative Proceedings," *Edgefield Advertiser*, May 31, 1877.

229 **"to politically guillotine"**: James Connor, quoted in W. Lewis Burke, "Post-Reconstruction Justice: The Prosecution and Trial of Francis Lewis Cardozo," *South Carolina Law Review* 53, no. 361 (2002): 372.

229 **"eyes became dilated"**: Ibid., 400.

230 **"organized frivolity"**: Robert M. Lusher, *Diary*, February 13, 1877 (unpublished manuscript), Louisiana and Lower Mississippi Valley Collections, Louisiana State University, Baton Rouge.

230 **"five or six more years"**: Annual Report of the Superintendent of Public Education, 1874 (New Orleans: The Republican Office, 1874), 11.

230 **"so as to prevent the Radical Board of Directors"**: Robert Mills Lusher, *Autobiography of Robert Mills Lusher* (unpublished manuscript) 25, Louisiana and Lower Mississippi Valley Collections, Louisiana State University, Baton Rouge.

230 **"unwise and unnecessary . . . obstacle"**: Annual Report of the Superintendent of Public Education (New Orleans: The Office of the Democrat, 1878), iv, The Historic New Orleans Collection.

231 **"I have earnestly sought to obliterate the color line"**: "Gov. Nicholls to the Commission," *Daily Picayune*, April 20, 1877.

231 **"personal observation and universal testimony concur"**: "School Board," *Daily Picayune*, June 23, 1877.

231 **"giv[ing] the best education possible"**: William B. Woods, *Bertonneau v. Board of Directors of City Schools*, Circuit Court, D. Louisiana, Nov. Term, 1878. law.resource.org/pub/us/case/reporter/F.Cas/0003.f.cas/ 0003.f.cas.0294.2.pdf

231 **"nine-tenths of both races"**: "School Board," *Daily Picayune*, June 23, 1877.

232 **according to (likely inflated) news reports, $20 million**: "The Color Line in Louisiana," *New York Times*, June 27, 1877.

233 **"We have come to you, sir"**: "Mixed Schools," *Daily Picayune*, June 27, 1877.

233 **"I have not before"**: Ibid.

233 **"I believe the constitution says"**: Ibid.

233 **"I disagree with you"**: Ibid.

234 **"Governor, that the rights, the liberties"**: Ibid.

234 **"I believe it dangerous in a community like this"**: Ibid.

235 **"an English lord"**: Daniel Sharfstein, *The Invisible Line: Three American Families and the Secret Journey from Black to White* (New York: Penguin Press, 2011), 62.

235 **"Governor, put your prejudices aside"**: "Mixed Schools," *Daily Picayune*, June 27, 1877.

235 **"If a point of violation"**: Ibid.

235 **"The colored committee"**: "The Color Line in Louisiana," *New York Times*, June 27, 1877.

236 **"that I accept the civil and political equality"**: "School Board," *Daily Picayune*, July 4, 1877.

236 **vote of fifteen to three**: Ibid.

236 **"no distinction shall exist among citizens"**: "He Asks for Mixed Schools," *New Orleans Times*, September 27, 1877.

237 **"for advanced colored students"**: Annual Report of the Superintendent of Public Education, 253.

237 **"It has long been apparent"**: Ibid., v.

238 **"a citizen of the United States"**: "Dissolved," *Daily Picayune*, October 24, 1877.

239 **"cannot assume either the tasks or the prerogatives"**: Ibid.

239 **"This case is one of great magnitude"**: Paul Trévigne, quoted in Mary Niall Mitchell, *Raising Freedom's Child: Black Children and Visions of the Future After Slavery* (New York: New York University Press, 2008), 224.

240 **"Your children are colored?"**: *State ex. Rel. Ursin Dellande v. City School Board*, No. 9784 (1878), (Earl K. Long Library, University of New Orleans).

240 **"not belong exclusively"**: "Mixed Schools," *Daily Picayune*, May 21, 1878.

241 **"to be educated [in any public school]"**: "The Courts," *New Orleans Times*, November 29, 1877.

242 **"Both races are treated precisely alike"**: Woods, *Bertonneau v. Board of Directors of City Schools*, Circuit Court, D. Louisiana, 1878.

10. FADE TO BLACK AND WHITE

245 **"The gallery is for colored people"**: Cornelius Chapman Scott to Tobias Scott, April 8, 1880, Cornelius Chapman Scott Papers (South Caroliniana Library, University of South Carolina, Columbia).

246 **"I shall not undertake to bring"**: Ibid.

247 **"If the public good requires such legislation"**: *Hall v. DeCuir*, 95 U.S. 485 (1878).

247 **"all persons within the jurisdiction of the United States"**: Civil Rights Act of 1875, 18 Stat. 335.

247 **thirteen of the 133 delegats**: Garnie W. McGinty, *Louisiana Redeemed* (New Orleans: Pelican Publishing, 1941), 222.

247 **"no qualification of any kind for suffrage"**: Louisiana Const. of 1879, art. 188.

248 **one of the ten largest cities in America:** United States Census 1880.

249 **"to invoke the Civil Rights laws is becoming very fashionable":** "Equal Rights in Trade and Travel," *New York Times*, November 29, 1879.

250 **"every act of discrimination which a person":** Civil Rights Cases, 109 U.S. 3 (1883).

251 **"I cannot resist the conclusion":** Ibid.

252 **"wild scene in the [Atlanta] opera-house":** "General Telegraph News: The Civil Rights Decision. Divided Feeling in Atlanta on the Vexed Question," *New York Times*, October 18, 1883.

252 **"A Radical Relic Rubbed Out":** "Civil Rights," *Atlanta Constitution*, October 16, 1883.

253 **"Our government is a farce":** Valeria W. Weaver, "The Failure of Civil Rights 1875–1883 and Its Repercussions," *Journal of Negro History* 54, no. 4 (1969): 371.

253 **"the most startling decision of the Supreme Court":** "The Civil-Rights Act," *Evening Post* (New York), October 16, 1883.

253 **"I myself would rather be deprived":** Ibid.

254 **"black and curly hair":** Ira Berlin, *Slaves Without Masters: The Free Negro in the Antebellum South* (New York: Pantheon, 1974), 365–66.

255 **"I attribute a great deal of our present depression":** *Journal of the Eighty-Sixth Annual Convention of the Protestant Episcopal Church in the Diocese of South Carolina* (Charleston: Walker, Evans & Cogswell, 1876), 60.

256 **"They call everybody a negro":** *South Carolina in 1876: Testimony as to the Denial of the Elective Franchise in South Carolina at the Elections of 1875 and 1876,* vol. 1 (Washington, DC: Government Printing Office, 1877), 234.

256 **"impossible to comprehend how so many intelligent people":** Charles Gayarré, *The Creoles of History and the Creoles of Romance: A Lecture* (New Orleans: Crescent Steam Print, 1885), 3, 2, 3.

257 **"descendants of the original Creoles of Louisiana":** Creole Association of Louisiana, *Charter, By-Laws & Rules of the Creole Association of Louisiana* (New Orleans: Crescent Steam Print, 1886), 14, 4, 14, The Historic New Orleans Collection.

257 **hundreds of mixed-race Louisianans became "white" every year:** John W. Blassingame, *Black New Orleans: 1860–1880* (Chicago: University of Chicago Press, 1973), 201.

257 **"proprietors are men of as pure Caucasian blood as any":** Rodolphe Desdunes, quoted in Blair Kelley, *Right to Ride: Streetcar Boycotts and African-American Citizenship in the Era of* Plessy v. Ferguson (Chapel Hill: University of North Carolina Press, 2010), 61.

258 **"promote the comfort of passengers in railway trains"**: *Official Journal of the Proceedings of House of Representatives of the State of Louisiana* (Baton Rouge: The Advocate, 1890), 60.

258 **"in communities where lawlessness exists"**: Kelley, *Right to Ride*, 63.

258 **"unconstitutional, un-American [and] unjust"**: *Official Journal of the Proceedings of House of Representatives*, 127.

259 **only sixteen**: C. Vann Woodward, "*Plessy v. Ferguson*: The Birth of Jim Crow," *American Heritage* 15, no. 3 (April 1964).

259 **"the prejudices of . . . intellectual dwarfs"**: *Official Journal of the Proceedings of House of Representatives*, 203, 202.

260 **"Chinamen and Dagoes"**: Ibid., 204.

260 **"more obnoxious than most colored persons"**: Ibid., 410.

260 **"When this bill shall have passed"**: "Speech of Hon. Henry Demas, on the Separate Car Bill, Delivered in the Senate, at Baton Rouge, La., July 8, '90," *Crusader* (New Orleans), July 19, 1890.

260 **"thousands good and true men petition you"**: Louis Martinet, quoted in "The Separate Car Bill," *Crusader* (New Orleans), July 19, 1890.

260 **"We'll make a case, a test case"**: Carolyn L. Karcher, *A Refugee from His Race: Albion W. Tourgée and His Fight against White Supremacy* (Chapel Hill: University of North Carolina Press, 2016), 254.

261 **"every manner of outrage"**: Kelley, *Right to Ride*, 71.

261 **"legal resistance"**: "The Violation of a Constitutional Right," Pamphlet, Citizens' Committee (New Orleans: The Crusader Print, 1893), 2, Amistad Research Center, Tulane University, New Orleans.

261 **"seat[s] in Congress or [the] opera-house"**: Booker T. Washington, Speech at the Atlanta Exposition, 1895, http://historymatters.gmu .edu/d/39/, accessed January 26, 2018.

263 **"There are the strangest white people you ever saw here"**: Louis Martinet, quoted in Otto Olsen, *The Thin Disguise: Turning Point in Negro History. Plessy v. Ferguson—A Documentary Presentation, 1864–1896* (New York: Humanities Press, 1967), 56–57.

264 **"the Jim Crow car is ditched"**: "Jim Crow Is Dead," *New Orleans Daily Crusader*, July 16, 1892.

265 **"as white as the average white Southerner"**: Untitled, undated clip on the arrest of Homer A. Plessy, *New Orleans Daily Crusader*, 1892, Rodolphe Desdunes Papers, Xavier University, New Orleans.

266 **"great research, learning, and ability"**: Olsen, *The Thin Disguise*, 14.

266 **"created no new rights"**: Ibid., 73.

267 **"singular coincidence that many of the very wealthy"**: "A Wealthy Negro's Suicide," *New York Times*, May 16, 1893.

268 *"Separate cars,* and *separate schools"*: Samuel F. Phillips, quoted in Olsen, *The Thin Disguise,* 106.

268 **"The claim that this act is for the common advantage":** Albion W. Tourgée, quoted in Mark Elliott and John David Smith, eds., *Undaunted Radical: The Selected Writings and Speeches of Albion W. Tourgée* (Baton Rouge: Louisiana State University Press, 2010), 333.

268 **"meant to undo all that slavery had done":** Ibid., 324.

268 **"the establishment of a statutory difference":** Ibid., 297.

268 **"Is not the question of race, scientifically considered":** Ibid., 297.

268 **"the autocrat of Caste":** Ibid., 326.

268 **"carry a certified copy of his pedigree":** Ibid., 335.

269 **"Justice is pictured blind":** Ibid., 310.

269 **"I was born of a New England Puritan family":** Henry Billings Brown, *Memoir of Henry Billings Brown* (New York: Duffield & Company, 1915), 1.

269 **"in the nature of things":** *Plessy v. Ferguson,* 163 U.S. 537 (1896).

270 **"if enforced according to their true intent":** Ibid.

270 **"There is no caste here":** Ibid.

270 **"Notwithstanding this decision":** *Report of Proceedings for the Annulment of Act 111 of 1890* (New Orleans: Thomas & Panalle, n.d.), 7, Amistad Research Center, Tulane University.

271 **"the judgment this day rendered will, in time":** *Plessy v. Ferguson,* 163 U.S. 537 (1896).

272 **"there [i]s not a full-blooded Caucasian":** "ALL NIGGERS, MORE OR LESS!" *News and Courier* (Charleston, SC), October 17, 1895.

272 **"We think . . . that any candid mind":** *State v. Treadaway,* 52 So. 500 (1910), quoted in Charles Frank Robinson II, *Dangerous Liaisons: Sex and Love in the Segregated South* (Fayetteville: University of Arkansas Press, 2003), 91.

272 **"a person of the negro or black race":** Virginia R. Domínguez, *White by Definition: Social Classification in Creole Louisiana* (New Brunswick, NJ: Rutgers University Press, 1993), 29.

273 **"white, black, mulatto, quadroon [or] octoroon":** All of the census race questions from 1790 to the present are compiled at www.racebox.org (consulted February 8, 2017).

273 **the number of African-American policemen in Charleston:** William Archer, *Through Afro-America: An English Reading of the Race Problem* (London: Chapman & Hall, 1910), 170.

273 **about half the city force:** Bernard E. Powers, *Black Charlestonians: A Social History, 1822–1885* (Fayetteville: University of Arkansas Press, 1999), 242.

273 **nearly two hundred:** W. Marvin Dulaney, *Black Police in America* (Bloomington: Indiana University Press, 1996), 17.

274 **"Colored . . . republicans may here be allowed to vote":** *Congressional Record Containing the Proceedings and Debates of the Special Sessions of the Senate of the Forty-Seventh Congress*, vol. 12 (Washington, DC: Government Printing Office, 1881), 120.

274 **"Only one member (a doctor) was dark-brown":** Archer, *Through Afro-America*, 170, 172–73.

274 **funded at plausibly comparable levels:** George Brown Tindall, *South Carolina Negroes: 1877–1900* (Columbia: University of South Carolina Press, 1952), 216.

275 **"demonstrat[e] the superiority of the white man":** Harry Wilson, quoted in William Ivy Hair, *Carnival of Fury* (Baton Rouge: Louisiana State University Press, 1976), 139.

275 **"There are colored persons of wealth":** Kelley, *Right to Ride*, 95, 94.

276 **"divid[e] their cars by a wooden partition":** "Mr. Stanley Presents an Ordinance to Separate Races," *Daily Picayune*, September 12, 1900.

276 **"I regard the proposed separate car ordinance":** "Railways Oppose Separate Car Law," *New Orleans Times-Democrat*, October 20, 1900.

276 **"tamper with existing conditions?":** Ibid.

277 **"Under the ordinance":** Ibid.

277 **"this absurd proposition":** Ibid.

277 **"a dangerous game to play":** *Southwestern Christian Advocate*, quoted in Kelley, *Right to Ride*, 95–96.

277 **a vote of twelve to four:** "Separate Cars Measure Beaten," *Daily Picayune*, October 24, 1900.

277 **"The measure is brought forward":** *Southwestern Christian Advocate*, quoted in Kelley, *Right to Ride*, 102.

278 **"for the purpose of determining upon some concerted course of action":** "Negroes Take Action," *Daily Picayune*, July 31, 1902.

278 **"almost everyone said it looked ridiculous":** "Screens Separate the Races in Street Cars," *Daily Picayune*, November 4, 1902.

278 **"[hearing his response,] the conductor's face wore":** "New 'Jim Crow' Law Becomes Operative," *Times-Democrat* (New Orleans), November 4, 1902.

280 **"flexible" plan:** "Race Separation on Street Cars," *Charleston Evening Post*, July 22, 1912.

280 **"was not likely to cause any race feeling":** "Mayor Favors Flexible Plan," *Charleston News and Courier*, July 26, 1912.

280 **"At one time, mulattos who looked like white[s]":** Mamie Garvin Fields with Karen Fields, *Lemon Swamp and Other Places: A Carolina Memoir* (New York: Free Press, 1983), 64.

280 **"We used to get together in pairs":** Ibid., 65.

281 **"There are no races":** W. E. B, Du Bois. "The Superior Race," *The Smart Set*, April 1923.

CONCLUSION: LIVING THE LIE

285 **"fine command of English":** "Prof. Greener's Lecture," *News and Courier* (Charleston), November 26, 1907.

285 **"keys to all of the [executive offices as well as] important messages":** "'Willis,' Aged University Janitor, Oldest Employe and Himself Alumnus, Stricken on Campus Early, and Dies." *The Record* (Columbia) January 28, 1927.

286 **"No names!":** Michael Robert Mounter, "Richard Theodore Greener: The idealist, statesman, scholar and South Carolinian" (unpublished PhD diss., University of South Carolina, 2002), 487, South Caroliniana Library, University of South Carolina, Columbia.

287 **Homer Plessy, was officially "white":** United States Census, 1920.

287 **"a mulatto, who had evidently inherited":** Thomas Dixon Jr., *The Clansman: An Historical Romance of the Ku Klux Klan* (New York: Doubleday, 1905), 93.

288 **"placard[s of] the Civil Rights Bill":** Ibid., 353.

289 **"inns, restaurants, hotels, eating houses":** Charles McClain, "California Carpetbagger: The Career of Henry Dibble," *Quinnipiac Law Review* 28, no. 4 (2010): 954.

289 **"all principals be directed to receive all colored children":** Robert J. Swan, "Thomas McCants Stewart and the Failure of the Mission of the Talented Tenth in Black America, 1880–1923" (unpublished PhD diss., New York University, 1990), 160, Brooklyn Historical Society.

290 **"Notwithstanding this decision":** *Report of Proceedings for the Annulment of Act 111 of 1890* (New Orleans: Thomas and Panalle, n.d.), 7, Amistad Research Center, Tulane University.

BIBLIOGRAPHIC NOTE

291 ***New battles.—After Buddha was dead":*** Friedrich Nietzsche, *The Gay Science*, ed. Bernard Williams, trans. Josephine Nauckhoff (Cambridge, UK: Cambridge University Press, 2001), 109.

291 **"It's up to you":** James Baldwin, quoted in *James Baldwin: The Price of the Ticket*, documentary film, directed by Karen Thorsen (Nobody Knows Productions, Maysles Films, Inc., 1990).

INDEX

Page numbers in *italics* refer to illustrations.

academics:
  after Civil War, 55
  desegregation of, *see* schools,
    desegregation of
  for free people of color, 19
  race restrictions in, in New
    Orleans, 24
  racism in curriculum in, 227
  and streetcar desegregation, 103
  University of South Carolina, *see*
    University of South Carolina
Academy of Music (Charleston,
    South Carolina), 181–82, 279
"accident of color," 147
ACERA (American Citizens' Equal
    Rights Association), 258
activism:
  antiracist, xvii, xviii
  in Charleston, 83–85
  for desegregation, 182
  for equal rights, 42–44, 83–84
  following Black Code, 73–74
  in Jim Crow era, 289–90
  see also protests
"Act to Protect All Citizens in Their
    Civil and Legal Rights, A" (Dib-
    ble), 288–89
Adams, Dock, 219
Adams, Thomas E., 73, 102
African-Americans:
  attending constitutional conven-
    tions, 107–8, 112–14, 118–19
  and Benjamin Butler, 39–40
  in Charleston after emancipation,
    49
  and civil rights legislation, 192
  in Congress, 175
  and desegregations of schools, *see*
    schools, desegregation of
  and police brutality, 59
  as police officers, 180–81, 273–74
  protests by, 83–85, 101; *see also*
    activism
  resegregation fought by, 232–34, 278
  as soldiers, 88–89; *see also* Native
    Guards

African-Americans (*continued*)
  traditions of, in New Orleans, 100
  violence against, for political activ-
    ity, 74–76, 119–20, 218, 224
  and voter intimidation, 247
  voting rights, *see* African-American
    suffrage; voting rights
African-American suffrage:
  Bertonneau/Roudanez fight for,
    45–46
  and 1868 Louisiana state constitu-
    tion, 108
  and Fifteenth Amendment to the
    U.S. Constitution, 121
  following Black Code, 64, 66, 74
  and New Orleans Riot, 76
  see also voting rights
Alabama, 94, 118
Alcorn University, 161
Américains, 10, 17
  and Mardi Gras, 142
  against resegregation, 276
  rise of, 20–21
  and school desegregation, 139,
    141–42
  on whiteness, 201–2
American Citizens' Equal Rights
  Association (ACERA), 258
American Revolution, 5
Anderson, Robert, 31, 33, 50
Anglo-Americans, 11, 17
"Anglo-Saxon," 201, 269
Antoine, Caesar C., 145
Arabs, as white, 202
Archer, Thomas, 274
Arthur, Chester A., 267
"Aryans," 227
Asian-Americans, as white, 260
Atlanta Constitution, 252–53
Atlantic Monthly, 113
Avery Institute, 154

Badger, Algernon, 144, 204
Banks, Nathaniel, 42, 44, 47

Barksdale, Ethelbert, 218
Baldwin, James, 291
Barnwell, Robert W., 158
Barracks School, 126–27
Baton Rouge, Louisiana, 248
Battery (neighborhood), 12–13
Battle of Shiloh, 37
Beaumont, Gustave de, 21–22
Beauregard, Pierre Gustave Toutant,
    29, 31–32
  and destruction of Charleston, 153
  on Radical Reconstruction, 79
  return to New Orleans, 56
  and streetcar desegregation, 99,
    103
  and Unification Movement, 146–
    47, 149, 202
Belden, Simeon, 238
Benson, John G., 188
Bertonneau, Arnold John, 286–87
Bertonneau, E. Arnold, *xix,* xxii
  civil rights court case with, 241
  lobbying for voting rights, xxi–
    xxiii, 44–46
  in Native Guard, 36
  and passing for white 286
  Sumner meeting with, 45, 89
"big tent of whiteness":
  Arabs under, 202
  Asian-Americans under, 260
  and binary terms, 259
  Hispanic-Americans under, 201
  Italian-Americans under, 260
  Jews under, 201, 253, 288
  Mediterranean-Americans under,
    201
  multiethnic congealment under,
    201–2, 259
  and racial passing, 234–35
  Spaniards under, 202
binary terms:
  Américains' notion of, 201
  development of, xvii–xviii; *see also*
    race, defining

and mixed-race populations, xvii, 6, 256
in New Orleans, 20
and one-drop rule, 273; *see also* one-drop rule
rejection of, 185, 259
and streetcar desegregation, 255
see also "big tent of whiteness"
biracial populations, 34, 61–62; *see also* mixed-race populations
biracial women, as head of households, 92
Birth of a Nation, The (Griffith), xvi, 288
black:
biological definition of, 62
legally, defining, 62
see also African-Americans
Black Code, 59–79
in Charleston, South Carolina, 59–63, 71
Congress fighting, 69–71
Johnson's view of, 67–69
mixed-race populations fighting, 63–64
in New Orleans, 64–65, 71
Northern backlash to, 66–67
overturning, 71
repeal of, 77
rights after overturning of, 77–79
violence after overturning of, 71–76
"black Negroes," 280
Booth, Edwin, 249
Booth, John Wilkes, xxii, 50, 68
Boseman, Benjamin, 155
Bowers, Mary P., 91–92, 96
Boyd, David F., 171, 211
Bradley, Joseph, 250
Brewer, Fisk P., 162, 168–70
Brooklyn, New York, 289
Brooks, Preston, 46, 114, 177, 199
Brown, C. F., 259
Brown, Henry Billings, 269

Brown, John, 25
Brown, William G., 139, 230
Brown Fellowship Society, 6–7, 19, 51, 62–63, 155, 256
Brown v. Board of Education of Topeka, 290
Bureau of Refugees, Freedmen, and Abandoned Lands, 69, 91–92, 94
Butler, Benjamin Franklin:
and Civil Rights Act (1875), 192, 208
mocking of, 144
occupying New Orleans during war, 38–41
on school desegregation, 127–28
and streetcar desegregation, 44, 88
Butler, Matthew, 220, 221

Cable, George Washington, 103, 139–41
Cain, Richard Harvey:
and Civil Rights Act (1875), 198
and civil rights protest, 220
at constitutional convention, 112–13
on race riots, in Charleston, 120
and Rutherford B. Hayes, 226
and school desegregation, 193
Cardozo, Benjamin Nathan, 288
Cardozo, Francis Lewis, 54–55, *57*
arrest of, 229–30
and Avery Institute, 154
at constitutional convention, 111–13, 116–18, 119
and desegregation of schools, 155, 164–66
in Jim Crow era, 287
and Republican Party reconstruction, 83–84
and streetcar segregation, 93–94
Caribbean, mixed-race children in, 4
Carillon, Le, 149–50, 201–2
"carpetbaggers," and Reconstruction state constitutions, 107, 114
Cassanave, Felix, 98

"Caucasian":
   and Creole, 256
   defining, 259
   and one-drop rule, 272
   and race determining, 188, 206
   and race mixing, 276
   and white supremacy, 128; *see also*
      white supremacists
"Celts," 162, 253
Charleston, South Carolina:
   activism in, 83–86, 182
   Black Code in, 59–63, 71
   civil rights enforcement in, 181–87
   after Civil War, 49–51
   during Civil War, 37–38, 48–49
   in colonial times, 3–4
   1868 South Carolina state consti-
      tutional convention in, 111–19
   elections in, 224–26
   in mid-nineteenth century, *1*
   mixed-race in, 12–15, 18–20, 280
   during Red Shirts violence, 221–22
   resegregation in, 273, 279
   streetcar segregation in, 83–86,
      88–89, 91–95, 279–81
   voter suppression in, 274
Charleston Browns, 12–14
   Black Code response by, 62
   after Civil War, 52
   and Howard University, 164
   and resegregation, 280
   supporting white power structure,
      27–28
   see also Charleston, South Caro-
      lina
Charleston City Railway Company,
   94–95
Charleston Daily Courier, 84–85
Charleston Daily News, 93
Charleston Daily Republican, 182
Charleston Mercury, 112–13
Chase, Salmon P., 52
Chesnut, Mary Boykin, 20
Chicago Tribune, 67

Citadel Green, 83–85, 95
citizenship, revocation of, xxi, 25–26;
   see also Dred Scott (court case)
City Railroad Company (New
   Orleans), 98–99
Civil Rights Act (1866), 69–71, 90,
   93, 96
Civil Rights Act (1875), 178–79, 190,
   192–99, 215, 245–47, 249
Civil Rights Cases (1883), 249–53
civil rights legislation, 175–211
   and African-Americans in political
      seats, 175–78
   court enforcement of, 182–90
   police enforcement of, 179–82, 226
   press against, 209–10
   response to, 208–9
   Senate debates for 193–98
   and school desegregation, 208
   Sumner push for, 178–79, 190–92
   and White League, 200
"Civil Rights of the Negro in the
   United States, 1865–1883" (Lofton), xv
Civil War, 31–56
   activism during, 42–44
   disputed meaning of, xxii–xxiv
   fight for equality following, 50–52
   free people of color position during,
      34–37
   mixed-race leaders in, 31–34
   mixed-race populations during, 34
   and Native Guard, 36–41
   racial landscape following, 52–56
   and streetcar access, 88–90
   voting rights during, 44–46
Claflin University, 227
Claiborne, William C. C., 9, 11
Clansman, The (Dixon), 287–88
Clay Club, 23
Cleveland, Grover, 267
Colfax massacre, 215–17
Colored Committee on Mixed
   Schools, 232

Comité des Citoyens, 260–63, 270–71, 290

Commission on Public Fraud (South Carolina), 228

Committee of One Hundred, 144–49

Committee on Education, at 1868 South Carolina state constitutional convention in Charleston, 116

concubinage, see plaçage

Confederate cause, free people of color support of, 34–36

Congo Square, 100

Conner, James, 223

constitutional conventions, post–Civil War, 107–21
  in Charleston, 111–19
  and desegregation of schools, 109–11, 115–18
  and desegregation of public accommodations, 108–9
  in New Orleans, 107–11, 119
  racial landscape of, 107–8, 111–12, 114

"contraband of war," slaves as, 38

contracts, labor, 65

Conway, Thomas, 128–29, 134, 136–37

Cooper, Ashley, 13

Corrupt Bargain, 226

Courcelle, Charles J., 180

Creoles of color, 9, 16
  as black, 27–28, 202
  civil rights of, 24
  after Civil War, 52–53, 55–56
  during Civil War, 38–39
  and desegregation of schools, 126
  and 1868 Louisiana state constitution, 107–8
  fight for civil rights by, 98–99
  mocking of, 123, 143–44
  and one-drop rule, 256–57
  as police officers, 181
  against resegregation, 276

and resegregation, 234, 237–38, 260

and streetcar rights, 88

Unification Movement resistance by, 149–50

see also New Orleans, Louisiana

Creole Association of Louisiana, 257

Crescent City White League, 201–2

Daily Phoenix (Columbia, South Carolina), 149, 158, 160, 167

Daily Picayune, The (New Orleans):
  on civil rights, 98, 200
  on free people of color, 26
  on Mardi Gras of 1873, 143
  and resegregation, 243
  on school desegregation, 140
  and soldier recruitment, 36

Daily True Delta (New Orleans), 90

Daily Union-Herald (Columbia, South Carolina), 157, 170

Darwin, Charles, 142–43

Davis, Jefferson, 31, 176

DeCuir, Josephine, 187–88, 246–47

DeLarge, Robert Carlos, 63, 83, 105, 112–13

Dellande, Ursin, 239–40

Democratic Party, 121
  African-Americans supporting, 222
  controlling Congress, 208
  and racial violence, 222–23
  and resegregation, 228
  and school desegregation, 172
  and voter intimidation, 218–19
  and White League, 202–3

Desdunes, Daniel, 263–64

Desdunes, Rodolphe, 257–58

desegregation:
  of Academy of Music (Charleston, South Carolina), 181–82
  and arguments over public safety, 93
  historical records of, xvi, 227
  of schools, see schools, desegregation of
  of streetcars, 101–3

Dibble, Henry:
  and desegregation of schools,
    136–38
  in Jim Crow era, 288–89
  and Nicholls court case, 97, 102
  and Sauvinet court case, 186
  and White League, 205
Dixon, Thomas, Jr., xvi, 287
Dostie, Anthony P., 74
Douglass, Frederick, 68
Dowling, J. J., 265
Dred Scott (court case), xxi
  effects of, 25, 59
  invalidating, 71
  and Revels, 176–77
  and transit systems rights, 88
Du Bois, W. E. B.:
  civil rights studies by, xvi
  on 1868 South Carolina state con-
    stitutional convention, 114
  on interracial marriage, 16
  on Louisiana Republican Party
    formation, 47
  on race, 281
  on social/economic differences
    among African-Americans in
    Louisiana, 108
Dubuclet, Antoine, 187
Ducloslange, P., 99
Ducoslange, Eugene, 205
Dumas, Francis E., 119
Dunn, Oscar J., 119
Dunning, William A., xvi
Durham, James J., 166–67
Dyer, Thomas W., 135

Eckhard, Sydney, 85–86, 91, 222
Eight Box Law (South Carolina), 248
elections:
  after Civil War, 64–65
  disputed, 175, 225–26, 274
  resegregation after, 230–42
  and voter suppression, 217–25
Elliott, Robert Brown, 116–17

emancipation, racial landscape fol-
    lowing, 50–53
Emancipation Proclamation, xxi, 42
"enticement," crime of, 65
equality, racial, see racial equality,
    fight for

Fairfield Herald (South Carolina),
    156
Farragut, David, 37
Ferguson, John Howard, 264
Fifteenth Amendment to the U.S.
    Constitution, 121, 175, 192, 217,
    225, 248–49
Fleet, Genevieve, 163
Fool's Errand, By One of the Fools, A
    (Tourgée), 262
Ford, John T., 182
former slaves:
  equal rights for, 53
  fight for equality by, 108
  free people of color collaborating
    with, 48, 62–63
  see also African-Americans
Forrest, Nathan Bedford, 120, 139
Fort Sumter, 31
Fourteenth Amendment to the U.S.
    Constitution, 71, 77, 216, 238,
    268
Franklin, Benjamin, 115
Freedman's Bureau, see Bureau of
    Refugees, Freedmen, and Aban-
    doned Lands
free people of color:
  as Charleston Browns, see Charles-
    ton Browns
  following Civil War, 51
  and Dred Scott, 25–26
  former slaves collaborating with,
    48, 62–63
  and interracial marriage, 16
  as middle class, 4–5, 12–13
  as New Orleans Creoles, see Cre-
    oles of color

in New Orleans, 10–11
and race mixing, 6–7, 16
see also African-Americans

Garrison, William Lloyd, 45
Gayarré, Charles, 256
George, James Z., 218
Georgia, legislators in, 119
Gibson, Randall Lee, *213,* 235
Gordon, George H., 240
Grace, John, 279–80
Grant, Ulysses S., 75, 121, 144,
    215–18, 225
Great Betrayal, 226
Great Compromise, 226
Greene, Belle da Costa, 286
Greener, Richard Theodore, *283*
    and civil rights legislation, 199,
        211, 253–54
    Red Shirt violence against, 221
    return to University of South Car-
        olina in 1907, 285–86
    on Sumner death, 199
    and University of South Carolina,
        162–64, 168
Griffith, D. W., xvi
Guillaume, Joseph, 99

Hahn, Michael, xxiii, 46, 74
Haitians, immigration of, 10–16
Hamburg, South Carolina, 219–20
"Hamites," 227
Hampton, Wade, 222–28, 244
Harlan, John Marshall, 251–52,
    270–71
Harlan, Robert, 251
Harper's Weekly, 75–76, 205–7
Harris, W. C., 259–60
Harvard, Greener attending, 162–63
Hayes, Rutherford B., 225
Hayne, Henry E., 35, *151*
    and the desegregation of the Uni-
        versity of South Carolina, 159,
        193

at 1868 South Carolina state consti-
    tutional convention, 112–13, 116
switching sides in Civil War, 48
Hayne, Paul Hamilton, 160
Hayne, Robert Y., 19, 35, 159–60
Hays, Harry T., 73
Heath, Edward, 99–100, 102, 180
"Hebrews," 253; *see also* Jews
Higgins, E. A., 278
higher education, desegregation in,
    110; *see also* University of South
    Carolina, desegregation of
Holloway, Richard, 181
Holmes, Thomas M., 62
Horton, Jotham, 75
Howard, John, 136
Howard University, xv, 164–66, 285
Humane Brotherhood, *see* Society of
    Free Dark Men
Hunt, Caleb, 175

immigration, 191–92
industrialization, after Civil War, 51
integration, *see* desegregation
interracial marriage and cohabita-
    tion, 15–16, 23–24, 61, 64–66,
    70, 77, 190, 255–56, 268, 272
Invisible Empire (Tourgée), 262
Isabelle, Robert, 134–36, 182, 183
Isabelle, William R., 135–36

Jefferson, Thomas, 8, 9, 27, 43, 192,
    219, 254
Jenkins, Maria, 88
Jennings, Elizabeth, 87–88
Jews:
    civil rights for, 14, 250
    nineteenth-century view of, 33–34
    against resegregation, 276
    and segregation, 253
    as white, 201–2, 206, 288
Jim Crow, xvii
    binary racial terms from, xvii–xviii
    and bloodline policing, 271

Jim Crow (*continued*)
   and railcar segregation, 261–65
   and streetcar segregation, 275-81
   white civil rights supporters slan-
     dered during, 107
Johnson, Andrew, 67–71, 73, 78, 121,
   176

Keating, Josephine, 206–7
Keelan, James, 43
King, Edward, 22, 159–60, 166, 181,
   189–90
Ku Klux Klan:
   murders of African-American
     policemen by, 273
   formation of, 120
   Tournament of Roses parade and,
     287
   Rainey threatened by, 179
   and voter intimidation, 172
   and White League, 200

labor contracts, for freed slaves, 65
Lacroix, Victor, 76, 107
land rights, 53, 63
la raza, 3
Latin America, colonial racial system
   of, 3
Laurens, Edward, 14
Lee, Robert E., xxii, 49
"legally black," defining, 62
"legally white," 19
legislation, civil rights, *see* civil
   rights legislation
Leslie, Charles P., 116
Lewis, John L., 37
Lincoln, Abraham:
   assassination of, xxiii, 50, 67
   background of, xxii
   election of, 26
   and Emancipation Proclamation,
     xxi, 42
   perception of, 43
   on racial purity, 66
   and voting rights, xxiii, 45–46

literacy, and voting rights, 64
Lofton, Williston Henry, xv–xvi
Longstreet, James, 203–4
Louisville Bulletin, 253
Louisiana, *see* New Orleans, Louisiana
Louisiana Civil Code (1808), 23
Lowndes, Thomas Pinckney, 79
Loyal National League of Louisiana, 43
Lusher, Robert Mills, 128–29, 138–
   39, 230–31, 236–37
Lynch, John R., 194–96

Mardi Gras, 142–43, 230
Marks, Isaac Newton, 145–46,
   148–49
Marr, R. H., 216
marriage, interracial, *see* interracial
   marriage
Martinet, Louis A., 232, 236, 257,
   260, 262
Mary, Aristide, 145, 232–34, 260, 267
McInnis, Daniel, 85–86, 91
McKinlay, William J., 112–13, 223
Melton, Cyrus D., 158
Memphis, Tennessee, 72
Menard, John Willis, 175
Metropolitan Police, 144, 180, 203–4,
   216
Mettasca, Josephine, 126–27
middle class, mixed-race as, 4–5, 8
miscegenation, *see* interracial
   marriage
Mississippi:
   Black Code in, 61
   1868 state constitution, 118
   school desegregation attempt in,
     161
   voter intimidation in, 118, 218
Mississippi Plan, 218
Mistick Krewe of Comus, 142–44, 230
Mitchell, William "Willis," 285
mixed-race populations, 3–28
   and ACERA, 258
   attending constitutional conven-
     tions, 107–8, 112

in Charleston, *see* Charleston, South Carolina
during Civil War, 40–43, 44–45, 47, 48
Confederate support by, 34–36
in Congress, 175-179, 192–99
development/acceptance of, 3–6, 8–18
and *Dred Scott,* xxi, 25–26
in Jim Crow era, 280–81, 285–90
in New Orleans, *see* New Orleans, Louisiana
and one-drop rule, 256–57, 286
race classifications of, 21–22, 254–55, 271–73
and resegregation, 280–81
restrictions to, 7–8, 17–21, 23–25, 47
see also biracial populations
Mobile, Alabama, 94, 181
mob rule, 71–72, 204; *see also* race riots
Monfort, Eulalie Marie Adelaide, 241
Monroe, John T., 73, 76
"Moors," 202
Morgan, J. P., 286
Moses, Franklin J., Jr.:
arrest of, 229
and Confederate service, 33–34, 50
at constitutional convention, 114
and desegregation of schools, 155–56, 162, 171
Mossof, J. H., 188
"mulatresses," in Charleston and New Orleans, 92
"mulatto":
and Black Codes, 61
blacks aligned with, 52
defined, 254
in 1890 census, 273
and interracial marriages, 16, 20, 70, 254
and school desegregation, 171
"mustee," defined, 254

Nation, The, 52, 210, 253
Native Guards, 39–41
"Negro," defining, 259, 272; *see also* African-Americans
Newman, J. K., 276
New Orleans, Louisiana:
biracial rights in, 10
Black Code in, 65, 71
civil rights enforcement in, 183–84
after Civil War, 52–53, 55–56
during Civil War, 35–38, 42–48
defining race in, 272
desegregation of schools in, *see* schools, desegregation of
elections in, 175, 224–26
and 1868 Louisiana state constitution, 107–11, 119
free people of color, 10–11
higher education desegregation in, 161
middle class in, 9
in mid-nineteenth century, *1*
mixed races in, 8–9, 15–16, 20–24
one-drop rule in, 256–57
police department in, 180
race restrictions in, 23–25, 64–65
race riots in, 74–75, 78
racial landscape of, xxi
removal of capital from, 248
resegregation in, 231–42, 273–74, 275–79
streetcar and railcar segregation in, 87, 89–90, 93, 95–103, 258, 260, 275–80
White League in, 200–205
New Orleans Bee, 102
New Orleans Republican, 96, 207
New Orleans Riot, 74–75, 78
New Orleans Times, 79, 101, 146
New Orleans Tribune, 47–48, 71, 77, 90, 96, 145
New York City, 44, 87–88, 289
New-York Evening Post, 78
New York Herald, 70–71
New York Stock Exchange, 190–91

New York Times:
Civil Rights Act (1875), 209–10, 249–50
on resegregation, 235–36, 252
on school desegregation, 154, 170–71
on streetcar desegregation, 93
Nicholls, Francis T., 224–26, 231, 233–36, 260, 266
Nicholls, William, 97–98, 102, 136
Nietzsche, Friedrich, 291
North Carolina:
and interracial marriage, 190
and Reconstruction Act, 78–79

Oberlin College, 114, 162
"octoroon," 119, 254, 273
Ogden, Frederick N., 203
one-drop rule:
defined, xvii, 254
Greener on, 253
and mixed-race populations, 114, 286
and police department integration, 180–81
and racial outing, 234
and resegregation, 240–41, 272–73
in South Carolina, 255–56
"oriental," 34
Origin of Species, The (Darwin), 143
Orr, James L., 60, 63

Pascal, Leonville, 127
Peabody, George, 129
Penn, Blanche, 206–7
Penn, Davidson, 203
Perrin, Emilien, 277
Phelps, Albert G., 277
Phillips, Samuel F., 267–68
Pike, James, 191
Pinchback, Pinckney Benton Stewart, 109
plaçage, 9, 15–16, 23, 92, 256
Plessy, Homer Adolph, 264–67, 287, 290

Plessy v. Ferguson, 266–68, 279, 290
police brutality, 59
police departments:
and desegregation, 179–82
and resegregation, 273–74
political representatives, African-Americans as, 175–78
and civil rights legislation, 192
Joseph Hayne Rainey, 178
after resegregation, 274
Hiram Rhodes Revels, 175–77
white supremacists fighting, *see* voter suppression
Potens, Aimée, 41
Prostrate State, The (Pike), 191
protests:
for desegregation, 85–86, 98–101
against integration, 162, 166, 209
following Red Shirts massacre, 220–21
against resegregation, 278
against school integration, 138, 158
for voting rights, 73–74
see also activism

"quadroon," 24, 53, 189, 254, 279

race:
court cases debating, 185, 188–89, 268, 270
defining, 3–4, 185, 201–2, 272–73
development of inferiority in, 5
mixing of, 4; *see also* mixed-race populations
and one-drop rule, 254
and resegregation, 254–55
views on purity of, 66
race riots:
in New Orleans, 74–75
in New York City, 44
in Memphis, 72
racial equality, fight for:
following Black Code, 62–64
in Charleston, 49; *see also* Charleston, South Carolina

and desegregation, *see* desegregation

in New Orleans, *see* New Orleans, Louisiana

public vs. private, 157

racial inequality, incidences of:

and civil rights legislation, 184–85, 187, 195–97

race riots, *see* race riots

after resegregation, 245–46, 249–50 and school desegregation, 157, 171

and streetcar segregation, 89

Radical Reconstruction, 79, 128, 134, 175, 263

Radical Republicans, 45, 70, 76–77

Rainey, Joseph Hayne, 177–78, 194, 220, 226

Randolph, Benjamin Franklin, 114–15, 120

Ransier, Alonzo J., 112–13, *173,* 182, 197–98, 287

Rapier, James, 196–97

Reconstruction Act, 77–78, 118

Red Shirts, 219–21, 225

Regulators, 205–8

Reid, J. M., 99–100

Reid, Whitelaw, 52–53

Republican Party:

and desegregation of colleges, 154

and desegregation of schools, 128, 172

and elections, 224

elections of, in Charleston, 119

forced out of office, 228–29

founding of in Louisiana, 47

founding of in South Carolina, 83

freedmen in, 53

and race wars, 222–23

and Red Shirts violence, 221

resegregation, 230–42

and Civil Rights Act (1875), 246–47

court cases fighting, 249–53, 261–67

Creoles fighting, 256–59

and one-drop rule, 253–56

of schools, 226–28, 274

of streetcars, *243,* 259–60, 264, 275–76

of theaters, 245–46

and voter suppression, 248–49

Revels, Hiram Rhodes, 175–77

Rey, Henry, 76

Reynolds, J. L., 158

Rhett, Edmund, Jr., 60

Rightor, Nicholas H., 238–41

Rivers, Prince, 219

Rivers, William J., 162

Roberts, Sarah, 45, 66

Rogers, William O., 128–30, 230–31, 236–37

Rollin, Frances, 93

Rollin, William, 19

Roudanez, Jean Baptiste:

background of, xxii

on Committee of One Hundred, 145

lobbying for voting rights, xxi–xxiii, 44–46

Sumner meeting with, 89

Roudanez, Louis Charles, xxii, 41–42, 54, 180, 234–35

Ruby, George T., 234

St. Amant, Joseph, 258

St. Phillip's Episcopal Church (Charleston, South Carolina), 6

Sauvinet, Charles St. Albin, 129, 183–87, 247

"scalawags," 107, 114

scholarships, for student recruitment, 167

schools, desegregation of, 125–72

and *Brown v. Board of Education of Topeka,* 290

in constitutional conventions, 109–11, 115–18

enforcing, 134–38

failed attempts at, 125–33, 161

in Louisiana, 125–49

reversal of, *see* resegregation

schools, desegregation of (*continued*)
  and student recruitment, 164–68
  threats to, 226–27, 230
  and Unification Movement,
      144–49
  University of South Carolina, *see*
      University of South Carolina
  and White League resegregation,
      205–8
  white supremacists fighting, 128,
      164, 172
  see also academics
Scott, Cornelius Chapman, 164–65,
    167, 227, 244–46
Scott, Robert, 91, 94, 120
Scribner's Monthly, 159
segregation laws:
  in New Orleans, 21
  in schools, *see* schools, desegrega-
      tion of
  for streetcars, *see* streetcar sys-
      tems, segregation on
  in theaters, 245–46
  and transit systems, *see* streetcar
      systems
"Semites," 227
Separate Car Act (Louisiana),
    258–60
Sheridan, Philip, 75, 102
Sherman, William Tecumseh, 153
Sickles, Daniel, 67, 79, 95
slavery:
  free people of color supporting, 17,
      20
  post–American Revolution, 5
  sexual exploitation/race-mixing
      during, 4
slaves, as "contraband of war," 38
Sloan, R. Gourdin, 159
Smalls, Robert, 88–89, 221, 226
social racial equality, 157, 170,
    209
Society of Free Dark Men, 51
Soloman, Hardy, 229

Soulié, Bernard, 36
South Carolina, *see* Charleston,
    South Carolina
South Carolina Gazette, 4
Southwestern Christian Advocate,
    275, 277–78
Spaniards, 202
Spartanburg Herald, 218
Stanton, Edwin, 40
Stanton, Elizabeth Cady, 192
"star car," *81*
  development of, 87
  fights against, 90, 96, 99
  see also streetcar systems, segrega-
      tion on
State of South Carolina v. Cantey,
    19, 62
Stevens, Alexander Hamilton, 26–27,
    69
Stewart, Thomas McCants, 165–66,
    170, 199, 289
Stewart, William Morris, 177
Straight University, 161
streetcar systems, segregation on,
    84–103
  in Charleston, 83–86, 88–89,
      91–95
  and Civil Rights Act, 90
  company response to fight against,
      94–95
  court cases against, 86–88, 91–94,
      97–98
  end of, 101–3
  in New Orleans, 87, 89–90, 93,
      95–103
  protests against, 85–86, 99–101
  reintroduction of, 275–81
  and soldiers of color, 88–90
student recruitment, after desegre-
    gation, 164
suffrage:
  African-American, *see* African-
      American suffrage
  women's, 192

suicides, of African-American leaders, 267, 275
Sumner, Charles:
   death of, 199
   and equal rights legislation, 178–79, 190–92
   and legislative access, 113
   Revels defended by, 177
   and Sarah Roberts suit, 66
   streetcars discrimination in the District of Columbia banned by, 88
   voting rights pushed by, 45–46

Teachers' Institute, 140
Tennessee, school segregation in, 172
Terry, J. R., 43
"Teutons," 162
Thirteenth Amendment to the U.S. Constitution, 190, 268
Thirteenth Louisiana Volunteer Infantry Regiment, 37
Tilden, Samuel, 225
Tocqueville, Alexis de, 21
Tourgée, Albion Winegar, 261–63, 267–69
transit systems, see streetcar systems, segregation on
Trévigne, Paul, 41, 46, 237–39
Trumball, Lyman, 190

Unification Movement, 146–50, 202
United States v. Cruikshank, 216–17
United States v. Reese, 217, 247
University of South Carolina:
   desegregation of, 153–72, 193–94
   Greener return to, 285–86
   resegregation of, 226–28
Upper Girls School, 205–6
U.S. Colored Infantry, 48
U.S. Supreme Court:
   against civil rights, 215
   and Civil Rights Cases (1883), 249–53, 266
   and DeCuir case, 247
   and Dred Scott, 25, 88, 176
   and Fifteenth Amendment, 217
   and Fourteenth Amendment, 216
   and Plessy v. Ferguson, 267, 269
   and Sauvinet case, 247
   and streetcar resegregation, 246–47
   and United States v. Cruikshank, 216–17
   and United States v. Reese, 217
   on voting rights of African-Americans, xxi–xxii
Union, L' (New Orleans newspaper), 41, 46

Vance, Robert B., 193
Vickers, George, 176
Villeré, Marie Antoinette, 32–33
Virginia, race defined in, 254–55
voter suppression, 118–20, 218, 224–25, 248–49, 274
voting rights:
   Bertonneau/Roudanez lobby for, xxi–xxiii, 45–46
   during Civil War, 47–48
   defining race, 185
   in District of Columbia, 77
   and Eight Box Law, 248–49
   and Fifteenth Amendment interpretation, 217
   fight for, after Civil War, 54
   and literacy, 64
   and New Orleans Riot, 76
   restrictions in, 17, 23
   and streetcar access, 90
   and voter intimidation, 118–19
   for women, 192
   see also African-American suffrage

Waite, Morrison Remick, 217, 246
Walker, James, 266
Walker, Joseph A., 184
Walmsley, R. M., 276

Washington, Booker T., 261
"white" (term):
    defining, 201–2
    development of, xviii
    as inherited aristocratic status,
        5–6
    legally, 19
white indentured servitude, decline
    of, 5
White League, 200–205
"white Negroes," 280
whiteness, big tent of, *see* "big tent of
    whiteness"
whites:
    against desegregation, 116–17
    equality disagreements among,
        108
    and Reconstruction state constitu-
        tions, 107, 114
    view of Charleston, 51
white supremacists:
    against African-American political
        activity, 120

Cable on, 141
and Colfax massacre, 215–17
counterrevolution by, 248
and desegregation of schools, 128,
    164
fighting civil rights legislation,
    200
and multiracial constitutional con-
    vention, 73
on racial purity, 66
and Reconstruction Acts, 78
and resegregation, 232, 252
Wickliffe, George M., 109–10
Wilkinson, Lydia, 93
Williams, J. J., 259
Wilson, David, 108–9
Wilson, Harry, 275, 277–78
women of color, 84, 92
women's suffrage, 192
Woods, William B., 241–42
Wormley, James, 225
Wright, Jonathan Jasper, 156–58,
    228